I0877210

Approaches to Teaching Austen's *Persuasion*

Edited by
Marcia McClintock Folsom
and
John Wiltshire

Modern Language Association of America
New York 2021

© 2021 by The Modern Language Association of America
All rights reserved
Printed in the United States of America

MLA and the MODERN LANGUAGE ASSOCIATION are trademarks
owned by the Modern Language Association of America.
For information about obtaining permission to reprint material from
MLA book publications, send your request by mail (see address below)
or e-mail (permissions@mla.org).

Library of Congress Cataloging-in-Publication Data

Names: Folsom, Marcia McClintock, editor. | Wiltshire, John, editor.
Title: Approaches to teaching Austen's Persuasion / edited by Marcia McClintock Folsom and John Wiltshire.
Description: New York : Modern Language Association of America, 2021. | Series: Approaches to teaching world literature, 10591133 ; vol 166 | Includes bibliographical references. | Summary: "Offers pedagogical techniques for teaching Jane Austen's Persuasion, including considerations of social class, gender, philosophy, disability studies, the author's life, and the history of the Napoleonic Wars. Gives syllabus suggestions for undergraduate and graduate courses in nineteenth-century English literature, the history of the novel, and women's writing."—Provided by publisher.
Identifiers: LCCN 2020050488 (print) | LCCN 2020050489 (ebook) | ISBN 9781603294775 (hardcover) | ISBN 9781603294782 (paperback) | ISBN 9781603294799 (EPUB) | ISBN 9781603294805 (Kindle edition)
Subjects: LCSH: Austen, Jane, 1775–1817. Persuasion. | Austen, Jane, 1775–1817—Study and teaching.
Classification: LCC PR4034.P43 A67 2021 (print) | LCC PR4034.P43 (ebook) | DDC 823/.7—dc23
LC record available at https://lccn.loc.gov/2020050488
LC ebook record available at https://lccn.loc.gov/2020050489

Approaches to Teaching World Literature 166
ISSN 1059-1133

Cover illustration:
Detail of *Miss Mary Tunaley* (1790–93), by Joseph Wright of Derby, England (1734–97). Oil on canvas, 77.2 x 64.1 cm (30 3/8 x 25 1/4 in.). Museum of Fine Arts, Boston. Gift of Mrs. Guy Lowell, 51.1528. Photograph © 2021, Museum of Fine Arts, Boston.

Published by The Modern Language Association of America
85 Broad Street, Suite 500, New York, New York 10004-2434
www.mla.org

For our grandchildren
August, Lorenzo, and Alejandro Folsom
Oscar, Angus, and April Wiltshire

CONTENTS

Part One

MATERIALS

Editions

Jane Austen died on 18 July 1817, and *Persuasion* was first published in one book with *Northanger Abbey* on 20 December 1817, by John Murray. It was titled Northanger Abbey *and* Persuasion, "[b]y the author of *Pride and Prejudice*, and *Mansfield Park*, &c," with a "Biographical Notice of the Author." The publication date on the title page was 1818. *Northanger Abbey* was published as volumes 1 and 2, and *Persuasion* as volumes 3 and 4. It was Jane Austen's brother, Henry Austen, who arranged for the publication of these two previously unpublished works and who wrote the "Biographical Notice of the Author" (Tomalin 272).[1]

For almost a century, *The Novels of Jane Austen*, first published in 1923 and edited by R. W. Chapman, has been the standard edition of all Austen's novels and was cited by scholars throughout the twentieth century and in the beginning of the twenty-first century. (*The Novels of Jane Austen* is referred to here as the Oxford edition.) Modern paperback editions are based on the Oxford edition and include the revisions done by Mary Lascelles for the 1965–66 impression of the Oxford third edition. In 2005 Cambridge University Press began publishing an annotated scholarly hardcover edition of the works of Jane Austen in nine volumes. The Cambridge University Press edition of *Persuasion*, edited by Janet Todd and Antje Blank, was published in 2006: recent and authoritative, it includes a long introduction, extensive endnotes, and a facsimile of the canceled chapters, followed by a transcription. The Cambridge edition of all Austen's works is an appropriate purchase for college libraries and for Austen scholars. An excellent hardcover edition of *Persuasion*, edited by Robert Morrison, was published by the Belknap Press at Harvard University Press in 2011. It is too heavy (and probably too expensive) to recommend for classroom use, but it is a great resource for teachers and general readers, extensively annotated on every page and illustrated with paintings reproduced in full color, maps, and documents. The canceled chapters are included in appendix A, "The Original Ending of *Persuasion*," as is the "Biographical Notice of the Author," by Henry Austen.

There are several very good paperback editions of *Persuasion*, including the one published by Oxford World's Classics and edited by James Kinsley; the one published by Penguin Classics and edited by Gillian Beer; the one published by Broadview Press and edited by Linda Bree; the one published by Anchor Books, edited by David M. Shapard, and titled *The Annotated* Persuasion; and the one published in the Norton Critical Editions series and edited by Patricia Meyer Spacks. All but the Norton retain Austen's division of the book into two volumes of twelve chapters each, and for that reason, we do not recommend the Norton, which numbers all chapters consecutively. The dramatic scene, in chapter 12 of volume 1, where Captain Frederick Wentworth suddenly leaves—"when the horses were baited, he was off"—is the startling last line of that chapter, and the scene's drama is obscured when the two-volume division is lost.

Of particular interest to teachers and general readers are the introductions and notes to the other four paperback editions, by Deidre Shauna Lynch for the Oxford World's Classics edition, by Beer for the Penguin edition, by Bree for the Broadview edition, and by Shapard for the Anchor edition. The Oxford World's Classics edition includes the canceled chapters and three appendixes on contextual issues. The Broadview edition has a chronology and nine relevant and helpful appendixes, including the canceled chapters, Henry Austen's "Biographical Notice of the Author," and well-chosen excerpts of poetry by James Thomson, Walter Scott, and Lord Byron. The Broadview edition is especially useful for courses where *Persuasion* is read with Romantic poetry, as suggested by Anna Dodson Saikin's essay in this volume. *The Annotated* Persuasion preserves the division into two volumes and is helpfully annotated and illustrated on facing pages of the text. This might be a particularly good choice of paperback edition for classes where students would be interested in following the notes as the novel unfolds. It includes a chronology, many helpful maps, and numerous black-and-white illustrations. However, it does not include the canceled chapters.

An interesting variation among the editions is the way the first two sentences of the novel are printed: they are either kept exactly as they appear in the 1818 first edition or emended to make one long sentence. The first edition of the novel divides the first two sentences between the words "contempt" and "As." The Oxford third edition, edited by Chapman, prints those two sentences as one, with a comma separating "contempt" and "as" (J. Austen, *Novels* 5: 3). The first of the notes in this edition explains that "the correction was made by [Thomas Babington] Macaulay" (5: 292). The resulting sentence makes sense as a long and even ponderous introduction of the pompous Sir Walter Elliot:

> Sir Walter Elliot, of Kellynch-hall, in Somersetshire, was a man who, for his own amusement, never took up any book but the Baronetage; there he found occupation for an idle hour, and consolation in a distressed one; there his faculties were roused into admiration and respect, by contemplating the limited remnant of the earliest patents; there any unwelcome sensations arising from domestic affairs, changed naturally into pity and contempt, as he turned over the almost endless creations of the last century—and there, if every other leaf were powerless, he could read his own history with an interest which never failed—this was the page at which the favourite volume always opened:
>
> "ELLIOT OF KELLYNCH-HALL. . . ." (5: 3; vol. 1, ch. 1)

The various phrases, separated by commas and semicolons, capturing the slow shifts in Sir Walter's moods, suggest how the Baronetage provides Sir Walter with amusement, occupation, and even consolation by allowing him to compare his "ancient and respectable" family with more recently created titles and families (5: 4). One essay in this volume, Margaret Case's "Baronets and the Baronetage: Close Reading the Opening Chapters of *Persuasion*," carefully explains how a class can be led to understand this opening statement about the Baronetage and the language of Sir Walter's pride as he compares his name and family history with those of other baronets.

Among the many modern editions of *Persuasion*, some print the opening as one long sentence: the Oxford edition, the Belknap Press edition, the Oxford World's Classics paperback edition, and the Anchor paperback edition. Other editions do not emend the opening but instead leave it divided into two sentences, as it appears in the first edition: the Cambridge edition and the Penguin, Broadview, and Norton paperback editions.

After leading a class through the very helpful exercises suggested in the essay by Margaret Case, an instructor might find it interesting to talk about why some editors think the first two sentences in the first edition should be emended to one sentence, and why other editors might prefer to leave them as originally printed. Since Jane Austen did not live to take her manuscript to the publisher, it is possible to argue that Henry Austen, who brought the manuscript to Murray to be published, thought the first sentence was too long and therefore too difficult. Or maybe the printer thought it would be better shortened.

Students might discuss which editorial decision most effectively captures Sir Walter's relation to this social register of English landed gentry. A skilled student reader might argue that it makes sense that Sir Walter would enjoy escaping from "any unwelcome sensations arising from domestic affairs" by feeling "pity and contempt" for the baronets who were more recently named, and that such feelings would arise "as he turned over" the pages of the Baronetage. Discussing these two versions of the opening paragraph of the novel will give a teacher the opportunity to point out how important it is always to pay close attention to Austen's punctuation.

The teachers whose essays are included in this volume have used six different editions in their classes, and no doubt, most of the paperback editions will continue to be assigned in courses because of considerations of cost, readability, and appropriateness of the introduction (or even of the book's cover). All citations to *Persuasion* in this volume are to the 2006 Cambridge edition. Citations include the volume number and the chapter number, so passages can be readily located in other editions of the novel. If students use an edition with chapters numbered consecutively, teachers may help them convert the consecutively numbered chapters to chapters by volume. For instance, since chapters thirteen through twenty-four are in volume 2, subtracting twelve from any chapter in that range in a single-volume edition of *Persuasion* gives the equivalent chapter number in volume 2.

Critical Reception

An anonymous review of *Persuasion* that appeared in *British Critic* in March 1818 mentioned both *Northanger Abbey* and *Persuasion* and showed a preference for *Northanger Abbey*. The reviewer writes that although *Persuasion* has some parts of "great merit," it is "in every respect a less fortunate performance," and complains that "its moral tendency [is] to encourage young women to disobey their seniors" (Review 314). But soon after, in an anonymous review published in the *Quarterly Review* in January 1821, the young clergyman Richard Whately offered intelligent observations on Austen's last novel. He poignantly notes his regret at her death "in the prime of life, considered as a writer," and also notes that the volume Northanger Abbey *and* Persuasion was "the first publication to which her name is prefixed" (Whately, Review 323). As with his astute comments on the suffering of Fanny Price, Whately's observations about Anne Elliot's feelings in the early scenes are extremely perceptive. He accurately describes Anne's anguish when Wentworth returns: "Nothing can be more exquisitely painted than her feelings. . . . First, dread of meeting,—then, as that is removed by custom, renewed regret for the happiness she has thrown away" (331–32). He registers Anne's acute observations of Wentworth: "her involuntary sympathy with all his feelings, instant comprehension of all his thoughts, of the meaning of every glance of his eye, and curl of his lip, and intonation of his voice." Whately writes that the scene of Anne's conversation with Captain Harville "is exquisitely beautiful" (332), and he cites much of it.

From Jane Austen's death through the mid-Victorian period, though the author's reputation grew, there was little published criticism of *Persuasion*, except for some powerful short comments about Austen's writing. For example, in an unsigned 1852 essay in the *Westminster Review*, G. H. Lewis declares, "First and foremost let Jane Austen be named, the greatest artist that has ever written." He goes on to acknowledge that there are "heights and depths in human nature Miss Austen has never scaled or fathomed," but "though her world is restricted, it is complete" (337). In his 1859 essay "The Novels of Jane Austen," he especially highlights Austen's "rare gift of dramatic creation of character" (346), focusing his discussion on *Pride and Prejudice*, *Mansfield Park*, and *Emma*. Shorter comments about Austen written by nineteenth-century English and American writers are collected in the first volume of Ian Littlewood's *Jane Austen: Critical Assessments* (423–37). In 1862, Julia Kavanagh, a popular novelist, wrote perceptively about the novel, saying that it "shows us the phase of her literary character which she chose to keep most in the shade: the tender and the sad," and comparing Anne's suffering to that of Elinor in *Sense and Sensibility*: "Here we see the first genuine picture of that silent torture of an unloved woman, condemned to suffer thus because she is a woman and must not speak" (Kavanagh 372).

Finally, in the twentieth century more criticism of *Persuasion* began to be published. In 1911 the great Shakespearean critic A. C. Bradley gave a lecture that judiciously commented on all six of Austen's published novels, compared them, and located the specific merits of each. His appraisal of *Persuasion*'s "special and distinctive charm" identifies in the novel an "open romantic sympathy" that distinguishes it from the earlier novels. The conversation between Anne and Captain Harville, and its effect on Captain Wentworth, is "the only passage in Jane Austen's works which I could honestly describe as 'moving'—moving from the mingled sense of pathos and beauty" (215). Bradley also speculated that if Jane Austen had lived longer, she might have expressed more fully a love of nature that she sometimes held in check because of her "keen sense of the absurdities" attending upon an expression of that love; if she had lived, we might "have seen that she was nearer to the poets of her time than she now appears" (216). The essay in this volume by Lynda A. Hall explores *Persuasion* in the context of Augustan and Romantic thinking and suggests how the novel might be taught as both a Romantic work and a response to Romanticism.

Bradley's lecture was followed by Reginald Farrer's essay on Austen's work, which was published in 1917, the one hundredth anniversary of Austen's death. Though offering clear evidence of something wrong in some places with the tone and some of the plotting in *Persuasion*, Farrer offers surprisingly strong support to those who consider the last novel to be Austen's best:

> Anne Elliot suffers, tensely, hopelessly, hopefully. . . . And the result is . . . for such as can feel at all, there is more intensity of emotion in Anne's calm . . . than in the wildest passion-tatterings of Maggie Tulliver; . . . and that culminating little heartbreaking scene between Harville and Anne (quite apart from the amazing technical skill of its contrivance) towers to such a poignancy of beauty that it takes rank . . . as one of the very sacred things of literature that one dares not trust oneself to read aloud. (Farrer 197)

The publication in 1923 of R. W. Chapman's Oxford edition of Austen's novels elevated them to the status of serious, classic works. The fifth volume in the Oxford edition is Northanger Abbey *and* Persuasion, which contains two frontispieces, both entitled "Comforts of Bath"; a chronology of *Persuasion*; "A Biographical Notice of the Author," by Henry Austen; "The Original Version of the Concluding Chapters of *Persuasion*," with notes by Chapman; illustrations of "Milsom Street," "Lyme Regis," a "Landaulet," "Interior of the Concert Room," and "Pulteney-Street and Laura Place"; an index of characters, including "Feigned Places" and "Ships"; and a general index for all the novels that has three sections: "Of Literary Allusions," preceded by a note by Chapman's later editor, Mary Lascelles; "Of Real Persons (Not Being Authors)"; and "Of Real Places." The care and completeness of Chapman's edition of *Persuasion* made possible the scholarly study of the novel that followed.

One astute later-twentieth-century critic, A. Walton Litz, wrote about *Persuasion* in his 1965 book *Jane Austen: A Study of Her Artistic Development* and in a 1975 essay, "*Persuasion*: Forms of Estrangement," which was published in a collection edited by John Halperin. In the essay, Litz carefully revises some of his earlier interpretations. The essay identifies the "deeply *physical* impact of *Persuasion*," the subtlety of the novel's assimilation of Romantic poetry, and the important differences between the mood and language of the first and second volumes (223). Litz also points out that Austen's last novel is different from Austen's other novels in its "sense of the moment—both historical and personal—at which it was written" (231). A short piece by Brian Southam, "*Persuasion*: The Cancelled Chapters," published in *The Jane Austen Companion*, edited by J. David Grey, briefly compares the canceled chapters with the novel's brilliantly revised ending, succinctly proving that the basis of Austen's conscious art is her deliberate rethinking of her work (322–23).

John Wiltshire develops an important argument about the novel in "*Persuasion*: The Pathology of Everyday Life," the fourth chapter of his 1992 book *Jane Austen and the Body*. The chapter contrasts Sir Walter Elliot, who "equates value only with handsomeness, and who has . . . no inner life or moral sense" (165), with the novel's own interest in the forces of time, change, and decay and its repeated exploration of physical injury, disability, disease, and vulnerability. The chapter also highlights the importance of nursing in the novel, the connection between nursing and femaleness, and the ways people cope with injury, loss, or deprivation. In this volume, the essay by Sylvia A. Pamboukian further highlights the novel's remarkable emphasis on women as nurses, and Talia Schaffer points out the medical context of the novel, examining injuries, illness, and disability as part of that context. In his book, Wiltshire also analyzes the subtlety of Austen's presentation of Anne's "self-reflection and self-consciousness" as "a strength, a resource" (178). The essay in this volume by Timothy Peltason suggests how to teach Austen's experiment with a new kind of writing that she developed in order to reveal the inner life of Anne.

Several of the paperback editions of *Persuasion* published in the 1990s and early 2000s offer useful and important introductions to the novel. The introduction by Bree in the 1998 Broadview edition emphasizes the importance and precision of the novel's placement in time—in the summer, fall, and winter of 1814 and early months of 1815—while noting the many ways that events from the past cast shadows over the present. In this volume, the essay by William Nelles suggests how students might map the chronology of the novel and outlines how teachers might help them create "time maps" of specific chapters.

The 1998 Penguin Classics edition offers an introduction by Beer that begins with an excellent long discussion of the word *persuasion* and its meanings. An essay in this volume by Melissa J. Ganz suggests structuring class discussions around debating persuasion: that is, around the concept of persuading. Julie Ann Melnyk's essay in this volume also offers strategies for teaching the many instances of persuasion in the novel. Beer's introduction includes the sections "Kinships and Commonwealths," "Plots and Property," and "Revision and Return," briefly but perceptively touching on key issues in the plot and in the novel's "poignant and dizzying" conclusion (xxix). In the introduction to the 2004 Oxford World's Classics edition, Lynch characterizes Austen's last novel as a "voyage of discovery," echoing Virginia Woolf's claim in the essay "Jane Austen," and calls it "a work of exceptional innovation and experiment, one in which Austen heads somewhere new" (Lynch, Introduction vii; Woolf 147). In particularly vivid language, Lynch discusses the novel's interest in the past and the present and, in the section "The Power of Precedents," its exploration of inherited titles; in the section "'No . . . Examples in Books': An Unscripted Future," Lynch examines the "amazing conversation" between Anne and Captain Harville that brings Lynch to her final argument: that when the longed-for happy ending arrives, "this climax takes form, thrillingly, as a scene of reading" (xxxi).

Brian Southam's important and carefully researched book *Jane Austen and the Navy* (first published in 2000, with a revised and corrected second edition published in 2005) places the last three of Austen's novels in the context of the experience of Austen's brothers Francis and Charles in the British navy and in relation to Austen's knowledge of their lives. The last two chapters of his book, "*Persuasion*: The Righting and Re-writing of History," and "The Aftermath of *Persuasion*," are indispensable reading for teachers and readers especially interested in Austen's handling of the naval characters in the novel and her allusions to naval experience. The essays by Monica F. Cohen and Sheila Johnson Kindred in this volume offer distinctive approaches to teaching about Austen's presentation of the navy in *Persuasion*.

In the first of Southam's two chapters on *Persuasion,* Southam provides chilling details about the ubiquity of flogging and other punishments on naval ships and about the near presence of the sick and wounded, which might complicate the debate between Mrs. Croft and her brother, Captain Wentworth, about women living on shipboard. In "The Aftermath of *Persuasion*," Southam considers later readers of the novel, including Richard Simpson, a Shakespeare scholar who singled out the naval characters, and fascinatingly, Charles Darwin, the Darwin sisters, the Wedgwood and Fitzroy families, and an American admirer of Jane Austen, Eliza Susan Quincy, "of distinguished Founding Father stock," who wrote to Admiral Francis Austen asking for more information about his sister Jane (315).

Southam's thoughtful comments on Charles Darwin's firsthand knowledge of *Persuasion* leads to another critic, Peter W. Graham, and his 2008 book *Jane Austen and Charles Darwin: Naturalists and Novelists*. The book offers four interconnected essays that each work out observations about how these two writers and thinkers excelled in reading the world by looking closely at social and natural phenomena. Graham offers perceptive analyses of relationships in the Musgrove family (66–67), marriages in *Persuasion* (and in all the Austen novels) and in Darwin's life (87–132), and the meanings of the many encounters and events that take place in the Lyme Regis chapters of *Persuasion* (vol. 1, chs. 11–12; Graham 169–79).

In the 2007 book *A Revolution Almost beyond Expression: Jane Austen's* Persuasion, Jocelyn Harris offers detailed suggestions about what in Austen's reading and her life can be perceived as the origins of the novel; Harris carefully sorts out the differences between the canceled chapters (10 and 11) and the rewritten chapters 10, 11, and 12; and she analyzes Austen's rewriting of the ending. Her chapter on the relation between Walter Scott and Austen is searching in its knowledge of the works of both authors and in its astute appraisal of Austen's implied attitude toward Scott as revealed in *Persuasion*. Likewise, Harris's chapters on Lyme Regis and Bath are steeped in information about the place of both towns in early-nineteenth-century English thought and experience. Harris's short final chapter convincingly captures the complicated intertextuality of the novel's ending, which blends Shakespearean rebirth and Romantic hope, joy, and a "revolution . . . almost beyond expression" (193). In this volume, the essay by Catherine J. Golden offers excellent guidance to teachers whose students can read *Persuasion* "through the lens of place." Golden provides a Web-based assignment that enables students who have toured Bath and Lyme Regis in person to reflect on their experiences, and she discusses an activity in which students tour the towns virtually.

Films

There have been three film adaptations of *Persuasion*. All three are British productions. The first, which dates from 1971, was originally shown on TV in a series of episodes. In 2004 it was remastered and reformatted as a DVD by the BBC. The 1995 version, also made as a television drama for the BBC with WGBH/Boston, was received with such acclaim that it was subsequently released in cinemas worldwide, with success. The 2007 *Persuasion* was made for showing on British commercial television, in collaboration with WGBH/Boston, and later released on DVD. These films, and the indebtedness of the later films to the earlier ones, are discussed in the sections of the introduction called "Embodiment and Sexuality" and "The Films of *Persuasion*."

The 1971 *Persuasion*, directed by Howard Baker, written by Julian Mitchell, and featuring Ann Fairbank as Anne Elliot, runs for 225 minutes. It is interesting to compare with later versions. The screenplay for the 1995 film was written by Nick Dear and published by Methuen Film in 1996. This screenplay is useful for teachers, as is the brief introduction by Dear. The film, directed by Roger Michell, stars Amanda Root as Anne Elliot, Ciarán Hinds as Wentworth, and Sophie Thompson as Mary Musgrove and includes a distinguished supporting cast. It runs for 107 minutes. The essay in this volume by Abigail Burnham Bloom, "Teaching *Persuasion* with the Michell Film Adaptation," focuses on this, the most successful film of the three. David Monaghan's compelling and detailed analysis of the "Movement Motif" (129) in both the novel and the Dear and Michell film offers specific observations of the film's technical strategies and explores the implicit meanings of the decisions made to change aspects of Austen's text.

The 2007 production, starring Sally Hawkins as Anne Elliot, was directed by Adrian Shergold from a script by Simon Burke and runs for ninety-three minutes. It is available, as is the 1995 *Persuasion*, on DVD. Most contributors to this volume, and most teachers, do not attempt to show a complete film during class time. Alternative ways to use films are to make them available to students to view on their own, or to show selected short scenes during class.

Digital Resources

There is a large and expanding body of digital resources for Austen's novels and for related study that can help teachers and students. Several essays in this volume suggest how teachers might use these resources in teaching *Persuasion*. In particular, the essay by Golden, "Placing *Persuasion*," offers an activity involving customized virtual tours of Bath and Lyme Regis that enable teachers to demonstrate how Austen roots her novel in both the built and the natural worlds. Following these tours, students will come to understand that the world of *Persuasion* is filled with places where the author lived and traveled, including the streets, buildings, and outdoor spaces where she places her characters. The essay by Peter J. Capuano, "Teaching *Persuasion* in Multiple Contexts," includes a detailed analysis of free indirect discourse and guides teachers and students to *Austen Said: Patterns of Diction in Jane Austen's Novels*. This Web site offers a cutting-edge digital platform developed by Laura White and her team at the University of Nebraska-Lincoln, which enables students to explore Austen's diction, including unique word usages (by novel, character, class, gender, age, and role) and the frequency of their use. The Web site's visualization section allows users to see patterns of indirect speech and free indirect discourse, including the intensity of scale of free indirect discourse, at a glance.

The "Cambridge Companions" Web pages make available e-books in the collection Cambridge Companions to Literature and Classics, which offer "thousands of comprehensive and accessible essays on major authors, periods and genres, written by experts and designed for student readers." These volumes place writers "in literary and historical context; their major works are analyzed . . . and their influence on later writers assessed" ("Cambridge"). There are two editions of *The Cambridge Companion to Jane Austen*, both edited by Edward Copeland and Juliet McMaster. The 1997 edition contains an essay by John Wiltshire on the three Chawton novels (*Mansfield Park*, *Emma*, and *Persuasion*), and the 2011 edition contains an essay by Penny Gay on *Emma* and *Persuasion*. The Web site is accessible to individual and institutional subscribers.

"A Hyper-concordance to the Works of Jane Austen" is an extremely useful online resource that allows users to search for words in Austen's works, which are included in their entirety. Lines in each work are numbered. Search results list every line of text where the search term appears in a given work, allowing users to see at a glance the context for each instance of the term. Access is free (Matsuoka).

"Jane Austen and Time: A Study of Her Uses of the Almanac" is a remarkable series of Web pages by Ellen Moody. Moody has created detailed calendars or time lines for all six of Austen's published novels and also for "The Watsons," "Lady Susan," and the fragment "Sanditon." She has also created a chronology of Austen's writing life. The purpose of these pages, as the writer explains, is to enable readers to "use these calendars to understand the novel that is in front of them more clearly, to see what is literally there. The calendars are also intended to help people writing about and teaching Austen who want to reach her text in the most fundamental way." Access is free, but no part of the Web site may be reproduced without the express permission of Moody.

Jane Austen's Fiction Manuscripts is an extraordinary digital archive of some 1,100 pages of writing in Jane Austen's hand. Of particular interest is the only surviving example of canceled chapters from just one of Austen's published novels, in this case *Persuasion*. The canceled chapters are discussed in the introduction to this volume, in the section "Comparing the Canceled Chapters with the Ending of the Novel." In addition, this archive gives interested readers access to manuscripts written by Austen from her childhood to the year of her death. Transcriptions of the manuscripts, including their corrections, are also viewable. This is a unique and fascinating resource for all Austen readers. Access is free.

The Jane Austen Society of North America publishes an annual print journal, *Persuasions*, and an online journal, *Persuasions On-line*, that usually appears twice a year. Both journals are peer edited, and the essays are of excellent quality. On the society's Web site, readers can access an index to past issues of the online journal and tables of contents for the print journal. Some full articles of the print journal are available. A search filter on the "Publications" page permits readers to search for essays about specific novels or for essays on particular topics, like courtship, health, money, religion, travel, or parents and siblings. Access is free.

The blog *Jane Austen's World* explores English culture and society during the Regency period. The blog includes a page called "Teacher/Student" that offers resources on Austen that target high school readers; the page is copyrighted (Sanborn).

JSTOR is one of the world's best sources for academic content. Users may search its list by academic discipline. *JSTOR* is not free to the public, but some of its resources are open access, meaning a subscription is not required to view them. There is a large open-access file on Austen criticism. Subscribers may join for a specified time, or libraries can subscribe. Many instructors will be able to access the site through an institutional subscription.

The Republic of Pemberly, one of the most familiar of the Austen Web sites, includes on its "Jane Austen Information Page" a vast collection of texts written by Austen, including her letters and juvenilia, academic articles, and modern take-offs and spin-offs of her work. "The Republic of Pemberly Discussion Group" can be found on *Facebook*. *The Republic of Pemberly* has extensive source listings and essays on every one of the novels. For example, the section on *Persuasion* includes a full concordance of every use of the words *persuade*, *persuasion*, *persuadable*, and *persuaded* in the novel as well as an analysis of the meanings of *persuading*, as "influencing others," and of *persuasion*, as "one's beliefs." The Web site might make an interesting companion to the essay by Julie Ann Melnyk in this volume. Access is free.

NOTE

[1] The short essay by Jane Austen's brother Henry is reprinted in H. Austen, "Biographical Notice" [*Memoir*], "Biographical Notice" [J. Austen, *Novels*], and "Biographical Notice" [J. Austen, *Persuasion*].

Part Two

APPROACHES

Introduction

Marcia McClintock Folsom and John Wiltshire

Background

According to a note by her sister, Cassandra, Jane Austen began writing the novel later called *Persuasion* on 8 August 1815 (J. Austen, *Works*; see page facing 242).[1] This was seven weeks after the battle of Waterloo finally brought an end to the war between Britain and France that had been waged at sea and on land since 1793. Napoleon Bonaparte, the French commander in chief, had in fact resigned earlier, on 5 April 1814, and had been sent in exile to the isle of Elba, off the coast of Italy. In March 1815 he had escaped, used his status as a popular hero to gather an army of supporters around him, and resumed fighting. The renewed conflict is called the Hundred Days War, and it ended when his army was vanquished at Waterloo.

These historical events are present by implication in Jane Austen's novel. The time span of *Persuasion* begins, quite specifically, in "the summer of 1814" (9; vol. 1, ch. 1) and ends in February 1815. This is the period when Napoleon was in exile on Elba. His apparent defeat allowed naval officers to come ashore, as they do in the novel, and to pursue marriages, as Captain Frederick Wentworth does, because the long war was thought to be over. *Persuasion* is the only work by Jane Austen in which the action is dated so precisely. Perhaps this dating makes it a historical novel, a form inaugurated by Walter Scott's very successful *Waverley* in 1814, which, as its subtitle states, is set in the Scotland of "sixty years" before. Austen, perhaps in response to Scott, writes a historical novel set in a momentous time period that had only just passed. Her first readers would have certainly known that the lull in the war that provides the setting of the novel would come to an end a month after the action's apparently happy closure.

Important circumstances in Jane Austen's personal life also lie in the background of *Persuasion*. Two months after Austen began work, her brother Henry fell ill, and she stayed on in London to care for him. In early 1816, members of her family began to suspect that she herself was unwell, and in May of that year the two sisters, Cassandra and Jane, made the long journey to Cheltenham Spa so that Jane could try the supposedly medicinal waters. On 18 July 1816, she thought she had finished writing, and wrote "Finis" at the end of her manuscript. This was exactly a year before her death.

Jane Austen's nephew James Austen-Leigh wrote in his *Memoir* of 1871 that Jane went to bed depressed the night after signing off at the end of her manuscript. About the concluding reconciliation scene between Anne and Wentworth, Austen-Leigh writes, "[s]he felt it tame and flat." "This weighed upon her mind," he writes, "the more so probably on account of her weak state of health" (147), but just two weeks later, in better spirits, she entirely refashioned the closing chapters of the novel, and on 6 August the novel as we know it was completed. And, as Austen-Leigh remarks, "[p]erhaps it may be said that she has seldom written anything more brilliant" than the two chapters that replaced chapter 10 of the second volume in the draft (148). The discarded, or canceled, chapters (chapters 10 and 11 of the original manuscript) have survived, a precious document whose many corrections and passages struck out are testimony to the difficulties the ailing Jane Austen had in completing the story to her satisfaction. The canceled chapters are discussed below.

Though her health remained very uncertain, in a letter to her favorite niece, Fanny, on 13 March 1817 Jane Austen gives an assurance that "I have a something ready for Publication, which may perhaps appear about a twelvemonth hence" (*Jane Austen's Letters* [Le Faye, 3rd ed.] 333). This seems an oddly contradictory sentence. "Ready for Publication" suggests that the novel had been written out in the form of a fair copy, meaning that it was ready for the publisher to read and for the printers to work from. Only one fair copy of a work by Austen survives, the early "Lady Susan": in the preface to the first publication of "Lady Susan," in 1925, R. W. Chapman describes the state of the manuscript as "beautifully written" and "almost free from correction and revision" (Chapman, Preface). William Gifford had read *Emma* for its publisher, John Murray, in October 1815, presumably from a fair copy: the novel was published in December of that year.

So if *Persuasion* was "ready," and the manuscript was clear of corrections, why the "twelvemonth" before publication? *Emma*, a much longer novel, was published nine months after it was finished, and there are no indications that Jane Austen or Henry, her agent in London, approached the publisher in the six months after the writing was finished in August 1816. It is therefore possible that the "perhaps" in her letter signaled that she was uncertain about her future, or indeed that *Persuasion* was not in fact quite "ready."

The novel was published posthumously in one volume together with *Northanger Abbey* on 20 December 1817, though the title page reads "1818." Apparently, Jane and Cassandra had consulted about the title, and "The Elliots" seems to be what they had decided on. It was probably Henry Austen who decided to publish the two novels together. The final and much better title also appears to be his decision.[2]

Free Indirect Discourse in Persuasion

Jane Austen has many different means of acquainting us with her characters, but the most important is the mode or technique she developed that is variously called free indirect speech or free indirect discourse. The British novelist Julian Barnes gives a useful working definition of this practice. He writes that it is that "way of dipping into a character's consciousness—for a paragraph, a sentence, a few words, sometimes for just a single word—showing things from his or her point of view, and then dipping out again" (71).[3] To put this another way, free indirect speech represents characters' inner lives through the words they say to themselves, but the author gives no tangible signs that she is moving out of an impartial, perhaps objective, mode, and no indication when she slips back out of the character's viewpoint into her default narrative mode. Whether it's called free indirect speech or free indirect discourse, this mode is attended to, illustrated, and discussed in several essays in this volume. We offer here an overview, focused on instances that might be especially useful for teachers opening discussion of this important, tricky matter with a class.

Austen's use of free indirect discourse became more sophisticated over her writing career, and in *Persuasion* it is more flexible and more subtle than in any of her previous novels. This presents a teaching challenge, but also a teaching opportunity. Whether a passage—a sentence or a few words—is to be assigned to a character can often be a matter of opinion and can lead to lively discussion in the classroom. Here is an example, from the novel's second chapter. The wily lawyer Mr. Shepherd is seeking to persuade Sir Walter Elliot to settle in Bath:

> Sir Walter had at first thought more of London, but Mr. Shepherd felt that he could not be trusted in London, and been skilful enough to dissuade him from it and make Bath preferred. It was a much safer place for a gentleman in his predicament—he might there be important at comparatively little expense.—Two material advantages of Bath over London had of course been given all their weight. . . . (15; vol. 1, ch. 2)

The film script of the 1995 production of *Persuasion* has Shepherd speaking directly here to Sir Walter, saying that Bath would be "an altogether safer place" for "a gentleman in his predicament" and that "In Bath, I think, you might be important at comparatively little expense" (Dear 8). But aren't these expressions rather too incautious, even impolite, for this skillful negotiator to use? Isn't it more likely that this is a sentence that Shepherd says to himself, and doesn't it reveal his real attitude, since—as the narrator has previously indicated—he stands to lose money himself if Sir Walter does not in fact "retrench"? After this dipping for a moment into the character's thoughts (only the two dashes indicate that the point of view is shifting) we are brought back to the narrator with "of course." Although this passage includes free indirect speech (Mr. Shepherd's), the passage as a whole might appropriately be called free indirect discourse since it contains Mr. Shepherd's speech within the author's narrative voice—which skeptically comments on the whole transaction. Students can enjoy tracking these shifts, which occur throughout the novel and which involve the inner speech of a whole range of characters—not only Anne Elliot, but also Lady Russell, and surprisingly enough, Mary Musgrove and Charles Musgrove, and even for a page, Captain Wentworth—without bothering about what technical term to use. One good result of calling students' attention to this feature though, as contributors to this volume point out, is that they learn how important it is to read Austen's work attentively.

There is another, more important example of free indirect discourse in chapter 2. Lady Russell also votes for Bath:

> Lady Russell was fond of Bath in short, and disposed to think it must suit them all; and as to her young friend's health, by passing all the warm months with her at Kellynch-lodge, every danger would be avoided; and it was in fact a change which must do both health and spirits good. Anne had been too little from home, too little seen. Her spirits were not high. A larger society would improve them. She wanted her to be more known.
> (16; vol. 1, ch. 2)

After the summarizing introduction within the first sentence, the paragraph renders Lady Russell's private opinions. Meeting it for the first time, readers will certainly gather that Lady Russell cares for Anne and feels responsible for her happiness. But there is something about the decisive style of her thought, its categorical mode—"*every danger would be avoided*; and it was *in fact* a change which *must* do both health and spirits good" (emphasis added)—that might ring alarm bells and let the reader know that this is Lady Russell's inner voice. The sharp, abrupt rhythm of the four last sentences suggests Lady Russell's temperament even more potently: she knows her own mind and is confident that she is right. Even a first-time reader of the novel might feel a touch of skepticism, especially as it seems that the phrase "she wanted her to be more known" implies that Lady Russell, without admitting it to herself, is thinking of finding Anne a husband in Bath.

The cunning of this mode of narration here is that, without overt authorial intervention, the unsuspecting reader will be inclined to take Lady Russell's opinions at face value. Even late in the novel, in Bath, when Anne has come to the conclusion that Lady Russell's opinions often diverge from her own, there is nearly a whole paragraph in which her ladyship's approval of Mr. William Elliot is presented with such plausibility and conviction that a reader might well be taken in. Again, there is an introduction that begins as an authorial statement and glides imperceptibly into free indirect speech:

> As Mr. Elliot became known to her, she grew more charitable, or more indifferent, towards the others [Sir Walter and Elizabeth]. His manners were an immediate recommendation; and on conversing with him she found the solid so fully supporting the superficial, that she was at first, as she told Anne, almost ready to exclaim, "Can this be Mr. Elliot?" and could not seriously picture to herself a more agreeable or estimable man. Every thing united in him; good understanding, correct opinions, knowledge of the world and a warm heart. He had strong feelings of family-attachment and family-honour, without pride or weakness; he lived with

> the liberality of a man of fortune, without display; he judged for himself in every thing essential, without defying public opinion in any point of worldly decorum. . . . (158–59; vol. 2, ch. 4)

The balance and authority of these cadences take the reader into the "composed mind" of Lady Russell, which has just been mentioned. This transition is so convincingly achieved that a reader might easily be persuaded of the correctness and impartiality of her judgment—persuaded, perhaps, as the younger Anne had been persuaded by Lady Russell's arguments eight years before. On reflection—and students might be asked to look carefully at this inner speech—they might detect how thoroughly the dowager Lady Russell has herself been seduced by the younger man's smooth "manners."

Even more subtle use of free indirect discourse occurs in the fourth chapter of the novel when, after passages conveying Sir Walter's, Mr. Shepherd's, and Elizabeth's inner speech, the narrative turns to focus on Anne Elliot and invites readers into the heroine's consciousness. Or does it? Here is an example of the skilled modulations of Austen's style:

> How eloquent could Anne Elliot have been,—how eloquent, at least, were her wishes on the side of early warm attachment, and a cheerful confidence in futurity, against that over-anxious caution which seems to insult exertion and distrust Providence!—She had been forced into prudence in her youth, she learned romance as she grew older—the natural sequel of an unnatural beginning. (32; vol. 1, ch. 4)

The first phrases of this short paragraph plainly align the author or narrator in sympathy with her heroine's unspoken thoughts and feelings. But with the word "that"—"that over-anxious caution which seems to insult exertion and distrust Providence!"—the sentence becomes a generality that leads us away from Anne's own particular consciousness and that possibly makes us wonder retrospectively whether the whole sentence isn't to be attributed to the author. Is the second sentence here a rendering of Anne's thought, or is it an intervention of the narrator's? Its aphoristic wit doesn't sound quite like Anne's style. Nevertheless, most readers will probably feel that the overall effect of the paragraph is to express sympathetic identification with the heroine. This might be called "focalization": the author's focus is on Anne, though the style or voice is not hers.

Such blending of the narrative voice with the heroine's consciousness has led some critics to argue that sacrificing a vantage point outside the character's consciousness means the loss of the ironic or satiric point of view that is characteristic of Austen's art. There is certainly often a fusion (sometimes more like an interlacing) of *Persuasion*'s authorial consciousness with the inner life of Anne. But irony is not absent from a passage like the next one, which clearly remains within Anne's consciousness. She has just seen off her sister and brother-in-law to a dinner party to meet Wentworth:

> They were gone, she hoped, to be happy, however oddly constructed such happiness might seem; as for herself, she was left with as many sensations of comfort, as were, perhaps, ever likely to be hers. She knew herself to be of the first utility to the child; and what was it to her, if Frederick Wentworth were only half a mile distant, making himself agreeable to others!
>
> She would have liked to know how he felt as to a meeting.
>
> (62–63; vol. 1, ch. 7)

This is an early example in the novel of Anne's inner strategies. There is more than a touch of self-pity in the thought that she ought to get used to the loss of "comfort," a thought that is evidently intended to help her steady or brace herself. This thought is followed by an attempt at consolation in the thought of being useful, which is itself followed by a valiant defiance of the feelings that threaten to overwhelm her. But the shift to the next paragraph is dramatic: "She would have liked to know how he felt as to a meeting." Comically, this thought upsets Anne's attempt to keep a steady, controlled state: this is an early instance of what happens again and again in a novel that explores the ultimately unavailing techniques by which Anne seeks to control or repress her feelings. While the passage certainly explores Anne's inner life with sympathy, it indicates an ironic or comic contrast between her thoughts and her emotions.

Students might be encouraged to debate whether the close association of the author with her character in these passages results in sentimentality. The essay by Peter J. Capuano discusses this issue and directs readers to the very useful Web site *Austen Said* (described in the "Materials" section of this volume).

The Psychology of Anne Elliot

Nothing is more likely to arouse controversy in a classroom—as it has among *Persuasion*'s critics—than questions about Anne's inner life. Are her private ways of dealing with her situation admirable or not? Doesn't she resign herself too easily to the role of inferior, or doormat, the role of someone always "glad to be thought of use" and "glad to have anything marked out as a duty" (36; vol. 1, ch. 5), whether that duty is to be a piano accompanist while others dance or a nursemaid while her sister and brother go out for the evening, to always keep herself apart, or to do what others demand? How can we be interested in a heroine who is always sacrificing her own feelings?

Among critics, Anne's inner life (at least for the first volume of the novel) has been described as involving "self-mortification" (Miller 72) and "something very like masochism" (Bree 24), and though few readers would probably go that far, the presentation of a heroine who is continually repressing her own feelings, and more or less blaming herself for having such feelings, does perhaps invite such responses. Other readers will argue that Anne's self-discipline is admirable. Doesn't she display stoic courage in the face of sorrow—sorrows of several kinds? Isn't that why the narrator treats her with such sympathy? But then (the reply might be) doesn't this lead the novel, surprisingly for Jane Austen, into sentimentality?

But there are other ways of looking at this problem. Anne is a woman whose situation in life is dreadfully sad. She is not poor, of course, but her world is dreary and confined. It is unexciting, unstimulating, and barren. (Austen does not insist on this but indirectly conveys the emptiness of a genteel life in the country through the prefatory account of Anne's sister Elizabeth's plight in the novel's first pages [7; vol. 1, ch. 1].) Anne is lonely and ignored by her immediate family, but most important, she carries the psychological scars of a terrible mistake. She has thrown away her chance of happiness. And she is now, at twenty-seven, unlikely to marry at all. Perhaps in modern terms Anne is depressed—but her depression is not clinical or morbid; it is proportional to her situation. When Captain Wentworth reenters her life, the wound of her mistake eight years ago reopens. A teacher might suggest that Austen is interested in how Anne Elliot deals, from then on, with her powerlessness, and might call students' attention to the ways in which Anne exercises the only power available to her by attempting to take control of her inner life.

For Anne's inner life is the site of a continuous and often losing battle. This inner battle is played out through Austen's free indirect speech, which is now capable of conveying the struggles of a sensitive and responsive selfhood. A clear example of this is the passage that follows Anne's first meeting with Wentworth after the rupture between them. The dizzying effect of their encounter is brilliantly conveyed and often commented on by critics. Recovering slightly from the encounter, Anne thinks, "They had been once more in the same room!"—an upsurge of irrationality, of feeling. "Soon, however, she began to reason with herself, and try to be feeling less": calling upon her reason is a characteristic move for Anne and the default strategy of her inner struggle (64; vol. 1, ch. 7). Austen then moves into the free indirect speech mode to show Anne telling herself not to be so silly: "How absurd to be resuming the agitation which such an interval had banished into distance and indistinctness! What might not eight years do? Events of every description, changes, alienations, removals. . . ." These thoughts are forced and lack any conviction, so there follows a choric intervention by the narrator:[4] "Alas! with all her reasonings, she found, that to retentive feelings eight years may be little more than nothing." Then Anne's natural longings surge again, "Now, how were his sentiments to be read?" only to be chastised again by the rational, sensible self: "the next moment she was hating herself for asking the question" (65; vol. 1, ch. 7).

One variation of this struggle between natural feeling and the reasoning mind occurs on the walk to Winthrop. "Anne's object was, not to be in the way of any body"—which might be read as a strategy of the rational self but from another point of view looks rather like a symptom of defeat or depression. She seeks to "occupy her mind" with memories of poetry, to commune soothingly with herself, but this effort fails when she overhears Wentworth and Louisa talking about matters that involve and (presumably) agitate her. "Anne could not immediately fall into a quotation again" is all that is said (91; vol. 1, ch. 10). This understatement, with its smallest touch of irony, invites the reader to fill in what Anne must be feeling. Teachers will readily find other instances of Anne's struggle to control her feelings. But when she overhears more of the talk between Wentworth and Louisa, which bears on her own conduct in the past, she experiences again "extreme agitation," and no wonder (96).

Wentworth disappears from the novel at the end of volume 1 (in chapter 12) and does not reappear again until chapter 7 of volume 2, when Anne catches sight of him walking down the street in Bath. In the intervening chapters Anne has become significantly more independent and more in control of her own actions. She silently but categorically disagrees with Lady Russell, defies her father by visiting Mrs. Smith, is interested in Mr. Elliot, and keeps up her end of the conversations with him. When Anne gets news of Louisa's engagement to Benwick, which leaves Wentworth "unshackled and free," Austen depicts another variation on Anne's inner struggle. Her "heart beat in spite of herself"; "She had some feelings which she was ashamed to investigate. They were too much like joy, senseless joy!" (182; vol. 2, ch. 6). She's happy, but once again her habit is to school herself; part of Anne's temperament, readers understand, habitually seeks to dampen down anything akin to self-release.

When Anne sees Wentworth, through a window, coming down Milsom Street, this battle within her takes a remarkable turn:

> She now felt a great inclination to go to the outer door; she wanted to see if it rained. Why was she to suspect herself of another motive? Captain Wentworth must be out of sight. She left her seat, she would go, one half of herself should not be always so much wiser than the other half, or always suspecting the other of being worse than it was. She would see if it rained. (190; vol. 2, ch. 7)

At this moment Anne breaks free of her ingrained self-doubt and self-censorship and even analyzes it—one half of her, the reasoning self, always watching over the other half, her natural impulses, which consist of her responses, feelings, and desires. Well, she thinks, I do know I'm kidding myself about checking to see if it's raining, but I'll do what I want to do anyway. The comedy of this knowing self-deception signals Austen's authorial delight in this psychological breakthrough. From now on, Anne takes a more determined role, and the focus shifts to the outward events and mishaps that threaten her happiness.

Anne is a quite different heroine from either Elizabeth Bennet or Emma Woodhouse, who are both healthy, ebullient, and self-possessed young women who have the world before them. In *Persuasion*, Austen perhaps returns to a character she portrayed in *Sense and Sensibility*, Elinor Dashwood, who tries to quell her own emotions, behave with composure, and respond to excruciating situations with restraint. But Austen doesn't fall into the trap of allocating critical commentary on dislikable characters to Anne as she does to Elinor. In her last months, Austen considered what humans can do in the face of loss, sorrow, and sadness. In *Persuasion*, she extends a long and subtle presentation of one character's inner struggle and asks the reader to recognize a kind of heroism that isn't usually called heroic.

Embodiment and Sexuality

It does not take long for student readers of Austen to recognize that her novels take place in a very different world from their own. The formality of her language, the construction of her sentences, the politeness, even ritual, of the manners, and the apparently complete absence of sex and its discussion all can seem strange and uninspiring. When in *Persuasion* Wentworth remembers that "[h]e had been most warmly attached" to Anne, it's not likely to convey anything exciting to a student in the twenty-first century who is reading the novel for the first time (66; vol. 1, ch. 7). So it may come as an intriguing surprise to them if a teacher of *Persuasion* suggests that there is a good deal of interest in bodies and embodiment in this novel and even invites them to notice how powerful its depiction of sexual attraction is.

Persuasion certainly differs from Austen's earlier novels in its attention to the human body. This is clear from its opening chapters. Both Sir Walter Elliot and his eldest daughter, Elizabeth, pride themselves on their youthful good looks and take this to be a sign of their social superiority. They judge Anne too by her body: in her father's eyes she is now "faded and thin," even "haggard" (6; vol. 1, ch. 1). Looks are important throughout the novel, but still more important is a motif that they initiate, of the human body's vulnerability. Physical injuries happen or have happened to three people: the young Musgrove lad, who is brought home after a bad fall; Captain Harville, who has been lamed at sea; and most seriously, Louisa Musgrove, who, jumping precipitately from the Cobb, suffers a concussion on the stones below. Mrs. Smith, invalided and dependent in Bath, is a signal example of how illness and time can drastically change a life. There are many deaths in the background: Lady Elliot died when Anne was fourteen, Fanny Harville died while her fiancé was abroad, Dick Musgrove died at sea, and Mr. Elliot wears mourning for his wife. These deaths are not incidental: they exert their presence in crucial scenes of the narrative. The essay by Talia Schaffer in this volume examines the ways that the disabilities and injuries in the novel can in various ways create communities of caring. Another contributor to this volume, Sylvia A. Pamboukian, examines Austen's presentation of several women characters who assume roles as nurses. Other contributors point out, too, that there are answering responses to these bodily assaults: responses of both nursing and mourning. Anne mourns, Captain Harville mourns, and Mrs. Musgrove mourns; the melancholy Captain Benwick is only the most dramatic mourner in the novel.

In contrast to these many instances of injury, decline, and loss, Captain Wentworth is presented as the epitome of good looks, health, vigor, optimism, and allure. He had been irresistibly "full of life and ardour" on his first appearance in Anne's life and is hardly changed when he reappears eight years later (29; vol. 1, ch. 4). As Anne muses sadly, "The years which had destroyed her youth and bloom had only given him a more glowing, manly, open look" (65; vol. 1, ch. 7). Wentworth is given a physical presence in the early scenes of the novel by many small touches: he goes out "a shooting" with Charles Musgrove (89; vol. 1, ch. 10); indoors, while the ladies remain seated, he sometimes gets up abruptly and moves about the room.

In Anne's first conversation with Mrs. Croft, students may notice that Anne is "electrified" when Mrs. Croft mentions "her brother," and that she can't help thinking that Mrs. Croft must mean Frederick (52; vol. 1, ch. 6). But Mrs. Croft means his elder brother, Edward, and Anne has then to recover and manage her initial shock. The use of the word "electrified," itself startling, conveys the sense of Anne's arousal, a surprise that is felt through her body like an electric current. And later, when Wentworth appears in person, students may notice that every time Anne is even moderately close to Wentworth, Austen suggests that she is aroused, made nervously excited by his presence. This is a new phenomenon in the English novel, and even in Austen's work—that a woman should be depicted as excited by the proximity of a man. Even in a casual moment, as when Wentworth gets up "almost instantly" and moves to sit with Mrs. Musgrove, the phrase "They were actually on the same sofa" (with Mrs. Musgrove between them) conveys in the unnecessary word "actually"—which dips for a moment into Anne's consciousness—the absurd thrill, the frisson that she experiences. She interprets every look on Wentworth's face, every "glance of his bright eye" or "curl of his handsome mouth" (73; vol. 1, ch. 8). But this arousal is difficult to manage, especially when he comes closer to her. Anne experiences—not for the first or last time—"painful agitation" when he comes up behind her and lifts the troublesome little boy from off her back: a contrivance of Austen's narrative art that brings their bodies very close together, without them quite touching (87; vol. 1, ch. 9).

On the walk back from Winthrop, Wentworth sees that Anne is tired, and he athletically clears the "hedge in a moment" to persuade his sister to offer Anne a lift in the carriage (97; vol. 1, ch. 10). Then he "obliges" her to be "assisted" to her seat. This language is decorous, but not quite so when the focus turns to Anne's feelings: "Yes,—he had done it. She was in the carriage, and felt that he had placed her there, that his will and his hands had done it, that she owed it to his perception of her fatigue . . ." (98; vol. 1, ch. 10). It is extraordinary how much depth Austen is able to find in "felt"—a word that might slip by as a conventional acknowledgment but here will also convey something transmitted between the two bodies as they now meet. And then the excited "that" mimics in the rhythm of its reiteration the pounding of Anne's heart.

It is useful to compare this incident in the novel both with Nick Dear's script for the 1995 film *Persuasion* and with its rendering in the actual movie. Both Dear and Roger Michell, the director, seem to have grasped how momentous this apparently slight moment actually is for Anne.

This is how the film script presents it:

> WENTWORTH (quietly). Please.
>
> ANNE experiences a maelstrom of sensations as WENTWORTH lifts her briskly and courteously up into the gig. She has felt his touch, his smell. . . . In an instant she is seated. (Dear 42)

Which piece of writing, students might be asked, makes Anne's feelings the more telling? Dear's notion that Anne senses Wentworth's "smell" is a violent extrapolation from the text but expressive as a response to the covert sexual energy of this scene. This would be impossible to convey in film, but Dear is presumably seeking to convey to the director his belief that this scene in the novel has erotic importance.

In the film, Ciarán Hinds, who plays Wentworth, is seen glancing briefly back at Anne struggling along alone behind him. Then the Crofts offer her a seat in their carriage. In close-up, the face of Anne, played by Amanda Root, becomes beautiful as she recognizes their kindness but modestly declines. Again, in fleeting close-up, Wentworth's face is seen close to hers. In the next shot—again in close-up—where his white-gloved hand appears against the rich folds of her dark velvet cloak, on her rump or perhaps her back, Wentworth is lifting her upward. The polite word in the script, "Please," is omitted, a recognition of his decisive style, often described in the novel as his taking action "instantly" (73; vol. 1, ch. 8). Students may debate whether the film's rendering of the incident matches the quiet turbulence conveyed in Austen's prose. There is more discussion of this incident in the section on films.

What is conveyed by the impact of this moment on Anne—something way beyond the realm of courtesy and politeness? That Wentworth has been aware of Anne's exhaustion after the lengthy walk is an item in the script that signals his renewing feeling for her (what one might call his moral development), but the action is also an inscription of his appeal to her, of his vitality, strength, and virility.

Some students may resist the notion that there is a sexual subtext to such incidents in the novel. But it is not difficult to see what is in play during the remarkable moment a few chapters later when Anne and Wentworth, climbing the steps from the beach at Lyme, encounter a "gentleman": "Anne's face caught his eye, and he looked at her with a degree of earnest admiration, which she could not be insensible of. . . . It was evident that the gentleman (completely a gentleman in manner) admired her exceedingly." The language again is decorous and controlled. But "earnest admiration" must mean that the man is making his attraction to her evident, and the aside that credits him with being a gentleman suggests that she has quickly appraised him, too, and responds to him. Wentworth catches the meaning of this interplay immediately and here again "instantly" turns to her with a "glance of brightness" (112; vol. 1, ch. 12) that, like the glance of his "bright eye" (73; vol. 1, ch. 80) that she recognizes earlier in the novel as typical of him, is now restored through his intuition at what the gentleman is feeling. The triangle is completed when Anne is warmed with pleasure at Wentworth's pleasure.

In his essay in this volume, Timothy Peltason traces Anne's ability to notice and appreciate the clear signs of Wentworth's approval. Lynda A. Hall, in her essay, also notes the way this scene shows Anne becoming aware of a return of her beauty in the bracing seaside air. It is incidents like these that make credible the change in Anne's character and hopes that the second volume of *Persuasion* initiates. Anne begins life in Bath with the knowledge that besides the renewed respect for her character that Wentworth feels, his "ardour" for her may also be revived (29; vol. 1, ch. 4). As Peltason explains, Austen shows how Anne gradually comes to enjoy the evident respect, affection, and admiration she attracts as the novel unfolds. Anne has clearly enjoyed her friendship with Captain Benwick, recognizes that the Crofts both like her, and seems to enjoy the attentions of Mr. Elliot, but his style, though assiduous and flattering, only reminds her of how much she prefers Captain Wentworth's. Anne has overcome her reticence and is ready for the moment when Wentworth unexpectedly arrives in Bath.

Romancing the Navy

In her 1814 novel *Mansfield Park*, Austen presents a scene in which the young midshipman William Price entertains the Bertram family with stories of his life at sea. "In the course of seven years he had known every variety of danger that sea and war together could offer," the narrator declares. No details are given, but the reader is left to assume that his "recital" includes enough of what are called "such horrors" to hold all his listeners (except Mrs. Norris) appalled and entranced (275; vol. 2, ch. 6). The historical and naval background is important in *Mansfield Park*, though it is less fully present in the novel's text than it is in *Persuasion* (see Folsom and Wiltshire 21–25). In *Persuasion*, there is a more extended scene than the one in the earlier novel, occupying almost the whole of chapter 8, in which Captain Wentworth also entertains a family audience with his seafaring career. The Musgroves, like the Bertrams, are quite ignorant about life on board ship, and Wentworth very evidently enjoys teasing the young ladies about their ignorance and boasting, more or less, about his career. He first tells them about his first command, a broken-down sloop called the *Asp*, in which he captured "privateers enough to be very entertaining" (71; vol. 1, ch. 8).

Privateers were "privately owned armed vessels commissioned by the government to fight against enemy ships" (355n5)—and hunting them down was part of the British response to Napoleon's continental system, as was blockading French ports. It would be "entertaining" perhaps because these ships would offer little, if any, resistance to capture. Wentworth goes on to tell his eager audience how he had "the good luck to fall in with the very French frigate he wanted" (71; vol. 1, ch. 8), the good luck being that this capture would bring honor, but more important for a man like Wentworth who was seeking his fortune, that the navy itself would be very likely to buy the captured vessel at market price. (A French frigate captured in 1809 had a total value for its captors of £25,000.) Admiral Croft later says he hopes that he'll "have the good luck to live to another war" (75).

The naval war, then, was an opportunity for brave and daring men like Wentworth to make their fortune. But two less glamorous facts lie behind Wentworth's gripping tale of danger and lucky escapes. The first is the cost to the ordinary crew. More than a fifth of the seamen would die in these engagements that were so "entertaining." Still more would suffer terrible injuries, so that a ship's deck resembled, as one officer wrote, "a slaughter house" (Parsons 86; qtd. in Southam, *Jane Austen and the Navy* [2nd ed.] 279). A woman on a ship might hear from night to morning nothing but the groans of the sick and wounded. True, the young Musgrove sisters exclaim in "pity and horror" at Wentworth's recital (J. Austen, *Persuasion* 71; vol. 1, ch. 8). But, as in *Mansfield Park,* none of the horrors—except the dangers to Wentworth—are mentioned. Of course, Austen is depicting a young man enjoying showing off before these naive country young ladies, but the novelist seems to be colluding with her character in presenting the naval war as an adventure. Even when death and injury are mentioned in the novel, they are treated lightly: the death of Dick Musgrove is treated with puzzling ambiguity, which may make readers uncomfortable, and Captain Harville's injury gets passed over.

The second less glamorous fact that seems to be concealed in *Persuasion* is that by 1814 the navy had certainly declined in public prestige and acclaim since the days of Nelson. This was partly because the British failed to defeat the Americans in the Atlantic war of 1812–14 and had to settle for an ignominious truce. But the decline was also, Brian Southam argues, because of weariness with the long war, increasing desertions, and a shortage of good timber for shipbuilding (*Jane Austen and the Navy* [2nd ed.] 270). More important, Austen and her readers would have known very well that it was the Battle of Waterloo on 18 June 1815 that changed everything, when British and Austrian troops under the command of the Duke of Wellington finally defeated Napoleon.[5]

Persuasion's last sentence celebrates "that profession which is, if possible, more distinguished in its domestic virtues than in its national importance" (275; vol. 2, ch. 12). The novel has indeed shown the domestic side of its naval figures (even to the extent of making Admiral Croft, who would be in his forties,[6] into a loveable old gentleman) but has passed over much of the truth about the cost of their "national importance." Austen may have felt an understandable desire to celebrate the navy, since two of her brothers were naval officers. However, just as she resisted the Prince Regent's librarian's suggestion that she should write a "Historical Romance," saying, "I must keep to my own style & go on in my own way," she knew that the domestic reception of naval events was her field, and that it was no business of hers to confront readers with grim details of naval life (*Jane Austen's Letters* [Le Faye, 3rd ed.] 312). Monica F. Cohen's essay in this volume explores Austen's presentation of the sailors' domestic side. Several other essays in this volume present ways of teaching about the navy: Paul Westover's essay suggests how students might read *Persuasion* as a wartime novel, and Sheila Johnson Kindred traces the evidence that Jane Austen's knowledge about the naval careers of her brothers Francis and Charles influenced the novel's presentation of naval officers and naval history.

The Films of **Persuasion**

Showing parts of a film of *Persuasion* to a class can be a dangerous business. Many students may superimpose their memory of the film they have seen over their memory of the novel. But if a class is shown scenes from not just one film version but two, then this problem is much less likely to occur, and instead a range of interesting issues will arise and can animate classroom discussion. This teaching method, in which Austen's original text is set against two film interpretations of a particular scene or passage, can prompt an exciting and exhilarating excursion into adaptation theory and can reward teachers with a means by which to encourage students to attentively read the text on which the films depend. Students will come to understand that different films give different interpretations of the novel. This approach to teaching the novel by comparing scenes from at least two films with the text is explored in the essay by Abigail Burnham Bloom.

Some preparation for this triangular study of three "texts" may be in order. Filmmakers setting out to make a new version of an Austen novel can't help but be aware of the previous films that have been made of Austen's books, and these films will influence them to give a decisively different account. It may be helpful to explain to a class that the climate in which a version of a classic was expected to stay as close as possible to the original novel has given way to one in which directors are praised for the originality of their conceptions. It may also be useful to tell the class (perhaps after discussion of the films) that all three films were originally made for television, and that the earliest BBC version, directed by Howard Baker, was screened in 1971.

The difference between a film and the text of *Persuasion* can be quickly demonstrated by showing the first scenes. The novel opens not with a dramatic exchange (as *Pride and Prejudice* does) but with two chapters that give necessary background information about the characters before the action begins with Mr. Shepherd's speech in chapter 3. The 1995 film opens very dramatically with a shot of oars in a choppy sea, quickly followed by a short sequence showing Shepherd and his daughter approaching Kellynch Hall. From this point brief scenes of life at sea are intercut with scenes at Kellynch. The 2007 film, directed by Adrian Shergold, in contrast opens with a focus on Anne Elliot, and the camera follows her as she hastily works through the big house to make an inventory of its contents.

The 1995 film's shots of seafaring life end with one in which Admiral Croft declares, "Gentlemen, the war is over," tells his officers that Napoleon has been sent to the isle of Elba, and adds, "Gentlemen, we are going home." This sets the ensuing drama within its specific historical context: the months of 1814–15 when the Napoleonic war seemed to be over. The next scene opens with Sir Walter declaring, "No, I will not have a sailor in my house." Students might be asked what the very different opening of the 2007 film achieves. Behind the credits, it depicts Anne as a quasi-servant, hard pressed and exhausted, her face anxious and sad. Is this an appropriate rendering of the marginal position of Anne that the novelist suggests by, for instance, delaying the focus on Anne for several chapters, and by hardly allowing her a few words?

Persuasion is a novel that depends on the inner life—that is, the inner words—of the heroine. Anne's unspoken thoughts and conflicted emotions are crucial to the narrative. One of the challenges facing a scriptwriter and a director of a film is how to convey this inner life in a medium that is dramatic and visual. In chapter 4, for instance, the novelist takes the reader into Anne's mind: in a long paragraph, Anne thinks about the past and how much she regrets taking Lady Russell's advice to break off the engagement with Wentworth. Austen emphasizes that Anne has never told Lady Russell of her change of heart: she could certainly be most "eloquent" about it (32; vol. 1, ch. 4), but she has denied herself that relief (31). The films need to get this crucial information about Anne's changed feelings across, and so two of them invent scenes in which, alone with Lady Russell, Anne tells her of her regrets. In the 2007 film she is more bitter (and even aggressive) than in the 1995 one. Students might be asked which version they feel is closer to the spirit of the novel.

One way to deal with the problem of the hidden inner life is to use the old-fashioned technique of voice-over. Voice-over is not used in the 1995 *Persuasion* until Wentworth's letter is presented and Anne reads it in his voice; Anne's voice is then added to Wentworth's to form a brief duet that wonderfully captures the affinity between the two characters. When voice-over is used in the 2007 film, it always feels awkward. The writer and the director can also invent incidents that allow the viewer to deduce Anne's thoughts and feelings from her actions. In the 1995 film, for instance, there is a short scene in which Anne is seen sorting through books with a maid in the attic of Kellynch Hall, where she comes across an old navy list with a letter folded into a paper boat inside it. She takes it out and glances across at the servant before putting it away. No words are spoken. The filming requires viewers to interpret the moment, which in turn requires that they imagine Anne's private life. By these means the consciousness of viewers may acquire the inwardness with the character that in the novel is achieved by the novelist's full relation of Anne's thoughts about the past. There is a very similar, very short scene in the 2007 film in which Anne opens a box that contains a wad of letters tied with ribbon. Students can be asked what meaning this moment conveys.

If students are shown only these first few scenes—less than twelve minutes of each film—and then return to the novel, they may appreciate how complex and interesting reading a novel against films and reading films against a novel can be. As mentioned earlier, another incident that can yield lively discussion occurs later on when Wentworth lifts Anne into the Crofts' carriage after he has seen her exhausted from the Winthrop walk. In the 2007 film he comes round the rear of the vehicle, lifts Anne up like a child, and virtually dumps her in the spare seat at the back. Her reaction is not shown. In the novel it is crucial.

As we have suggested, the makers of contemporary film versions of classics are encouraged to put their own interpretation on the source text, usually to make it seem more contemporary. All the films move material around, and the 1995 film uses bits of the canceled chapter 10 to heighten suspense toward the close. The 2007 film transfers the speeches Anne gives to Harville in the final reconciliation scene to a much earlier conversation with Benwick. It then replaces that famous scene in which Wentworth partially overhears Anne and Harville conversing passionately about love and writes his own passionate letter, with an invented conclusion. Anne is shown grasping Wentworth's proposal letter in her hand and literally racing against the clock, and the crowds, through the streets of Bath to find him and tell him, gasping, that she accepts him. Does this substitution of a quiet scene in an inn with a hectic chase that leaves Anne panting and breathless successfully remake her as a determined, modern, active heroine? Or does it inadvertently underline this film's established portrayal of Anne as a victim, the suppliant woman who must accept whatever fate delivers to her?

This and many other opportunities for lively controversy in the classroom are presented by the use of films. Overall, two more questions can be posed. The films present an Anne who gets happier, and prettier, but do they also show, as the novel does, how she grows away from habits of her inner life that have inhibited and constricted her, into an authoritative, articulate, and poised woman? And what happens in the films to the politics that *Persuasion* embodies, which, as contributors to this book show, are implicitly feminist and radical?

Was Persuasion *Ready for Publication?*

On 13 March 1817, Jane Austen wrote to her niece Fanny, "I have a something ready for Publication, which may perhaps appear about a twelvemonth hence" (*Jane Austen's Letters* [Le Faye, 3rd ed.] 333). This "something" would be the not-yet-titled *Persuasion*. But was her novel in fact "ready for publication"? Depending on the sophistication of the students in a particular course, it may be either an exciting strategy or a mistake to discuss in class the question of whether *Persuasion* was finished by the writer herself. For students who enjoy it, critical detective work, which entails looking for evidence of something missing, can be exciting. It can give the reader a sense of being in close touch with the writer and able to imagine the writer's own plans and ideas. Such critical detective work is especially rewarding for rereaders of Austen's *Emma*, since reading that book a second, third, or even tenth time allows readers to perceive hidden but clearly worked-out clues that lie beneath the apparently everyday surface of the novel.

With *Persuasion*, such thinking can illuminate the sadly touching evidence that Austen's life ended before she could do her usual vigilant revising that make all the pieces of her other novels fit together so perfectly. With *Persuasion*, perceptive readers can't help noticing some failures of consistency in the plot, and even some problems in the writing, and thinking that Austen would have resolved these issues if she had been well enough and had had the time to work on the whole manuscript.

If student readers are not used to the work of close reading, then introducing the idea that the novel may not have been finished by the writer may make them lose interest in the novel or dwell on things they don't like about it. A suggestion that the book wasn't quite done may also make them miss the satisfactions of following the novel's success in tracing Anne's growth, or the way the book's changes of location keep offering new experiences to Anne.

Still, the question of whether *Persuasion* was left unrevised is an interesting one, and it can promote lively discussion in a classroom. In the first place, there are passages in the novel that modern readers may well wish away—most notoriously the description of Mrs. Musgrove's "large fat sighings over the destiny of a son whom alive nobody had cared for" (73; vol. 1, ch. 8). One problem with this passage is the unkind crudeness of the language, which often disconcerts and offends student readers. But the real problem is the shift in the narrative to the author's point of view. No one in the family makes such a cruel suggestion about Richard, so that the claim that "nobody had cared for" him is a gratuitous intervention, one that is hardly remedied by the clumsy apology in the next paragraph. The passage is disturbing because slips like this one are similar to the narrative's other, more subtle shifts in point of view.

There are other places in the novel where the author or narrator seems to want to press views on the reader, and students might be asked if they can find them. The passage on the walk to Winthrop is one example, where the point of view seems firmly focused to reflect Anne's mind, until a crucial change comes at the word "that" in the phrase where autumn is called "that season of peculiar and inexhaustible influence on the mind of taste and tenderness" (90; vol. 1, ch. 10). Here is an authorial intervention unlike any other in Austen's earlier novels; however, it certainly does align the author's sensibility with her character's.

In her essay in this volume, "*Persuasion* as Transition," Hall identifies the paragraph about the environs of Lyme in volume 1, chapter 11, as a telling example of "Austen's use of natural images" and singles out the suggestion that "many a generation must have passed away since the partial falling of the cliff prepared the ground for such a state, where a scene so wonderful and so lovely is exhibited" (J. Austen, *Persuasion* 103; vol. 1, ch. 11), as a reference to what Hall describes as the "mutability of nature." This passage certainly accords with many other suggestions of mutability and change in the novel. But this brief mention is embedded in a sixteen-line sentence of onrushing authorial enthusiasm, in which "green chasms among romantic rocks" and "orchards of luxuriant growth" in "a scene so wonderful and so lovely" seem to contradict the melancholy that was apparent on the walk to Winthrop and instead overtly recommend, on the author's authority, that readers visit these beautiful places.[7] It seems likely that Jane Austen, rereading her manuscript, would have saved the momentary reference to geological change and shortened the rest of the paragraph. The surviving manuscripts of *Persuasion* and "Sanditon" show that she was not afraid to make such changes. In *Pride and Prejudice* she had specifically disowned any ambition to write travel-book descriptions ([Rogers] 266; vol. 2, ch. 19).

More significant perhaps are problems with plot details. When Mrs. Clay is first mentioned, Lady Russell is pleased that since Mrs. Clay has lost her husband and is left with the "burthen of two children," Elizabeth Elliot will obviously be prevented from inviting her to Bath (*Persuasion* 17; vol. 1, ch. 2). Sheryl Craig's essay in this volume points out that legal custody would have been held by Mr. Shepherd, so that, theoretically, Lady Russell was quite mistaken. This being the case, why does Austen emphasize Lady Russell's certainty that Mrs. Clay would have to stay behind to care for her children? In any case the children are never mentioned again. In a revision of the manuscript, Austen would surely have attended to this apparent contradiction.

Another small difficulty is that midway through the novel, Captain Harville is said to be "no reader" (106; vol. 1, ch. 11), but in the revised climactic chapter in which he talks so earnestly with Anne, he implies that he is a great reader: "I could bring you fifty quotations on my side of the argument," he declares (254; vol. 2, ch. 11). This difficulty could be gotten around, since we know that officers often took reading matter like Shakespeare and Milton on board, so Shakespeare's Cressida or Milton's Eve might have been in Harville's mind. Would he have "fifty quotations" though? If she had revised the manuscript, Jane Austen would surely have been careful to modify the suggestion that he was "no reader," perhaps by adding that he was no reader "on shore."

A more serious problem concerns the subplot of Mr. William Elliot and Mrs. Clay. There is no doubt that Austen conceived of Mr. Elliot as a far more thorough villain than any of her other antiheroes. Students may discover hints in the novel that he is conducting an intrigue with Mrs. Clay at the same time as he is making up to Anne in pursuit of the Kellynch estate, but these hints are so slight that even an attentive reader could miss them. For example, on the evening when Anne has arrived at the Elliot home in Bath, there is a knock at the door at the late hour of 10:00 pm. "Mrs. Clay decidedly thought it Mr. Elliot's knock. Mrs. Clay was right" (154; vol. 2, ch. 3). This must mean something to an author as careful as Austen, presumably that Mr. Elliot has told Mrs. Clay he'll be coming round. But is this enough to alert the reader to an intrigue? When it rains in Milsom Street, there is a question about whether Anne or Mrs. Clay should go in the carriage. "Mrs. Clay's civility rendered her quite as anxious to be left to walk with Mr. Elliot, as Anne could be" (190; vol. 2, ch. 7). This passage is a stronger hint. Students might be asked whether they think Mrs. Clay and Mr. Elliot are having an affair. The winding up of the novel leaves another matter unanswered. The rewritten chapters of *Persuasion*, like the original draft, give no opportunity for Anne to tell Lady Russell the truth about Mr. Elliot and thereby correct her totally mistaken views about him.

Persuasion was not Austen's last projected novel. She began writing "Sanditon" a few months after *Persuasion* was apparently completed. But "Sanditon," a satire on hypochondria written by a sick woman, had to be abandoned after twelve chapters. Perhaps, then, the manuscript of *Persuasion* was deliberately put aside for further revision, and the canceled chapters for reconsideration, before publication. One telling fact is that Henry Austen, whom Jane Austen had asked to read *Mansfield Park* before publication and to give his verdict on it, and who had shepherded *Emma* through publication in London, was not allowed to read the *Persuasion* manuscript and was not given much idea of what it was about. When Jane Austen died, the title had not been settled on. So if the author could only write to her niece that the novel "*might* perhaps appear" a year after it was "ready," does that mean she knew it would need some revision?

Comparing the Canceled Chapters with the Ending of the Novel

The fact that Austen's original manuscript version of chapters 10 and 11 of the second volume of *Persuasion* has survived provides a wonderful opportunity for teachers of the novel. Editions of *Persuasion* increasingly include a transcript of the so-called canceled chapters of the book, and students can see the manuscript itself on the Web site *Jane Austen's Fiction Manuscripts*. The diplomatic display on this site displays the original document, with its many crossings out and corrections, and on the left a transcription of the text, showing clearly what Jane Austen canceled and what she substituted. Reading through the manuscript in its original form now offers fascinating insights into Jane Austen's methods of composition.[8]

The discarded chapters, which were titled "Chap. 10" and "Chapter 11," were found in a drawer of Cassandra Austen's desk after Cassandra's death in 1845. Jane had finished the novel (or so she thought) with these two chapters and had written "Finis," with the date "July 18, 1816," at the end of the manuscript. The three replacement chapters (in modern editions, chapters 10, 11, and 12 of volume 2) were completed a little more than two weeks later. The manuscript version of these replacement chapters has not survived. The final version of chapter 11 includes the scene at the White Hart Inn, in which Anne and Wentworth are finally reconciled. It replaces the earlier draft of chapter 10, which interestingly is headed "July 8," suggesting, like the many corrections on the manuscript, that the author struggled over it for ten days.

These two versions of the climactic scene are quite different. In the earlier version, Anne finds herself trapped in a room, half overhearing a conversation, or dispute, between Captain Wentworth and Admiral Croft, in which Kellynch is mentioned. Then Wentworth, very embarrassed, and addressing Anne with forced formality as "Madame," has to ask her whether the rumor that she is going to marry her cousin, and that they may want to move to Kellynch, is true. Anne, overcome, struggles to speak but tells him that "there is no Truth in any such report." Wentworth can hardly believe it, so he asks her again. Face to face—"he was looking at her with all the Power and Keenness, which she beleived no other eyes than his possessed"—their eyes meet. Anne says nothing, but "[h]er Countenance did not discourage" and in a "silent, but a very powerful Dialogue;—on his side Supplication, on her's acceptance—" they recognize each other's love and are "re-united" (J. Austen, *Persuasion* 318).

Cassandra told her and Jane's nephew James Austen-Leigh that Jane felt this conclusion to be "tame and flat," but in many ways it's tense and exciting (Austen-Leigh, *Memoir of Jane Austen, by Her Nephew* 147). Jane Austen builds up the tension by having Anne already agitated by Mrs. Smith's revelations about Mr. Elliot and develops it still more by the series of chance incidents that lead to her finding herself in the same room with Wentworth. His embarrassment at having to ask her if the rumors are true that she will marry her cousin is very convincingly demonstrated, and this awkwardness for them both, especially given the misunderstandings that have preceded this scene, winds up the tension even further. Whether or not students respond to this tension, they will almost always agree that the "silent" and "powerful" dialogue is a feeble gesture at a conclusion.

There are other reasons for finding this scene disappointing. The most obvious one is that, especially in volume 1 of the novel, Anne has been presented in a characteristic feminine role as the listener, rather than the speaker, and this scene confirms that conventional role. Wentworth does the speaking: Anne can manage hardly a word. (Strangely, in the manuscript, Wentworth's "Supplication" is even given a capital letter; Anne's "acceptance" isn't.) In volume 1, Anne is often seen sitting—at the piano, listening to his yarns about his sea career, overhearing his praise of Louisa—while Wentworth has often been shown standing or walking about, even clearing a hedge. He is the active figure, as in this scene. Anne is the text's site of inner turbulence and distress, as is the case here, where she appears sitting and silently struggling with conflicting emotions.

In an article titled "The Final Chapters of *Persuasion*: Austen's Passionate Revision," Marcia Folsom offers an imaginative reconstruction of the decisions that Jane Austen needed to make when revising her original text. This article will be especially inspiring to student readers because it conveys the excitement and enjoyment Jane Austen must have experienced as she refashioned her earlier chapter 10 into a moving and utterly convincing reconciliation scene.

Students should certainly be invited to compare the two versions side by side. They will quickly see that all of the stereotypes of femininity and masculinity are overthrown in the new chapters. Austen was able to write a completely new and longer chapter 10 that brings together almost all the characters, except Lady Russell, and develops the plotlines, especially the intrigue of Mr. Elliot and Mrs. Clay. Chapter 11, set in one of the communal rooms that have been the main settings of the Bath sequence, picks up many of the motifs of the preceding chapter, but in strikingly new ways. Overhearing, for example, has characterized Anne's marginal position on several occasions. At the White Hart Inn, Anne again overhears the talk of Mrs. Musgrove and Mrs. Croft, in which she detects, as in other overheard remarks, implications for herself. Wentworth also overhears the conversation and apparently has some of the same thoughts. When Captain Harville motions to Anne to come stand with him at the window, the positions of man and woman are reversed: Wentworth is sitting, carrying out a duty for a friend (as Anne has carried out many a duty), and it is he who overhears some of the crucial dialogue between his friend Harville and Anne.

More important, as students will quickly appreciate, the barely speaking Anne of the original manuscript is replaced by an Anne who now speaks at length and with the eloquence that the novel earlier denied her: she commands the textual stage. More important still, Austen now creates an exchange in which the crucial issues about male and female social roles that have been touched on earlier in the novel—as in Anne's thought that Benwick, "as a man," will quickly overcome his grief (105; vol. 1, ch. 11)—but that have remained largely latent are now openly exposed. Anne speaks without apology of the constraints that the life of gentility imposes on a woman, and essentially engages in a conversational battle with Harville and wins it.

"Men have had every advantage of us in telling their own story . . . the pen has been in their hands. I will not allow books to prove anything," Anne declares (255; vol. 2, ch. 11). Essays in this collection by Magdalena Nerio and Sheryl Craig emphasize the possible affiliation between Austen and early feminists like Mary Wollstonecraft and the feminism implicit in Austen's treatment of nursing and disability. Do we hear the voice of Jane Austen herself in Anne's words? Students may well want to debate this matter. It's certain that a comparison of the conclusion of the novel with Austen's earlier attempt to round it off will suggest how extraordinarily gifted a writer Jane Austen was. Under duress, she could produce a chapter that must be counted among her greatest work. Doesn't the whole of the chapter reverberate with the author's knowledge that, despite the setbacks of her illness, she could command her pen as no previous woman ever had?

NOTES

[1] For an excellent short overview of Austen's life, see Fergus.

[2] The word *persuasion* is more powerful as a title than an allusion to the mostly discredited Elliot family would be. As we see in the long discussion of persuasion in Gillian Beer's introduction to the Penguin Classics edition of the novel (vii–xiv), and in the essay

by Melissa J. Ganz in this volume, the word is rich in debatable connotations. Also see Janet Todd's argument: "Henry Austen . . . probably chose the more suggestive *Persuasion*, which draws attention to the novel's pervasive theme of literary and social influence and suited the current fashion for abstract titles like Edgeworth's *Patronage* and Brunton's *Discipline*" (115).

[3] Barnes makes the common error of attributing this technique, known as *style indirect libre* in French, to Gustave Flaubert, who wrote nearly half a century after Jane Austen.

[4] We call this intervention *choric* to mean that it is a moment when the voice of the narrator blends in sympathy with the thought-speech of the character.

[5] In "Sanditon," the unfinished novel that followed *Persuasion* in 1817, a real estate developer regrets aloud that he has called his new home "Trafalgar House" because "Waterloo is more the thing now" (J. Austen, *Works* 6: 380).

[6] For more on estimating the age of Admiral Croft, see Southam, *Jane Austen* (2nd ed.) 274n.

[7] Students might be interested to know that this passage is used on Lyme Regis's tourism Web site (lymeregis.org).

[8] The manuscript chapters are now in the British Museum.

Teaching *Persuasion* in Multiple Contexts

Peter J. Capuano

Jane Austen's more well-known fiction has inspired strong attachments from many people (instructors and students alike), but *Persuasion* might be Austen's most dynamic and teachable novel. In fact, one of the many advantages of teaching *Persuasion* is that so many students—even the ones who come into my courses already professing their love for Austen's works—have never read the text before. They are much more likely to have encountered *Sense and Sensibility*, *Pride and Prejudice*, or *Emma*. The relative obscurity of *Persuasion*, therefore, lends collective freshness to the reading process that is lacking when, say, half the class is reading the material for the second or even third time. But it is not just the fact that *Persuasion* is the Austen novel my students are least likely to have read that makes it the most effective one to teach. In this essay I argue that *Persuasion*'s place as Austen's final novel has much to do with its pedagogical effectiveness in two different courses I often teach at the undergraduate level: History and Theory of the British Novel, 1700–1900; and Survey of Nineteenth-Century British Literature.

Teaching Persuasion *in a Genre Course*

In the novel genre course, *Persuasion* is preceded on the syllabus by several epistolary novels. This means that by the time we study *Persuasion*—roughly halfway through the semester—the class is already familiar with the relation between the epistolary form and realist detail. Our earlier readings in Ian Watt's *The Rise of the Novel* (9–59) and J. Paul Hunter's *Before Novels* (3–58) emphasize how and why early novel readers were drawn to works written in the form of letters, but the students have also experienced for themselves the way letters create necessary circuits of plot advancement, suspense, and characterization in Eliza Haywood's *Fantomina*, Daniel Defoe's *Robinson Crusoe*, and, most thoroughly, in Samuel Richardson's *Pamela*. I recall our attention to epistolarity as we begin to study *Persuasion* because even the most fanatical undergraduate Austen fans typically do not know that her fiction writing career was so solidly connected to the epistolary format. Therefore, I begin introducing the work of Austen by focusing on her juvenilia. Her notebook *Volume the Second*—most likely assembled not long after 1790—includes "Lesley Castle," the famous "Love and Freindship," and "Collection of Letters," all of which were composed in epistolary form. "Lady Susan," written around 1795, is also epistolary except for a conclusion written from an authorial perspective, which itself may have signaled a shift in Austen's fictional composition practice. Once we've established Austen's historical ties to epistolarity, students become more attuned to and eager to think through questions pertaining to her narratological choices in *Persuasion*.

Students enter the classroom on the first day and encounter the entry from the Baronetage (which forms the end of the novel's opening paragraph) on the blackboard:

> "ELLIOT OF KELLYNCH-HALL.
>
> "Walter Elliot, born March 1, 1760, married, July 15, 1784, Elizabeth, daughter of James Stevenson, Esq. of South Park, in the country of Gloucester; by which lady (who died 1800) he has issue Elizabeth, born June 1, 1785; Anne, born August 9, 1787; a still-born son, Nov. 5, 1789; Mary, born Nov. 20, 1791." (3; vol. 1, ch. 1)

I break the students up into groups of about five or six and charge each group to consider some of the reasons why Austen would choose to begin the novel with such a seemingly odd block of text. Putting aside for a moment the entry's status as a tangible point of pride for an irresponsible baronet (which we discuss far more in the course Survey of Nineteenth-Century British Literature), these small student discussion groups usually generate a number of very interesting observations.

One keen-eyed group of close readers wonders why there is a quotation mark at the title of the entry and then two more enclosing the body of the entry. Is this a mistake, or does the open quotation mark reveal something about the narrator's relationship to Sir Walter Elliot or the reader? I find that it is best to leave these questions unresolved for the time being. Another group notices that the first line, which mentions nothing between Sir Walter Elliot's birth date and his marriage date, serves beautifully to encapsulate Austen's bread-and-butter theme of marriageability. The third group notices how date-heavy the entry is. When prodded to comment on the possible significance of the many dates in this entry, one of the group's members has done the math quickly and reports that dates constitute sixty-two characters in the entry, while there are only thirty-five words that aren't related to dates. Her fellow group members come to her defense, saying that such an obviously unbalanced chunk of text has to be important, even if they cannot yet formulate why. The final group, having had the benefit of extra time and discussion before it presents, usually comes up with the most comprehensive observation. In one class, a particularly astute final group was able to weave into their own summative observation the other groups' comments about the reader's relation to the narrator, the importance of marrying correctly within one's class, and the emphasis on dates. This group likened the Baronetage entry to a metanarrative moment in which the reader receives a letter of sorts from the narrator that signals all the text's most important themes, including, among other things, the tension created, and the plotline signaled, when a widowed baronet has no male heir.

From here, it's no stretch to discuss with the class how the dates in the opening of *Persuasion* offer the same realistic flourish as the dates in Crusoe's diary in *Robinson Crusoe* and in Pamela Andrews's letters in *Pamela*—thereby creating an important link to the formal structures of novels we encountered earlier in the course. Such a discussion inevitably leads to conversation about Austen's choice to use a letter in *Persuasion*'s most climactic scene: where Captain Frederick Wentworth lays bare his romantic feelings for Anne while she participates in a dialogue about the equality of gendered affection with Captain Harville. It has been my experience that students very much enjoy discussing possible alternative scenarios to unravel what the form of the letter accomplishes. This is why I take the opportunity to show the class that Austen herself was unsure about how to make this crucial scene convincing. We consult the Web site *Jane Austen's Fiction Manuscripts* to investigate how Austen wrote a reconciliation scene in a chapter that was later canceled, in which Wentworth's now famous letter does not appear.

I think it is enormously productive to continue this line of inquiry—to discuss what isn't in the novel (and why) as much as what is. This is essentially a grand exercise in deforming the text, the effectiveness of which has been the subject of work by Lisa Samuels and Jerome McGann and by Steve Ramsay. These scholars advocate for deforming and reforming whole texts (stanzas in lyric poems) or pieces of texts (paragraphs in novels) as a means to gain access to latent energies that already exist within them but remain unrecognizable in their original form. Take, for instance, Wentworth's powerful and climactic letter to Anne near the end of the novel (257–58; vol. 2, ch. 11). I ask students to analyze why the letter is so powerful, and they typically respond with a myriad of very good reasons related to how Wentworth starkly relays his personal romantic feelings—for the first time—to Anne and reader alike. But what if we gave ourselves license to deform the letter into its component parts? I show the class examples from Samuels and McGann's work on deforming parts of Wallace Stevens's "The Snow Man" (40–45). Following this lead, one group sets out to list all Wentworth's verbs, and another isolates his use of first- and second-person pronouns. As this latter group deforms Wentworth's letter on the board, the results are astounding. Here's how the letter appears, shorn of all but its pronouns:

I I you
my You my I
me I
I myself you your
I
you I
I you
you I you you
my I
I I you
I I
me You I
You You

I I
I

I ask what such deformative diagramming of the letter helps us see. Students relish pointing out how this letter operates in contradistinction to so much of the physical and emotional distancing that makes up the bulk of the interactions between Anne and Wentworth up until this point. The concentrated use of "I" and "you" at last collapses this emotional and physical distance in dramatic fashion. Furthermore, the small but distinctly separated final cluster of three *I*'s in the letter's postscript also reinforces Wentworth's position that, as my students note, Wentworth has done all he can in baring his feelings and so demands action from the "you" that is Anne, since the ball is now in her court.

In another exercise in deformation meant to plumb the depths of Austen's characterization, I instruct students (in groups or individually) to formulate sentiments that would never be included in letters written by various characters. Over the years, I've seen student-constructed letters from Mary to her older sister Anne that essentially say, "marriage is so boring; don't do it!" Mock letters from Wentworth to Anne typically have Wentworth say something like, "good heavens, Anne, how can you *not* see that I still love you!?" We do these exercises not solely to add principles we learn to principles we know but also because "deforming" the original letter helps us imagine what we don't know in different, startling, and productive new ways.

This line of inquiry usually also provides a smooth segue into discussions about what other kinds of distinguishing moves Austen makes in *Persuasion* that reveal breaks from previously encountered eighteenth-century fictional models. An essential component of any study of the novel as a genre, of course, involves an awareness of the ways in which poetry dominated most serious literary discourse even into the nineteenth century. Therefore, by the time we encounter *Persuasion* on the syllabus, my students are fully cognizant of the uphill battle that prose fiction in general, and Austen's in particular, had to mount in the face of formidable poetic output that came mostly from men. It usually astonishes the class to learn that Walter Scott—one of the most popular historical novelists of the time—at first published his novels anonymously for fear they would mar his reputation as a poet. Students armed with this knowledge often alight upon Austen's direct engagement with the issue. But if they do not, I direct them to take a closer look at Anne's discussion with Captain Benwick at the end of chapter 11. A dejected Benwick has recently lost his fiancée, and the narrator describes the interaction in the following way:

> He was evidently a young man of considerable taste in reading, though principally in poetry; . . . and having talked of poetry, the richness of the present age, and having gone through a brief comparison of opinion as to the first-rate poets, trying to ascertain whether *Marmion* or *The Lady of the Lake* were to be preferred, and how ranked the *Giaour* and *The Bride of Abydos*; and, moreover, how the *Giaour* was to be pronounced, he shewed himself so intimately acquainted with all the tenderest songs of the one poet [Scott], and all the impassioned descriptions of hopeless agony of the other [Byron]; he repeated, with such tremulous feeling, the various lines which imaged a broken heart, or a mind destroyed by wretchedness, and looked so entirely as if he meant to be understood, that [Anne] ventured to hope he did not always read only poetry; . . . she ventured to recommend a larger allowance of prose in his daily study; and on being requested to particularize, mentioned such works of our best moralists, such collections of the finest letters, such memoirs of characters of worth and suffering, as occurred to her at the moment as calculated to rouse and fortify the mind by the highest precepts, and the strongest examples of moral and religious endurances. (108–09; vol.1, ch. 11)

Most critics suggest that Austen is referring to such moralists as Samuel Johnson, who in his *Rambler* essays, in Boswell's words, provided "bark and steel for the mind" (i.e., fortifying medicine; Boswell 117; qtd. in J. Austen, *Persuasion* 365n12). However, when my students make connections to *Robinson Crusoe* and *Pamela*, they understand that Austen's defense of prose as against poetry is a significant step toward the elevation of prose, even of prose fiction, as instigating a more realistic treatment of human emotional challenges than the outpouring of personal feeling in lyric poetry.

We then make the further connection back to the theoretical underpinnings of the course in which various critics describe the early novel's truth-based realism as providing the opportunity to feel like somebody else—something that occurs far less often in lyrical poetry. Students also really enjoy Austen's extended effort to show how reading realistic prose—whether by Samuel Johnson or Samuel Richardson—can help alleviate Benwick's personal suffering. When we encounter Benwick again in chapter 14, he is doing far better, and Charles Musgrove explicitly links his emotional recuperation to his prose reading: "His head is full of some books that he is reading upon your [Anne's] recommendation, and he wants to talk to you about them; he has found out something or other in one of them which he thinks—Oh! I cannot pretend to remember it, but it was something very fine—I overheard him telling Henrietta all about it . . ." (142; vol. 2, ch. 2). Witnessing Austen elevate other kinds of writing above poetry almost always helps students see the novel as an *emerging* form—all the more so because during this period, the novel was felt to be the "natural" realm of women writers. Such a view is very different from the way most students enter the class (automatically seeing the novel as the ascendant, gender-encompassing literary form that it has become today).

Of all *Persuasion*'s components that make it a rich novel to teach in a genre course, however, none is as important or as influential as Austen's pioneering use of free indirect discourse. Students always report that they feel unusually close to a number of characters in *Persuasion*, but they are usually not quite sure why. This is a particularly vexed pedagogical juncture that I encounter often while teaching courses in the history and theory of the novel: in order for students to understand and appreciate how various components of the novel genre unfurl, they need to focus on how and why earlier novelists developed new formal techniques. Austen's pioneering use of free indirect discourse is certainly one of these moments.

Before I provide a working definition for free indirect discourse, I find it useful to investigate where in the text students feel closer to certain characters despite the fact that the novel is narrated in the third person. Moving from novels like Richardson's *Pamela* to *Persuasion*, it is hard not to feel closer to characters whose emotional characterization is more complex, so I press my students to say more about how they interpret or internalize this sense of closeness in Austen's work. When pressed, students say they feel like they somehow know the essential characteristics and feelings of even the secondary cast in *Persuasion*. Most students, for example, report feeling an intense narcissistic, privileged, and even juvenile, whiny tone emanating from Sir Walter Elliot from the novel's outset. I ask the students to locate places in the text where this feeling emerges. A paragraph appearing early in chapter 2 comes up often, so I put it up on the board:

> How Anne's more rigid requisitions might have been taken, is of little consequence. Lady Russell's had no success at all—could not be put up with—were not to be borne. "What! Every comfort of life knocked off!

> Journeys, London, servants, horses, table,—contractions and restrictions every where. To live no longer with the decencies even of a private gentleman! No, he would sooner quit Kellynch-hall at once, than remain in it on such disgraceful terms." (14; vol. 1, ch. 2)

Reading such a passage closely reveals much about how the best narration in the novel operates. Where, I ask, do we see Walter Elliot's dismissive narcissism, whininess, and juvenility? Students point to Sir Walter's petulant dismissal of both Anne's and Lady Russell's suggestions: Anne's are "of little consequence," and Lady Russell's "could not be put up with" and "were not to be borne." Then we wonder aloud about the curious but very subtle twists of narrative dexterity on display here. Clearly, the class notes, the paragraph begins with a fairly straightforward third-person narration that is meant to describe Sir Walter's reactions to advice about how to retrench and save the dwindling family money. But students identify Sir Walter's voice ("could not be put up with," "were not to be borne") even in the supposedly straightforward narration. This leads us to scrutinize Austen's use of quotation marks. It feels like the narrator channels Sir Walter's actual voice to give us his thoughts on the matter. A particularly perspicacious student usually notices a problem at this point: if Sir Walter is actually speaking these lines, how do we explain the shift—from within the quoted remarks—back to third-person narration ("No, he would sooner quit Kellynch-hall")?

This complex, subtle, and utterly effective mode of narrative exposition, my class learns, is possible because of free indirect discourse (FID). My colleague Laura White provides as good a technical definition of FID as any I know:

> In FID, the narrator renders not merely the point of view of a given character (focalization) but gives the flavor of a character's speech or thought. In the most direct form of FID, the narrator ventriloquizes for the character; in other words, the reader senses that by changing third person pronouns to first person ones, one would have a rendering of the character's direct speech or thought. . . . The narrator is speaking, but the language is really [Sir Walter's], including his use of clichés and hyperbole.

At this point, I've found it helpful to break the class up into groups and ask them to collectively scour the text for similar moments of FID. This is a very useful exercise because FID is more art than science. It is never totally clear cut, and students returning from their group work often encounter a sense of equivocality about their chosen passages. For example, the passage above involving Walter Elliot is somewhat atypical of FID because of the quotation marks. To assess this sense of the narration's complex and subtle ventriloquizing of a character's inner thoughts, students often point to a passage at the start of chapter 8 where the third-person narrator fluidly slips into Anne's perspective. Though Captain Wentworth and Anne Elliot "were repeatedly in the same circle,"

> [t]hey had no conversation together, no intercourse but what the commonest civility required. Once so much to each other! Now nothing! There *had* been a time, of all the large party now filling the drawing-room at Uppercross, they would have found it most difficult to cease to speak to one another. . . . Now they were as strangers; nay, worse than strangers, for they could never become acquainted. It was perpetual estrangement. (68–69; vol. 1, ch. 8)

Partly because of Austen's use of exclamation points and italics, but also because of the general movement from exposition ("They had no conversation together") to intense emotional feeling ("Once so much to each other!"), students correctly identify this passage as aligning with Anne's inner thought process.

But this is a literary device, not a mathematical formula. Even most undergraduates, therefore, are happy to learn that a group of scholars at their institution, the University of Nebraska, have built a Web site dedicated to experimenting with language use in Austen's novels—a significant part of which is dedicated to visualizing FID in all the author's major works. In *Austen Said: Patterns of Diction in Jane Austen's Major Novels*, a team of digital humanists led by White have produced a gold mine for investigating complex word usage in Austen. Though there are multiple ways in which this site is pedagogically useful, I point my class to the section on visualizing FID in *Persuasion*. Here, students can test their hunches about where FID occurs (and to what degree) against where the digital humanists have identified it. The site divides Austen's novels into chapters, so one can click on any chapter of the (major) novels and see a color-coded representation of the text of that chapter (fig. 1).

When FID is being introduced, the text appears highlighted in yellow. Where the narrative is indirect (though not totally free), the text appears highlighted in a spectrum of light to dark gray. The lighter gray highlighting corresponds to the "less certain" and the darker gray to the "more certain" ends of the spectrum. FID is tracked similarly, from pink highlighting for "less certain" to red highlighting for "more certain." The important element to note, here, is that the digital humanists at Nebraska are by no means dogmatic about their findings or their visualizations on this Web site. In fact, they invite students and scholars to use the site to record and justify their own interpretations, and anyone may access the tool. Thus, student participation in this process is a ready-made and extremely productive pedagogical exercise.

By using *Austen Said*, students come to see that this mode of narration allows for a far deeper connection with a given character's interiority and psychological state. Participants in the course History and Theory of the Novel are, perhaps for the first time, in a unique position to register the gravity of such a new narrative technique; they have seen the one-hundred-year accretion of

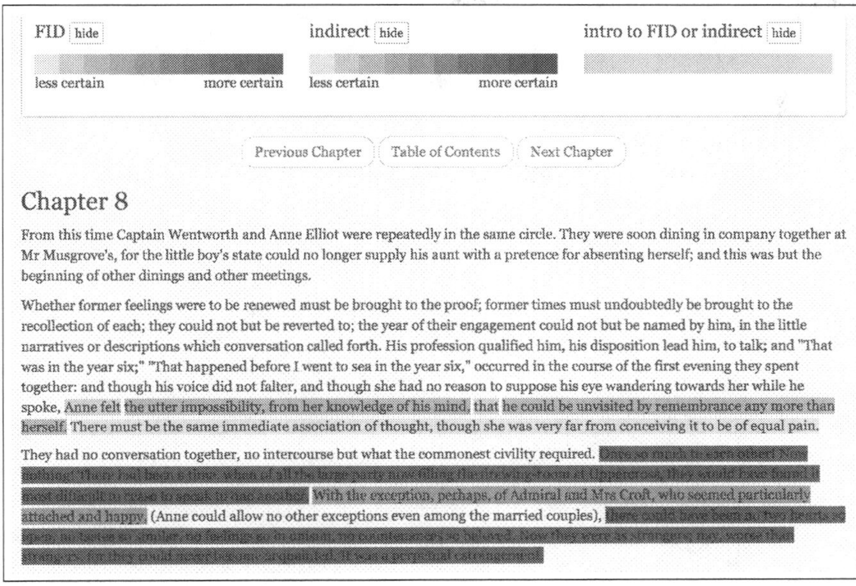

Figure 1. Screenshot of FID visualization from *Austen Said: Patterns of Diction in Jane Austen's Major Novels*.

more and more complex narration, from *Robinson Crusoe* up to *Persuasion*. As many students eventually surmise, and articulate in extremely accurate twenty-first-century parlance, FID was "a game changer" in the history of the novel. Furthermore, they continue to see the game changer in action, as it influences practically every novel on the syllabus after *Persuasion*: *Wuthering Heights*, *Hard Times*, *Madame Bovary*, and *The Picture of Dorian Gray*.

Teaching Persuasion *in a Nineteenth-Century Survey*

Reform is likely to be an overarching theme of any survey course on nineteenth-century British literature. The catastrophism and violence of the French Revolution was met with slow and gradual reform in England. These changes to the British social and cultural landscape involved not just the official Reform Bills (of 1832, 1867, and 1884) but also deeply systemic shifts in power that affected classes, professions, gender roles, the rights of property ownership, and other elements of social life. *Persuasion* is an ideal text to teach relatively early in a survey of the nineteenth century because it predicts, almost *avant la lettre*, many of these important cultural shifts. Although change, reform, and what we might call historical awareness are not typically the hallmarks of Austen's fiction prior to *Persuasion*, I teach this novel in my survey course precisely because of its engagement with the real current of history—specifically, the Napoleonic wars. Admiral

Croft has served in "the Trafalgar action" before the events of the novel begin (24; vol. 1, ch. 3). Moreover, Captain Wentworth has spent the eight years before the novel begins accumulating a fortune of 25,000 pounds in bounty payments for French vessels he captured during the war. Make no mistake: *Persuasion* is a love story just like Austen's other novels, but it is one that is predicated on "very specific social and economic circumstances, and those circumstances are profoundly affected by the outcome of the Napoleonic wars" (Cantor 128).

This, along with several other attendant dimensions of the text, makes *Persuasion* an anomaly in Austen's oeuvre. Taken as a whole, these dimensions anticipate changes that will come to British society much later in the century. Students are usually unaware that this is the only one of Austen's novels in which the action takes place in a specific historical moment (1814–15) close to the time of the novel's composition. Perhaps more important, *Persuasion* is the only one of Austen's novels to feature a male hero (Wentworth) who does not come from the landed gentry. This surprising anomaly is of a piece with many other pivotal social and economic "predictors" that I assure students will come to define the changing conditions of the nineteenth century. We witness one of these changes at the outset of the novel when the baronet Sir Walter Elliot is forced to rent out his ancestral estate to the navy's Admiral Croft. Such a dramatic shift in economic power predicts the larger pattern of events that will play out in the course of the century: namely, wealth becomes less and less tied to the landed gentry's ownership of land and more and more entwined with a professional middle-class claim to commerce. As Paul Cantor has put it, "Austen understands how in England a process of social and economic evolution accomplished more fully what political revolution attempted to bring about in France. . . . With the Napoleonic wars looming in the background of [*Persuasion*], the contrast between France and England is striking" (128).

It has been my experience that the idea of an emerging middle class is often confusing for North American undergraduates. This is partly because the sense of middle-classness has become more of an ideology than an economic category in the United States, where a vast majority of the population now consider themselves middle class (Martin).

As a result, there's some significant spadework to be done to convince students that the middle class did not always exist (i.e., that its emergence is the result of both historical and economic processes) and that the ruling gentry and the classes above them harbored an incredibly demeaning attitude toward the middle class. I direct students to pay particular attention to the dialogue at the end of chapter 3, where much of the delineation of class mentioned above is on display in the conversation between Mrs. Clay, Anne, and the Elliot family lawyer, Mr. Shepherd. Sir Walter is fumbling to ascertain where he has encountered the name of Wentworth before, and Mr. Shepherd (referring to Mrs. Croft's brother) mentions "the gentleman" who was a curate at Monkford. Sir Walter responds by saying, "I have no conception of whom you can mean, Shepherd; I remember no gentleman resident at Monkford since the time of old Governor Trent" (25; vol. 1, ch. 3). Once the confusion is settled and Sir Walter learns that his lawyer is referring to Mrs. Croft's brother, his dialogue is even more revealing: "Wentworth? Oh! Ay,—Mr. Wentworth, the curate of Monkford. You misled me by the term *gentleman*. I thought you were speaking of some man of property: Mr. Wentworth was nobody, I remember; quite unconnected; nothing to do with the Strafford family. One wonders how the names of many of our nobility become so common" (26).

Since there is so much to be gleaned about the British class system in this exchange, I usually write the passage on the board for close reading. Students usually notice Sir Walter's insistence on a specific meaning of "gentleman." In England at this time the term usually referred to someone who had a legitimate claim to land—very different from the term's use in North American culture. Furthermore, students today almost universally interpret the use of social titles, such as *Mr.* or *Mrs.*, as an indicator of respect. Indeed, this passage in the novel is a perfect place to teach Austen's foresight regarding the evolution of conventions of respectability in the nineteenth century. Power and respectability transfer during this time period from people with titles before their names (such as Sir, Baronet, Marquess, etc.) to people with titles after their names, as is the case in Robert Louis Stevenson's 1886 work *The Strange Case of Dr. Jekyll and Mr. Hyde*—a text I teach later in the semester, and one in which we encounter the protagonist described as "Henry Jekyll M.D., D.C.L, LL.D, F.R.S., &c." (11).[1]

So where, the students astutely ask, is the middle class in *Persuasion*'s depiction of the nineteenth century's first decades? This, I try to demonstrate to them, is where Austen's incorporation of the navy into the fabric of the narrative becomes even more ingenious. One of the central tenets of professional writing communities is to "write about what you know," and Jane Austen did just this. She did not have many real connections to the emerging middle-class industrialists and clerks who were beginning to transform (literally and figuratively) the British landscape in the second decade of the century. But she did have a connection to the navy through her brothers Francis and Charles. She would have known, as her depiction of Captain Wentworth's rise in status undoubtedly indicates, that the British navy was a far more meritocratic institution than the army—where commissions could still be purchased by wealthy families. That the navy was a meritocratic institution is underscored by the brief identification of Richard Musgrove's futile (and fatal) experience aboard Captain Wentworth's ship. Members of the navy during the Napoleonic wars were incentivized to capture enemy ships because they could collect payment for the sale of such vessels. Therefore, as Cantor has cogently argued about the "Navy men": "in their money-making, they exhibit the commercial and entrepreneurial spirit of the middle class, but in their service to their country, they display a patriotism that lifts them above purely mercenary means" (132). They are, in effect, treated as an acceptable professional prototype of the middle class—a treatment that eventually allows Wentworth to marry the daughter of a baronet.

Students are usually quick to note how Austen emphasizes the professionalism of members of the navy by contrasting it to the leisured lifestyles embodied by the Elliots and the Musgroves. It is worth noting, here, that each of the novel's final two sentences refers to the navy as a "profession" (275; vol. 2, ch. 12). In Austen's Regency England, to be part of the gentry class means doing very little in comparison to the naval officers who defend the nation. This distinction represents another colossal change. For centuries, the nobility's claim to rule had been based on military leadership. Preeminence in social and political matters went hand in hand with preeminence on the battlefield. This is certainly no longer the case in *Persuasion*, where baronets like Sir Walter and viscounts like Lord Dalrymple have left it to the Admiral Crofts and Captain Wentworths to ensure their safety from foreign invasion.

Once we've established the forward-looking, dare I even say progressive, thinking of Austen vis-á-vis the navy, I ask students to look for other dimensions of the text that seem similarly predictive of what they know about the trajectories of other social dynamics. This prompt usually leads to a discussion of the various ways in which women are treated in the novel. And since we've already invested so much analysis examining noble and middle-class social structures, students typically feel confident assessing Austen's treatment of women along these lines. First, we collectively think through Austen's descriptions of upper-class women's behavior. Elizabeth Elliot, who has inherited her father's narcissistic demeanor, seems genuinely incapable of maintaining a relationship with a would-be husband and, thus, remains single. Mary (Elliot) Musgrove appears indifferent toward her husband, overwhelmed by her children, and generally bored by her life among the landed gentry. Though Anne changes her views (and her actions) significantly over the course of the novel, students are often quick to point out that she allows herself to be persuaded by Lady Russell to break off her engagement with a financially unproven sailor.

Anne eventually displays many admirable qualities that separate her from her sisters, but until she does, the naval wife Mrs. Croft stands out as a harbinger of feminine assertiveness and independence. I ask the class where we see such qualities exhibited in the text. I should note, here, that since this is a survey course on nineteenth-century literature, at the start of the semester we read reactions to the French Revolution by Edmund Burke ("From *Reflections*") and Thomas Paine, but also selections from Mary Wollstonecraft's *A Vindication of the Rights of Men* ("From *A Vindication of the Rights of Men*") and *A Vindication of the Rights of Woman* ("From *A Vindication of the Rights of Woman*"). Since Wollstonecraft argues for the treatment of women as "rational creatures" (225)—using this exact phrase more than ten times in the latter work—my students almost always pick up on Mrs. Croft's use of the expression in the discussion with Captain Wentworth about whether women should be allowed on board naval vessels.

Here is the important dialogue from Mrs. Croft that students recognize as a précis of Wollstonecraft's argument: "But I hate to hear you [Wentworth] talking so, like a fine gentleman, and as if women were all fine ladies, instead of rational creatures. We none of us expect to be in smooth water all our days" (J. Austen, *Persuasion* 75; vol. 1, ch. 8). When read closely, this passage underscores much of what the students have come to associate as the differences between the English nobility and the emerging middle class. As students perceive it, quite accurately, Mrs. Croft is taking Wentworth down a peg. A "fine gentleman," in Wollstonecraft's words, doesn't treat women as rational creatures but instead "flatter[s] their fascinating graces, and view[s] them as if they were in a perpetual state of childhood, unable to stand on their own" (4). Students trace Mrs. Croft's remonstrance to several interactions between the Crofts in which they exhibit a more progressive, middle-class sense of marital partnership. Only a few pages after this scene, for instance, the narrator tells us that, unlike the splintering of activities by gender in upper gentry circles, "the Admiral and Mrs. Croft were generally out of doors together, interesting themselves in their new possessions, their grass, and their sheep, and dawdling about in a . . . gig" (79; vol. 1, ch. 9).

Once we've made the Crofts' interactions our focus, the class often delights in pointing out how Austen goes into greater detail regarding the reversal of typical gender roles when we encounter the Crofts driving in an actual gig. At the end of chapter 10, Admiral Croft nearly drives the gig into a post, but Mrs. Croft mock-heroically intervenes:

> "My dear admiral, that post!—we shall certainly take that post."
>
> But by coolly giving the reins a better direction herself, they happily passed the danger; and by once afterwards judiciously putting out her hand, they neither fell into a rut, nor ran foul of a dung-cart; and Anne, with some amusement at their style of driving, which she imagined no bad representation of the general guidance of their affairs, found herself safely deposited by them at the cottage. (99; vol. 1, ch. 10)

Here we have a stroke of brilliant Austenian irony at its finest: an admiral who succeeded in commanding vessels on the high seas during the war with France has to be helped by his wife in steering a gig out of "danger" on land.

This observation by Anne (by way of the narrator) provides a good opportunity to ask the class why Anne is so impressed by Mrs. Croft's words and actions. The question more often than not elicits responses about the transformation of Anne's character that takes place over the course of the novel. I then ask where we encounter this transformation in the text. One of the places where we see a definitive transformation, my students decide, is during the trip to Lyme when Louisa jumps and falls from the steps. While everyone else (naval officers included) react with stunned horror at what appears to be the death of Louisa, Anne acts with decisiveness and confidence. Mary hysterically screams "She is dead!, she is dead!" Charles Musgrove suddenly becomes "immoveable" by the horror, Henrietta similarly "los[es] her senses" and begins to faint, and even Captain Wentworth becomes queasy—summoning only the ability to exclaim, "Oh God! her father and mother!" (119; vol. 1, ch. 12). In the company of navy men who have fought bravely in the Napoleonic wars, Anne is the one who gives orders and restores calm to the scene. The narrator tells us that "Captain Benwick *obeyed* [Anne]" and that "every thing was done that Anne had prompted" (119; emphasis added). The Anne who engages in this kind of assertive behavior, we decide, is a far cry from the young woman who thought it best to yield to her family's belief that Wentworth was not a suitable match for a baronet's daughter.

Although Austen is not often thought of as a feminist, the exploration of gender relations in *Persuasion* is generally predictive of what eventually became known to the Victorians as the woman question. Many supporters of expanded rights for women later in the century, such as Harriet Taylor, Marion Kirkland Reid, and John Stuart Mill, drew on Mary Wollstonecraft's work. It is important for students to see that Jane Austen did so in her final published novel decades before these significant social reformers.

NOTE

[1] The various qualifications in Jekyll's name stand for, respectively, doctor of medicine, doctor of civil laws, doctor of laws, and fellow of the Royal Society.

Mapping the Chronology of *Persuasion*

William Nelles

Nearly a century ago R. W. Chapman and Sir Frank MacKinnon published the first chronologies for Jane Austen's novels in Chapman's classic 1923 Clarendon Press edition, *The Novels of Jane Austen*. The initial appeal of these chronologies, which consisted of summaries of datable plot events, lay primarily in the illumination they promised to bring to questions about Austen's methods of composition. Of particular interest were her revisions of "First Impressions," the original version of *Pride and Prejudice*. Critics had offered widely divergent theories about the scope and timetable of the revamp, and the chronologies seemed to offer a method for getting to the bottom of these questions. Chapman and MacKinnon's analysis of "Miss Austen's punctilious observance of the calendars of 1811 and 1812" throughout the novel suggested that the book had been thoroughly revised during those two years: "we must modify the assumption which is commonly made, though it rests on slender evidence, that *Pride and Prejudice* as we have it is substantially the same book as 'First Impressions'" (Chapman, "Chronology" 406). Chapman's conclusion was widely accepted and initiated a vogue for using almanacs to trace the course of Austen's revisions, especially for the earlier works. Scholarly interest in these chronologies pretty much dried up once the questions of dating had been carried as far as they could be, and for several decades the chronologies were by and large dismissed as period curiosities.

But the topic of chronology in Austen has attracted renewed attention in the twenty-first century. In the 2004 MLA volume *Approaches to Teaching Austen's* Emma, the editor, Marcia McClintock Folsom, defends the study of chronology as a "useful tool for students" (xxviii) that helps readers to see the "governing rhythms of the seasons beneath the novel's surface," recognize key features of "the novel's realism" (xxix), and link "the passage of time and Emma's growth into adulthood" (10). Folsom also includes a detailed chronology of her own in a section called "Teaching about *Emma*'s Chronology" (9–12).[1] For *Persuasion*, we now have two thorough chronologies of the novel's events, in Ellen Moody's online version from 2003 (Moody, "Calendar for *Persuasion*") and in David M. Shapard's *The Annotated* Persuasion (Shapard), and for biographical and historical dates, Deirdre Le Faye has published the exhaustive *A Chronology of Jane Austen and Her Family*, with some 15,000 entries filling 779 pages.

While these more comprehensive chronologies are primarily designed as tools for reference or research, a less detailed chronology—I offer an example below—can be a valuable resource for students, including first-time readers of *Persuasion*. At the most basic level, it can help students keep track of the major events in the plot and the main actions and movements of the more important characters (as short as the novel is, it still has some five dozen named characters). For *Persuasion* in particular, the only Austen novel in which the opening chapter is dated—to the summer of 1814—a chronology can be valuable in providing students with some of the indispensable historical context that informs the action within the novel and some of the biographical context that illuminates Austen's reasons for writing the novel.

Austen declared of *Pride and Prejudice*, with characteristically self-deprecating wit, "The work is rather too light & bright & sparkling . . . it wants to be stretched out here & there with . . . something unconnected with the story; an Essay on Writing, a critique on Walter Scott, or the history of Buonaparte . . ." (*Jane Austen's Letters* [Le Faye, 3rd ed.] 203).[2] As critics have long noted, while war is never explicitly mentioned in *Pride and Prejudice*, the backdrop of the militia camps, so important a part of the plot, reflects the date of the original composition of the novel, 1796, the year a French armada was narrowly prevented from invading Ireland by dangerous weather. In *Persuasion* (the first work she had written during a time of peace since the short pieces posthumously collected in *Juvenilia*), Austen brings the military background closer to the foreground; indeed, even though Napoleon is never explicitly mentioned in the novel, numerous critics have noted his importance for understanding the plot. The central action of the story begins when the Peace of Paris allows the British navy to come home after Napoleon's defeat, and its last datable event (the card party at Camden Place) takes place on 25 February, the day before Napoleon escapes from his exile on Elba and that peace ends. Perhaps even more striking is the fact that Austen began writing the novel the day after Napoleon was sent to his final exile on St. Helena and on the very day that the London papers announced it. Furthermore, the real experiences her brothers had as naval officers during the Napoleonic wars provided many of the details that she incorporated into the stories of Admiral Croft, Captain Frederick Wentworth, and the other sailors in the novel.

One can readily see from the chronology in the appendix at the end of this essay how the novel slows down and zooms in as we approach the climax of Wentworth's love letter: the list of datable events unrolls at first year by year, then month by month, and finally day by day. We can also see how tightly the historical context is tied to the characters' actions and motivations; for instance, the Peace of Paris triggers the reunion of Anne Elliot and Wentworth by allowing the sailors to come home. As William Deresiewicz puts it, "Subtly, covertly, without announcing as much, Austen makes the events of the novel coincide precisely with the period of Napoleon's first exile," synchronizing "the novel's personal drama of loss and love with the national drama of war and peace" (146–47). Critics have speculated that the final defeat of Napoleon helped to inspire Austen's writing of the novel itself, providing both a catalyst—"Napoleon's exile to St. Helena seems to have prompted her to begin writing *Persuasion*" (Harris 17)—and a theme: in Brian Southam's judgment, "Austen set out to write a determinedly morale-boosting novel, a story designed (with an eye on the sailor brothers) to show the Navy in its best light, recalling the great days of Trafalgar and St Domingo. . . . Opening as it does in the summer of 1814—with Na-

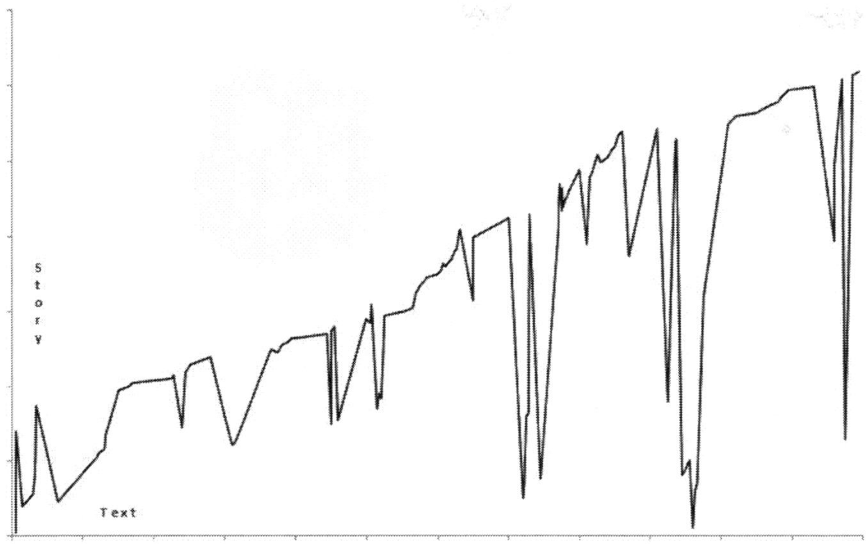

Figure 1. Time map of events in *Persuasion*, using data from Shapard. Created by Linda Williams.

poleon despatched to Elba and the Navy scaling down—*Persuasion* was also designed to show the profession in peacetime" (*Jane Austen* [1st ed.], 265).

I briefly explore here one more way to use the chronologies associated with Austen's novels. Narrative theorists have demonstrated that few, if any, stories are told in strict chronological order, and the study of these temporal anachronies has become a matter of considerable interest for narrative analysis.[3] The data gathered in the chronologies allow us to derive charts for depicting narrative sequence with a single line—a time map. The method is simple. Every chronology, in effect, assigns two coordinates to every event recorded: one for its place in the chronology and one for its place in the telling of the story. The chronologies list the events of the plot in strict chronological order, or in what narrative theory would call the order of the story (or fabula), and we can number these events consecutively to provide data for what will be the y-axis of our chart. But every chronology also provides page numbers for these events, which reflect the order in which the events are mentioned in the text (called *syuzhet*, or discourse order). These page numbers provide data for the x-axis of our chart. Entering the data from Shapard's chronology for *Persuasion*, for instance, produces the time map visible in figure 1.

Even at a first glance, a time map enables us to make some broad claims about the chronology of the novel. We may begin by observing that the earliest events in the story—indicated by "Walter Elliot, born March 1, 1760," and by the series beginning "married, July 15, 1784, Elizabeth," and continuing through the children's birthdates—are narrated by means of Sir Walter's perusal of the Baronetage on the first page of the text and include the crucial detail of the stillborn son that explains Mr. Elliot's claim on the entailed estate (3; vol. 1, ch. 1).[4] To note that the novel begins at the beginning may seem like a truism, but the novel presents an unusual narrative structure: narratives are far more likely to begin in medias res. As is typical of Austen's novels, no events prior to the ones introduced by this terse biographical sketch of the heroine's family will be mentioned. In the jargon of narratology, there are no "external" flashbacks, or analepses, that present events prior to this narrative beginning. As the map shows, however, there are frequent "internal" analepses, as the characters repeatedly rehash and rethink events that have been presented earlier in the novel, a feature that Folsom has called the "pattern of reviewing a past that exists within the novel itself" (*Approaches to Teaching Austen's* Pride and Prejudice 3).[5] In Deresiewicz's formulation, "Anne and Wentworth recover the future by recovering the past" (144). Kathryn Sutherland's analysis of the structure of the opening sentence of *Persuasion* leads her to an apt description of the structure of the entire work as highlighted by the time map, which announces in "the mounting crescendo of its repetitions what will be the mood and leitmotiv of the narrative as a whole—repetition and return, where lives like sentences revisit, reinhabit their earlier shapes" (285).

At a more detailed level, such time maps can help us assess the various factual and interpretive claims critics have made about the temporal progression of *Persuasion* and refine and extend even the most insightful analyses of Austen's method. David Lodge's argument, for example, that "Jane Austen's narratives rarely deviate from chronological order" might at first blush seem emphatically contradicted by the map, since each of the numerous downward spikes in the time map in figure 1 marks a flashback. But Lodge astutely stipulates three crucial exceptions to his own rule: "If there is a retrospective account of some event antecedent to the main action or a delayed explanation of some event in the main action, either it is incorporated into the time span of the main action in the form of a letter . . . or in dialogue, . . . or it is briefly summarized in a nonscenic way by the authorial narrator (e.g., the account of Anne Elliot's former relationship with Wentworth at the beginning of chapter 4 of *Persuasion*)" (173). We can test Lodge's hypothesis with a rapid survey of the ten most salient flashbacks listed in the time map, which are identified in figure 2. The authorial narrator's flashback in chapter 4, which is mentioned in the quotation from Lodge above and which is labeled as point 4 in the figure, is repeated (as always, with variations) at the end of volume 2, chapter 11, in dialogue between Anne and Wentworth (point 10). The same pattern is followed for the backstory of Anne's "old schoolfellow" Miss Hamilton (165; vol. 2, ch. 5), which is provided in a summary by the narrator (point 6), and for Mrs. Smith's backstory, which is provided in dialogue (point 7). Other flashbacks are communicated, consistently with Lodge's hypothesis, in a letter written by Mr. Elliot in 1803 (point 8), in which he mentions, among other events, his birthdate, having "lived three and twenty years in the world" (point 9).

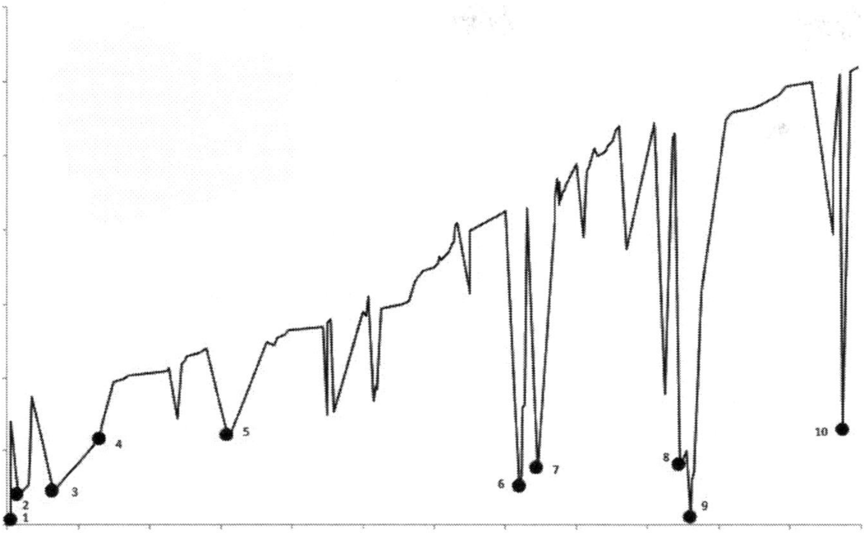

Figure 2. Flashbacks in *Persuasion*, using data from Shapard. Created by Linda Williams.

The map not only confirms the general accuracy of Lodge's list of Austen's devices for handling flashbacks but also helps us make some minor additions to it, including Austen's ingenious deployment of embedded texts other than letters to motivate flashbacks, as in the citations from the Baronetage already noted (points 1 and 2) and in the use of the Uppercross navy list to introduce the topic of Wentworth's stints on the *Asp* and the *Laconia* (point 5). Austen also relies on characters' thoughts to convey flashbacks, using free indirect discourse rather than dialogue, as when describing Lady Russell's belief that Anne would dislike moving to Bath with Sir Walter in part "from her happening to be not in perfectly good spirits the only winter which she had afterwards spent there" following her breakup with Wentworth (16; vol. 1, ch. 3; point 3). Free indirect speech is signaled here by, among other details, the erasure of Lady Russell's own agency in persuading Anne to dismiss Wentworth ("happening to be") and by the understating of Anne's grief as imperfectly "good spirits." The claim that the majority of the flashbacks are embedded within dialogue, characters' thoughts, or inserted texts helps account for the feeling so many readers have that the novels proceed in a linear fashion, though the novels are really no more or less disordered chronologically than most other novels. As Lodge sums it up, "[T]here is a minimal disruption of chronological order in Jane Austen's novels. We don't encounter in them the *effect* of flashback, in which the temporal progress of the main action is suspended and for a while effaced by the scenic presentation of an earlier event" (173; emphasis added).[6]

Apart from the critical and theoretical applications that time maps have for literary analysis, they may also contribute more generally to our students' ability to think about quantitative data. Michael C. Burke—among many others—contends that quantitative literacy must be addressed beyond its traditional disciplinary confines and proposes that "we begin by redesigning our freshman and sophomore writing programs in order to place a significant emphasis on working with quantitative data, and on the visual representation of that data." We can help with that work in our literature classes by teaching students to generate their own time maps, an activity that, among other things, demands that they become close rereaders of their target text. I offer students in most of my classes—not just classes on Austen—the option of producing a time map as one component of their research projects, and my experience has been that they enjoy the activity and learn a great deal from it. I ask them to construct their own chronologies from scratch, but students producing time maps of Austen's *Persuasion* could also build them from any of the chronologies published by Chapman, Moody, or Shapard; they could, in fact, assemble a time map merely by looking up the page numbers for the events listed in the Shapard chronology that are presented in this essay.[7]

NOTES

1 Most faculty members must regularly mimic Austen's practice in this regard, synchronizing their lesson plans with each term's academic calendar just as Austen coordinates the events of her novels with a current calendar, and this mimicry may be one of the underlying reasons why the idea of the chronologies resonates with so many of us.

2 That Scott and Napoleon Bonaparte were nearly inevitable examples rather than random ones is neatly confirmed by Jocelyn Harris's observation that Scott's famous review of *Emma* appeared in an issue of *The Quarterly Review* that also contained eight reviews of books about Bonaparte (74). Harris wittily, if hyperbolically, asserts that in *Persuasion* Austen "essentially writes here the history of Buonaparte that she threatened to insert into *Pride and Prejudice*" (17).

3 See Nelles and Williams for a general discussion of these matters, and Nelles on Austen's novels.

4 As Janet Todd and Antje Blank observe, "it was very unusual to record a still-born child. Debrett's *Baronetage* noted the deaths only of young children and infants" (J. Austen, *Persuasion* 335n6).

5 The distinction between internal and external analepses was articulated first by Gérard Genette (49). As with many issues in narrative temporality, there is ample opportunity to split hairs here: the opening paragraph of the novel (not reflected in the Shapard chronology used for this map) describes Sir Walter's habit of reading his own history in the Baronetage, so the subsequent flashback to the birth of Walter, as related in the page he then reads, could justifiably be considered an external analepsis, which is the path K. R. Ireland takes in her analysis of narrative sequence in the novel (211–13); she does, however, note that analepsis in "other Austen novels . . . is nearly always internal" (212).

6 This effect of linearity has misled numerous fine critics, including Ireland, who contends that in terms of temporal order "only *Persuasion* diverges at all significantly from the relatively unelaborated linear presentation which characterizes Austen's other nov-

els" (211). Having done time maps for all the novels, I can attest that the structure of *Persuasion* is quite similar to the others: *Northanger Abbey*, which is notably more linear than the rest, is the only outlier.

[7.] Linda Williams has created a series of step-by-step video tutorials designed to help students construct time maps: see Williams, *Time Maps: Part 1*, *Time Maps: Part 2*, *Time Maps: Part 3*, and *Time Maps: Part 4*.

APPENDIX: Chronology

Events in *Persuasion* are listed in roman type. EVENTS IN BRITISH HISTORY AND IN THE LIFE OF JANE AUSTEN APPEAR IN SMALL CAPS.

1760	1 March. Sir Walter Elliot is born.
1775	16 December. JANE AUSTEN IS BORN.
1780	Mr. William Elliot is born.
1784	15 July. Sir Walter Elliot and Elizabeth Stevenson are married.
1785	1 June. Elizabeth Elliot is born.
1786	FRANCIS AUSTEN ENTERS THE ROYAL NAVAL ACADEMY.
1787	AUSTEN BEGINS WRITING HER *JUVENILIA*.
	9 August. Anne Elliot is born.
1789	5 November. A stillborn son is born to Sir Walter and Lady Elliot.
1791	CHARLES AUSTEN ENTERS THE ROYAL NAVAL ACADEMY.
	3 June. AUSTEN WRITES THE LAST OF HER *JUVENILIA*, "AN ODE TO PITY."
	20 November. Mary Elliot is born.
1793	1 February. FRANCE DECLARES WAR ON GREAT BRITAIN.
1800	Lady Elliot dies.
1801–04	Anne attends school in Bath.
1801–06	AUSTEN LIVES IN BATH.
1802	Mrs. Smith (then Miss Hamilton) leaves the school.
	25 March. THE PEACE OF AMIENS SUSPENDS THE WAR WITH FRANCE.
1802–03	Sir Walter and Elizabeth seek out William Elliot.
1803	"SUSAN" (LATER TITLED *NORTHANGER ABBEY*) IS SOLD BUT NOT PUBLISHED.
	16 May. NAPOLEON BREAKS THE PEACE OF AMIENS.
	18 May. WAR WITH FRANCE RESUMES.
1803 or 1804	Mr. Smith and Miss Hamilton marry.

Chronology *(continued)*

1803 and 1804	The Austens visit Lyme Regis.
1804	Mr. and Mrs. William Elliot marry. Austen probably begins "The Watsons." 18 May. Napoleon is proclaimed emperor.
1805	Admiral Croft fights with the White Squadron in the Battle of Trafalgar. 3 October. Captain Francis Austen dines with Admiral Nelson aboard his ship, the *Victory*, but is dispatched to Gibraltar the next day, thus missing the battle. 21 October. Nelson defeats the French and Spanish fleets at the Battle of Trafalgar.
1806	6 February. The Battle of San Domingo occurs, in which the British defeat a French attack on the island. Frederick Wentworth is made commander after the Battle of San Domingo. Francis Austen earns the Naval Gold Medal for his part in the Battle of San Domingo as flag captain of the *Canopus*.
1806	Wentworth begins a six-month stay with his brother in the summer; his romance with Anne proceeds; Lady Russell persuades Anne to break off her engagement to Wentworth; and Wentworth is given command of the *Asp* and cruises the West Indies.
1807	Wentworth captures a French frigate.
1808	Wentworth is posted to the *Laconia* and cruises the Western Islands (the Azores). Walter Scott's *Marmion* is published.
1809	Anne refuses an offer of marriage from Charles Musgrove; Wentworth cruises the Mediterranean Sea. 7 July. Austen moves into Chawton cottage and begins revising *Sense and Sensibility* and *Pride and Prejudice* for publication.
1810	Scott's *Lady of the Lake* is published. 10 May. Charles Austen is promoted to post captain. 16 December. Charles Musgrove and Mary Elliot marry.
1811	February. Austen begins *Mansfield Park*. 30 October. *Sense and Sensibility* is published.
1812	Richard Musgrove dies; Captain Harville is wounded; Captain Benwick and Fanny Harville are engaged.

Chronology *(continued)*

1813 LORD BYRON'S *GIAOUR* AND *BRIDE OF ABYDOS* ARE PUBLISHED.

Mr. Smith dies.

28 January. *PRIDE AND PREJUDICE* IS PUBLISHED.

June. Fanny Harville dies.

July. AUSTEN FINISHES *MANSFIELD PARK*.

1814 21 January: AUSTEN BEGINS *EMMA*.

11 April. THE TREATY OF FOUNTAINBLEAU ENDS NAPOLEON'S RULE; NAPOLEON IS EXILED TO ELBA.

9 May. *MANSFIELD PARK* IS PUBLISHED.

30 May. THE PEACE OF PARIS IS SIGNED, FORMALLY (ALBEIT TEMPORARILY) ENDING THE NAPOLEONIC WARS.

June. Mrs. William Elliot dies.

(The current action of the novel begins and lasts eight months or so.)

July? Sir Walter concedes the need for retrenchment. Mr. Shepherd predicts, "This peace will be turning all our rich Navy Officers ashore. They will all be wanting a home" (19; vol. 1, ch. 3). Admiral and Mrs. Croft inspect Kellynch Hall and make an offer.

September. Sir Walter, Elizabeth, and Mrs. Clay leave for Bath in early September; Anne goes to Kellynch Lodge with Lady Russell for a week, then to Uppercross for two months, staying there into November.

29 September. The Crofts take possession of Kellynch Hall on Michaelmas.

October. Wentworth arrives at Kellynch Hall; Charles Musgrove is injured in a fall; Anne and Wentworth meet again at Uppercross after almost eight years.

November. The group from Uppercross goes to Lyme Regis; Anne and Benwick talk of "Mr. Scott and Lord Byron" (116; vol. 1, ch. 12); William Elliot sees Anne; Louisa's accident occurs; Wentworth stays in Lyme about a fortnight; Anne goes to stay with Lady Russell.

December. Wentworth goes to Plymouth for a week, then to Shropshire for several weeks. William Elliot arrives in Bath; Anne and Lady Russell visit the Musgroves during the Christmas holidays.

1815 January. Anne and Lady Russell go to Bath; Anne renews her friendship with Mrs. Smith.

1 February. Mary writes to Anne that Louisa will return home the next day; shortly after, Louisa's engagement to Benwick is

Chronology *(continued)*

announced; the Crofts come to Bath; Wentworth learns of the engagement from Harville and writes to his sister.

11 February? Anne and Admiral Croft stroll down Milsom Street in Bath.

15 February (Wednesday). Wentworth arrives in Bath.

16 February (Thursday). Anne encounters Wentworth at Molland's shop on Milsom Street.

17 February (Friday). Anne (with Lady Russell) sees Wentworth in Pulteney Street.

19 February (Sunday). Nurse Rooke finishes attending on Mrs. Wallis.

20 February (Monday evening). Nurse Rooke tells Mrs. Smith that Anne is to marry William Elliot.

22 February (Wednesday). Anne sees Mrs. Smith briefly and talks to Wentworth at the evening concert.

23 February (Thursday). Mrs. Smith acquaints Anne with William Elliot's real character; William Elliott says he will leave town Friday morning; the Musgroves and Captain Harville arrive in Bath and lodge at the White Hart Inn.

24 February (Friday). Charles and Mary Musgrove visit the Elliots; Anne returns with them to the White Hart; Harville and Wentworth show up; Mary sees William Elliott with Mrs. Clay; Sir Walter and Elizabeth leave invitations for their party.

25 February (Saturday). Anne spends the day at the White Hart with the Musgrove party; Wentworth writes his letter; Sir Walter hosts his party at Camden Place in the evening.

26 February (Sunday). NAPOLEON ESCAPES FROM HIS EXILE IN ELBA.

Soon after: Anne and Wentworth's engagement is announced; William Elliot and Mrs. Clay leave Bath together; there is dread of impending war; Wentworth secures Mrs. Smith's property in the West Indies.

20 March. NAPOLEON RETURNS TO PARIS; THE HUNDRED DAYS WAR BEGINS.

21 March. THE ADMIRALTY SUSPENDS THE DEMOBILIZATION OF THE FLEET.

29 March. AUSTEN FINISHES *EMMA*.

1 April. CHARLES AUSTEN IS ORDERED TO HUNT FOR ONE OF NAPOLEON'S SQUADRONS IN THE ADRIATIC SEA.

Chronology *(continued)*

18 June. The Battle of Waterloo ends more than twenty years of war with France.

15 July. Napoleon surrenders to the captain of the *Bellerophon* (later commanded by Charles Austen).

30 July. Byron publishes an anonymous, untitled poem, "Napoleon's Farewell."

30 July. Austen copies out Byron's poem and titles it "Lines of Lord Byron, in the character of Buonaparte."

7 August. Napoleon is moved to the *Northumberland* to be transported to his exile on Saint Helena.

8 August. News of Napoleon's exile is published in the London papers: "Bonaparte has sailed" (Southam, *Jane Austen* [2nd ed.] 271). Austen begins writing "The Elliots" (later published as *Persuasion*).

23 November. Austen thanks her publisher for loaning her Scott's *The Field of Waterloo*.

23 December. *Emma* is published.

1816 March. Scott's review of *Emma* appears in *Quarterly Review*.

18 July. Austen finishes the first draft of *Persuasion*.

6 August. *Persuasion* is completed.

"The Navy Who Have Done So Much for Us": Professional and Domestic Ideology in *Persuasion*

Monica F. Cohen

Class discussions about the role of the navy in *Persuasion* can highlight the radical cultural, political, and aesthetic shifts that make up the novel's central concerns. *Persuasion*'s naval figures acquire value in the culture of the novel by virtue of their skills in—surprise!—domesticity. Rather than recounting combats of clashing cutlasses and crashing cannons, enemy boardings, or sea chases, the novel introduces the navy to home audiences when Anne Elliot remembers Captain Frederick Wentworth answering questions about the quotidian details of life at sea, including its regulations, its food, its hours, its cooks and servants, and its knives and forks (vol. 1, ch. 8). This transposition of military values onto homemaking establishes a language for discussing the novel's poignant turn away from a social order organized around the ownership of land and toward one organized around acquired cultural capital and individual merit. Calling attention to the novel's deployment of maritime domesticity allows students to think about what is at stake in *Persuasion*'s radical swapping of the landed estate for the sea.

The only one of Austen's heroines to find her happy romantic ending far from the security of a Pemberley or a Mansfield Park, Anne Elliot recovers her beauty and her central place in the marriage plot at the same time that the navy enters the world of the novel with a social authority once reserved for the traditional landed classes. I use two scenes to explore the constellation of ideas that the novel associates with the cultural ascendency of the navy: Wentworth's storytelling at Uppercross, where a rapt audience of admirers invests him with both social and narrative authority, and the narrative sequence at Lyme Regis where Anne has new insights about the officers who inhabit the Harvilles's rented rooms. Read together, the scenes work well to anchor class discussions about how a sailor with "nothing but himself" (29; vol. 1, ch. 4) is transformed into the socially enfranchised romantic lead of an Austen novel.

Displaced from her ancestral home, Anne witnesses Wentworth's postwar social reentry when the Musgroves gather around the navy list (70; vol. 1, ch. 8), an exciting new addition to their library, while Wentworth regales them with his exploits at sea, "his profession" qualifying "him to talk" (68). Interestingly, the only danger Wentworth mentions facing in his time serving the nation during the Napoleonic wars seems to be a storm that could have overtaken his vessel and ended his gallantry. But he primarily talks about two dimensions of his naval career. The first is the structure of economic compensation that enabled men without social connections to make fortunes. Sailors like Wentworth received prize money: a share of the proceeds from selling the contents of captured ships or selling warships to the crown. Wentworth specifies that much of his luck in the war was financial, including when he captured a "French frigate" after capturing some mildly lucrative privateers and then making fast money cruising the Western Islands and sailing in the Mediterranean Sea (71; vol. 1, ch. 8). Prize money was sometimes controversial because profit seeking and military strategy did not always align, but the distribution of prize money was nevertheless a common means for compensating sailors whose salaries did not always reflect their sacrifices (Southam, *Jane Austen* [1st ed.] 128). Without overtly questioning this practice, the scene calls students' attention to the morally complicated theater of wartime moneymaking. It also calls attention to the new sources of wealth that were responsible for replacing landowners like the impecunious Sir Walter Elliot with navy men like the sensible Admiral Croft. Similar perhaps to the Antigua property that is the source of Sir Thomas Bertram's wealth in *Mansfield Park*, the wartime profit seeking that enriches Wentworth complicates his heroism in ways that students usually do not expect.

The second dimension of the naval career of Wentworth as it materializes in the scene at the Musgroves' takes shape in Anne's depiction of Wentworth as a charismatic conversationalist who answers the admiring Musgrove sisters with surprising "accounts" of daily life, reminding Anne of the time in their courtship when "she too had been accused of supposing sailors to be living on board without any thing to eat, or any cook to dress it if there were, or any servant to wait, or any knife and fork to use" (69; vol. 1, ch. 8). Filtered through Anne's registering consciousness, Austen's representation of the navy includes details designed to entertain young women who have little knowledge of maritime life, thus creating a way to establish Wentworth's domestic authority. Indeed, Mrs. Musgrove takes this discourse even further, depicting Wentworth as a virtual domestic manager when she credits him with turning her son, Richard, into "such an excellent correspondent, while he was under your care" (73). Even the cultivation of family responsibility seems to be a matter of naval leadership taking shape as surrogate parenting or teaching. While it is probably more accurate to say that Richard was under Wentworth's command, Mrs. Musgrove sees the arrangement as "care." While *Persuasion*'s naval officers might debate the wisdom of allowing women on board their ships as visitors or travel companions, Austen's use of female characters—Mrs. Musgrove, the Musgrove sisters, and Anne Elliot—as narrative lenses turns the representation of the floating community that is a naval ship toward domestic rather than military values.

The life in Britain's navy that Wentworth narrates for the consumption of the Musgroves contrasts interestingly with a similar scene in *Mansfield Park* when William Price also entertains a family circle with his adventures at sea. Like Wentworth, William has earned "a right to be listened to" by virtue of his naval profession (J. Austen, *Mansfield Park* 275; vol. 2, ch. 6). But whereas Wentworth mentions the war almost exclusively in terms of his career—the *Asp*, for example, "would be the making of me," and a sea battle was "good luck" because it pitted him against "the very French frigate I wanted," presumably for its financial value (J. Austen, *Persuasion* 71; vol. 1, ch. 8)—William, the passage makes clear, had "known every variety of danger, which sea and war together could offer," and thus tells of shipwrecks and battles (*Mansfield Park* 275; vol. 2, ch. 6). Whereas the Musgroves are filled with "pity and horror" at Wentworth's imagined death in a storm he luckily avoided (*Persuasion* 71; vol. 1, ch. 8), the "horror" experienced at Mansfield Park incites even the imperturbable Lady Bertram to "wonder any body can ever go to sea" while inspiring Henry Crawford with passionate admiration for "a lad who, before he was twenty, had gone through such bodily hardships, and given such proofs of mind" (*Mansfield Park* 275; vol. 2, ch. 6). Although Lady Bertram is the only character whose speech is quoted in the *Mansfield Park* scene, William's reported account of his time at sea is prompted by Sir Thomas's questions, in contrast with Wentworth's account in *Persuasion*, which is prompted by the questions of the Musgrove sisters. This shift in emphasis between the two novels is worth considering in so far as *Persuasion* seems to be using the navy to characterize its male hero in terms that depart from the commonplaces of adventure fiction—sea battles and shipwrecks. The difference emphasizes the domesticity that punctuates the novel's representation of Wentworth's naval career.

A classroom strategy can make this contrast between Austen's treatment of the navy in the two novels accessible to students. After briefly characterizing *Mansfield Park* for students unfamiliar with it, a teacher can circulate a handout of the scene where William Price talks about his life at sea, which can be examined alongside the abovementioned scene in *Persuasion*, and which is useful for organizing a class discussion about the contrast between a representation of the navy as primarily an expression of military adventure and a representation of the navy as primarily an expression of domestic values. Asking students to identify in each scene the language that is associated with naval service will bring the contrast into focus. In the *Mansfield Park* chapter, the emphasis is on "every variety of danger, which sea and war together could offer," and on "bodily hardships," "exertion," and "endurance" in William's stories (275; vol. 2, ch. 6). This language contrasts interestingly with Captain Wentworth's talk, in chapter 8 of volume 1 of *Persuasion*, about "the manner of living on board, daily regulation, food, hours &c." Students can also notice how each scene is focalized: in *Mansfield Park*, it is mostly through Sir Thomas, whereas in *Persuasion*, it is through Anne. These contrasts can help students think about how *Persuasion* uses the navy to bring domestic life into focus.

The language of "care" that Mrs. Musgrove introduces into the novel's depiction of the navy complicates its domesticity insofar as it emerges around the controversial detail of Richard Musgrove's death (J. Austen, *Persuasion* 73; vol. 1, ch. 8). Whether or not students agree with critics who have taken issue with Austen's callous depiction of "poor Richard" as a person who is "thick-headed, unfeeling, unprofitable" and whom no one was very sorry to lose (54; vol. 1, ch. 6), I think it is important to the novel that the Musgroves see Wentworth as a caregiver for their son and a preserver of family feeling. He is a hero to them explicitly because of his domestic responsibilities and not, at least not explicitly, because of his service in winning the war against France. Along these lines, I have found that short excerpts from D. W. Harding's chapter on *Persuasion* in *"Regulated Hatred"* (163–70) are useful here for teasing out the complexities of Wentworth's exchange with Mrs. Musgrove about Richard. As Harding points out, Wentworth's kindness to Mrs. Musgrove, his consideration for "all that was real and unabsurd in the parent's feelings" (J. Austen, *Persuasion* 73; vol. 1, ch. 8), balances critical awareness with genuine sympathy in speech that Harding calls a "mingling of tones" (165).

Interestingly, this mingling of discrimination and sympathy also characterizes both Wentworth and Anne as they each adjust to new environments: Uppercross, Bath, and Lyme Regis. In a novel that early on constructs its fictional world as a collection of "little social commonwealths" each with its own "matters of discourse," this mingling of tones as a matter of Austen's narrative style reflects what perhaps marks Anne and Wentworth as particularly modern characters: discrimination tempered by sympathy serves them both as a necessary disposition for the geographic, intellectual, and psychological mobility that characterizes their plotlines, bolstering their ability to navigate so many little commonwealths and to emerge as modern, cosmopolitan subjects. Like their narrator, Anne and Wentworth employ a mingling of tones as they move across the novel's various communities: Wentworth's consideration for all that was real and unabsurd in another's feelings matches Anne's willingness to learn the new discourses demanded by her "transplant[ation]" (*Persuasion* 46; vol. 1, ch. 6). In this sense, noting the inclusion of domestic details in the scene that depicts Wentworth's maritime profession helps students begin to identify the navy's role in the novel, the social values the navy heralds, and the worldview it cultivates. The sequence of events that features a depiction of Wentworth's discrimination mingled with sympathy originates in his domestic duties as a naval captain. Here students can also see how the work of characterization—the representation of Wentworth's personality—informs and is informed by a matter of style: the narrator's mixed tones.

This idea that there are alternative commonwealths and that these alternatives are welcome to both men and women informs the scene's final exchange about the navy: while Wentworth insists that he will never welcome women on board his ship, students are surprised that his sister, Mrs. Croft, uses the words "danger" and "suffer[ing]" to characterize the experience of women when they are not at sea in the company of their husbands (76; vol. 1, ch. 8). While Wentworth's sense of maritime domesticity seems to be all male at this early stage in the novel, it is also defensive, since women did indeed sometimes travel with the navy, even if this was not routine. Mrs. Croft's voice here works as a corrective: embedding her happy, companionate marriage in an evolving maritime culture, she suggests that the navy represents new opportunities for women as well as men. It is worth discussing in class why the novel depicts these new opportunities as socioeconomic for men and psychological for women. The differences the novel reveals between the opportunities the navy offers to men and those it offers to women could make students ask if emotional reward is an adequate compensation for real social and economic suffering. Thus, while the apparently egalitarian Croft marriage is one positive result of the social order on a sailing ship, the idea that the navy is good for women gets complicated in the episode involving Mrs. Smith. Here the structural inequality that prevents the poor and sick widow from straightening out her finances after the death of her reckless husband seems less intolerable when Wentworth intercedes on her behalf, an action that seems to suggest that the new social order will benevolently provide for dependent women. Wentworth's intervention, however, allows Mrs. Smith to gain from her dead husband's colonial holdings, an outcome that troubles Wentworth's heroism by implicating the navy, however associatively, in colonial exploitation. What gains there are for dependent women at home come at someone else's expense somewhere else.

The second significant place where the novel's professional navy cooperates with domesticity is the outing to Lyme and the narrative sequence that reinstates Anne at the center of the novel. When a group of young people take a short trip to Lyme, various previously unexplored attractions materialize, and the sequence provides the novel with a turning point. Not only does exposure to the sea air magically restore Anne to her youthful beauty, but Lyme is also where Anne witnesses sailorly skill—craft, contrivance, and ingenuity—applied to domestic space. In the Harvilles' rented rooms in Lyme Regis, Captain Harville applies maritime skills to make the lodging house rooms the "picture of repose and domestic happiness," as described in an unqualified paean to this new way of being in the world. Indeed, Captain Harville cultivates "the pleasanter feelings" that make the crafting of lodging-house furniture an expression of friendship and family by means of an expertise he gained through his professional career: "He drew, he varnished, he carpentered, he glued; he made toys for the children, he fashioned new netting-needles and pins with improvements; and if every thing else was done, sat down to his large fishing-net at one corner of the room" (106; vol. 1, ch. 11). Appearing without direct objects, the verbs coalesce around the idea of ongoing work while the cropped phrasing and rhythmic repetitions lyricize it. The fishing net, an apparently eternal work in progress, testifies to Harville's maritime career, but it can also be recuperated on a symbolic plane as a gesture toward the Gospels, wherein Jesus bids the fishermen to join the ministry as fishers of men (Matt. 4.18–20). While I hesitate to push this interpretation too far, the fishing net offers an occasion for the class to consider the novel's spiritual rhetoric, however spare. At the very least, the net associates this community of naval officers with an ethic of care that inflects their heroism with nonmilitary affiliations.

While the rented rooms contain "common necessaries" provided for "the common indifferent plight," the "ingenious contrivances" of Harville attest to the power of his professional expertise and shipboard work habits to convert the cramped space into "the picture of repose and domestic happiness" (J. Austen, *Persuasion* 106; vol. 1, ch. 11). It is interesting that many years later, Jane

Austen's brother Francis wrote, "I rather think parts of Captain Harville's [character] were drawn from myself. At least some of his domestic habits, tastes and occupations bear a strong resemblance to mine" (Le Faye, *Family Record*, 274). Domesticity as a picture may emerge here aestheticized and sentimentalized, but it is also imagined as a product of wartime work at sea, "connected as it all was with his profession, the fruit of its labours" (J. Austen, *Persuasion* 106; vol. 1, ch. 11). This partnership between professional and domestic ideology informs the novel's use of the scene to identify the direction of its romantic line of development, for it is here in the coastal community of Lyme that Anne meets Wentworth's affectionate brother officers and wistfully remarks to herself that they "would have been all my friends" (105), in a poignant revision of Elizabeth Bennet's similar musings in response to seeing Mr. Darcy's formidable estate, Pemberley, in *Pride and Prejudice*: "And of this place . . . I might have been mistress!" (J. Austen 272; vol. 3, ch. 1).

But while Elizabeth Bennet's mood in this *Pride and Prejudice* scene is the same as Anne's mood in the *Persuasion* scene, the two considerations of what might have been express very different political and social ideals. To be mistress of Pemberley is to join the vertical hierarchy of landowning families and to revitalize its traditions with new blood. To join a circle of friends is to aspire to a social order that is radically democratic in its reliance on the horizontal bonds that unite equals. Listing the attributes of these moments in the two novels provides a chance for students working together to contrast the qualities of a social order based on landed estates with a social order based on circles of friends. *Persuasion* represents the culture of landed wealth and the culture of the navy as being in competition. A large critical consensus understands this competition in terms of inherited versus merited privilege (Harris 107); economic recklessness versus economic sobriety (Copeland); and the superficiality of social calls among the fashionable versus genuine affection among naval officers (Green). Indeed, the novel represents the bonds that transform the brother officers into a viable community as resembling what sociologists call the substitute kinship tie (Duneier 175n4). This interest in alternatives to the biological kinship of the family suggests *Persuasion*'s anticipation of a significant principle of social organization in modern life: friends from work. While Wentworth is apparently close to his biological brother and sister, it is his "brother-officers" who appear at this pivotal moment in the plot (J. Austen 105; vol. 1, ch. 11)—it is their society and their values that are dramatized and their company that Anne aspires to. Here *Persuasion*'s complex representation of family and substitute kinship allows students in general education and survey courses to make connections to other texts, across time, culture, and genre.

A useful illustration of the tension between the culture of land and the culture of the sea inheres in the contrast between the navy lists, which the Musgroves are so proud of owning, and Austen's fictional version of the Baronetage, which opens the novel by introducing the Elliots through an entry that notes the stillbirth of their male heir on 5 November 1789, a date fraught with significance not only because it refers to the start of the French Revolution but also because it is Guy Fawkes Night in Britain. A class discussion comparing images of these two books usually encourages even the quieter students to participate (as I have found using visual material in class usually does). However precious it might be to Wentworth and however trendy it is among the Musgroves, the navy list was published as a set of inexpensive booklets printed in cramped lettering with tight margins on thin, low-quality paper and wrapped in a blue cover held together by glue (Barchas 210). Its "throwaway" format attests to its relation to news (211): issued monthly, its record of rankings during wartime changed rapidly. In this sense, it was the fast-paced literature of current events. By contrast, *The Baronetage of England* was published in a handsome leather-bound set of volumes and sold at eighteen times the price of the navy list (Barchas 210). While changes in the listings of *The Baronetage* also happened (when military heroes, for example, were made baronets), those changes occurred at a slower rate, thereby justifying the lavish materials devoted to the volume's reissues.[1] Nevertheless, as Barchas argues, Austen's tricky transposition of names complicates the relation between land and sea: the names of *Persuasion*'s naval heroes (e.g., Wentworth and Croft) are listed in *The Baronetage*, while many of the aristocractic characters in the novel are associated with naval enterprise (e.g., Carteret and Dalrymple; Barchas 206). This complication allows students to see the nuances in Austen's complex representation of cultural change. The new order of naval heroes might recapitulate—or at least preserve—pieces of the old order after all. The navy's domestic virtues thus invite students to wrestle with both the conservative and the subversive energies animating this complex novel.

NOTE

[1] See "Jane Austen in Austin" for an example of the edition of the navy list that the Musgrove family would have owned; see Debrett's for the kind of production values associated with Sir Walter's copy of the Baronetage.

The Influence of Austen's Naval Family Members on the Creation of *Persuasion*

Sheila Johnson Kindred

Jane Austen had a very personal understanding of the British navy and of naval families. She was vitally interested in the naval careers of her brothers Francis and Charles; she was also knowledgeable about the naval experiences of Charles's wife, Fanny Palmer Austen. An awareness of the wide-ranging world that Charles and Fanny and Francis made available to Jane Austen adds to our understanding of her remarkable ability to conceive of lives unlike her own with such deep, imaginative sympathy. The Napoleonic wars raged through most of Jane Austen's life, and the British navy was heavily engaged in them.[1] Francis served at sea during the wars. Charles and Fanny were also actively involved: they lived in naval ports and on warships, though they naturally had different responsibilities and perspectives because of their gender. Intriguingly, Jane Austen made a connection to North America through her familiarity with Charles's career and Fanny's involvement when Charles was assigned to the North American squadron from 1805 to 1811.[2]

This essay suggests how Jane Austen's naval family played a role in in the writing of *Persuasion*. The intimacy of Austen's relationships with her sailor brothers, and later with Charles's young wife, is suggested in the surviving letters, which provide insight into the detailed information Austen would have learned from them about the navy. There are parallels between their lives and experiences and the imagined lives of Captain Frederick Wentworth, Mrs. Croft, and Anne Elliot in the novel.[3] Austen was skilled in incorporating contextual details into her writing that were drawn from actual events in which her brothers were involved.

Jane Austen had closely followed her brothers' careers from when they began studies at the Royal Naval Academy, Portsmouth, through their years as midshipmen, and subsequent service and promotions to lieutenant and then post captain, a rank Francis achieved in 1800 and Charles in 1810. Thus, she had access to details about naval life for three decades of their careers. Not many letters from Jane Austen to Francis have survived,[4] but those that have reflect her keen interest in where he was stationed and how his career was progressing. She had a special bond with Charles. As the two youngest Austen children, she and Charles had grown up together in their father's vicarage in Steventon, Hampshire, until Charles left for his naval studies when Jane was fifteen. She affectionately referred to him as her "own particular little brother" (*Jane Austen's Letters* 38 [21–23 Jan. 1799]).

Jane Austen became connected to Fanny when Fanny married Charles in 1807. Fanny lived either in Bermuda or in Nova Scotia, as Charles's duties as a rising officer on the North American Station required. In June 1811, Fanny sailed with Charles and their two very young daughters across the North Atlantic to England, where he was commissioned as the captain of HMS *Namur*, the admiral's flagship at the Nore, which was the anchorage off shore from Sheerness, Kent. There Fanny courageously made a home for herself and her family on board the ship. Interspersed with the sometimes difficult, even dreary, living conditions at sea were occasions when Fanny and Charles joined Austen family gatherings in Hampshire and Kent.[5]

Jane Austen's association with Fanny Austen began by correspondence while Fanny was still in North America, and it was cemented into a closer bond when Fanny came to England. Charles and Fanny paid regular visits to Chawton, and Jane and Cassandra sometimes cared for their children. In becoming an Austen, Fanny joined a literary family whose members exchanged opinions by letters they passed around, though regrettably many have been lost. Fanny's own letters show her to be expressive, reflective, and willing to share her views. Through letters, and later through direct conversations, Jane Austen learned about Fanny Austen's role as an officer's wife in a naval world.

Austen began writing *Persuasion* on 8 August 1815, and by then she had plenty of sources of information about naval life. The Austen family regularly followed published naval news available in *Steel's Naval List*, the *Naval Chronicle*, and the *London Gazette*. Jane had lived in the port town of Southampton from 1806 to 1809, so she would have witnessed naval activity from shore.

Yet Jane Austen gleaned some of the most valuable information that would shape the writing of *Persuasion* from her contacts with her naval family members. Certainly, she would have been attracted to, and found more memorable, the personal narratives of individuals she loved and valued. In her correspondence with Charles, Austen learned about the many hazards of prize taking, that is, seizing an enemy vessel in order to get a share of the sale value of it and its cargo, ranging from the occasional lucky capture to experiences of regrettable loss, physical and financial as well as human, and all this from a brother whose activities in North American waters took place in the years shortly before she began to write *Persuasion*.[6] She could read about naval prizes in many sources, but it was much more immediate and poignant to learn directly from Charles about a promising prize taking that went wrong when the captured vessel never made it to port for adjudication.[7]

Francis, Charles, and Fanny were all effective communicators, both by letter and in person. Although only one of the letters that Charles wrote to Cassandra survives (a letter that also would have been read by Jane), it provides evidence of the immediacy of his descriptions. Jane Austen commented on Charles's writing skills, remarking "how pleasantly & how naturally he writes! and how perfect a picture of his Dispositions & feelings, his style conveys!" (*Jane Austen's Letters* 315 [26 Nov. 1815]). Unfortunately, no correspondence from Fanny to the Austen family has survived, but her extant letters to her own family, written in 1810 from Halifax, Nova Scotia, and from 1812 to 1814 from England, offer good examples of the lively and direct comments that characterized her accounts about naval life.[8] The appendix includes extracts from letters by Charles and Fanny that suggest how compelling they were as witnesses to the complexities of naval life.[9]

What Jane Austen learned from Charles likely inspired features of her portrayal of Captain Wentworth. There are numerous resemblances. Both men began prize taking as commanders of their own small sloops, Charles Austen's "dear old *Indian*" (C. Austen) and Frederick Wentworth's "dear old *Asp*" (J. Austen, *Persuasion* 71; vol. 1, ch. 8). Both were on foreign stations at the time (1805–06), the North American Station for Charles, and the West Indies for Wentworth (70; vol. 1, ch. 8). They were about the same age, serving as commanding officers for the first time, and were soon posted to their own frigates, Charles Austen to HMS *Cleopatra* in 1810, and Frederick Wentworth to the "*Laconia*" in 1808 (268; vol. 2, ch. 11). Like Charles, Wentworth enjoyed the company of his brother officers both in port and at sea, where he also hoped they would profit from capturing enemy vessels and their cargoes and earning prize money. There is even a similarity in their appearances. Charles Austen was known for his "charm of manner [and] handsome face."[10] Wentworth is first described as "a remarkably fine young man" (28; vol. 1, ch. 4), and emphasis is placed on his "glowing, manly, open look, in no respect lessening his personal advantages" (65; vol. 1, ch. 7).

As to the amount of prize money accrued, Wentworth came out much better than Charles Austen did. Although Charles collected more than £540 from the capture of the French privateer *La Jeune Estelle* in September 1808,[11] and probably received about £350 more from favorable decisions in six other cases, his prize money was reduced by fees, and also by costs in those instances when the judgments of the Vice Admiralty Courts of Bermuda and Halifax were not in his favor.[12] Charles Austen's net income from prize money was a far cry from Wentworth's impressive sum of £25,000. The difference is significant in the plot of *Persuasion*. Making a fortune by taking prizes was hazardous but offered a unique opportunity for men in the navy to increase their incomes and advance their prospects. Jane Austen understood well how prize taking might improve the social standing and marital prospects of a successful captain. When Captain Wentworth returns to Somerset in 1814, he has obtained rank and wealth enough to overcome Sir Walter Elliot's objections to his suit to Anne.

Fanny Austen was as able as Charles to inform Jane Austen about naval life, and crucially, her contribution was from a female point of view. Some of her experiences seem to have found their way into the lives of Austen's female characters, including Mrs. Croft and Anne. After Charles was sent to a European war zone in July 1810, Fanny confesses that "Captain Austen's sudden departure, & the uncertainty about his returning [completely] upset me. If he is not here by the middle of Sepr. I shall give him up."[13] Her distress is palpable. Later, a joyful Fanny writes: "I have been made happy by the return of my beloved Charles, which, after the arrival of the July [Mail] Packet, I had quite despaired of."[14] Fanny's situation is reminiscent of Mrs. Croft's when the then captain Croft was away at sea and Mrs. Croft had no way of knowing how he was faring (71; vol. 1, ch. 8).

Jane Austen's awareness of Fanny's life within the naval world may also be reflected in Austen's portrayal of Anne's feelings. In her letters, Fanny reports on the support she received from naval officers and their families in both North America and England. On the North American Station, Fanny and Charles enjoyed the supportive friendships of Charles's colleagues—Captains Edward Hawker (who was godfather to Fanny and Charles's daughter Cassy), Frederick Hickey, and Samuel Pechell as well as other officers—and the thoughtfulness of Admiral Sir John Warren (Charles's commander in chief). Fanny also observes that Admiral Sir Thomas Williams, Charles's superior in England, possessed a "warmth of manner which you rarely meet with."[15] Similarly, when she is in Lyme, Anne meets with generous examples of naval collegiality from Captain and Mrs. Harville and notes Wentworth's kindness to the grieving Captain Benwick.[16] She recognizes their deep friendships: "'These would have been all my friends' was her thought; and she had to struggle against a great tendency to lowness" (105; vol. 1, ch. 11).

Fanny's marriage to Charles involved Fanny in his career in an immediate way, including the many serious risks of his naval world. Her feelings veered between keen satisfaction and deep anxiety. Her happy family life within the naval community was mixed with periods of worry over the hazards her husband faced when he was away at sea in wartime as well as over the uncertainties of employment in the naval profession and, thus, their financial stability. As Charles's appointment as captain of the *Namur* approached its end, Charles hankered for active sea service once more, and he thought that a posting to the North American Station might be coming his way. There he would have opportunities to accrue prize money while the war with America continued. Fanny reflects on their situation more ambivalently: "[I] do not know how I shall reconcile myself to Capt. Austens going to Sea again: . . . however, . . . it is but right that he should endeavour to be in the way of making a little money while there is an opportunity."[17] Desirable as greater financial security would be, Fanny was unhappy in the realization that a North American posting would entail separation from Charles and the attendant anxiety about his safety, along with the rupture of the intimate family life aboard the *Namur* that she was trying so hard to sustain. One is reminded, too, of Lady Russell's fears about "the chances of a most uncertain profession" (29; vol. 1, ch. 4).

Anne is free of thoughts about the joys and miseries of naval life known to Fanny Austen until the end of *Persuasion*, when she is reunited with Captain Wentworth. Their marriage promises to be very happy, yet Jane Austen reflects Fanny's experience as a naval wife in a faintly ominous concluding observation about her heroine: "The dread of a future war [was] all that could dim [Anne's] sunshine. She gloried in being a sailor's wife but she must pay the tax of quick alarm for belonging to that profession . . ." (275; vol. 2, ch. 12).

Jane Austen was adept at using factual naval references to develop her narrative. She included references to real sea battles in *Persuasion*. She placed Wentworth in the action at San Domingo (6 February 1806) when an English squadron defeated a French one off the southern coast of that Caribbean island. She was particularly familiar with that battle as her brother Francis, then captain of HMS *Canopus*, was a participant. In the novel, Wentworth's promotion to commander is made plausible by his effective performance at San Domingo (28; vol. 1, ch. 4). Moreover, by bringing Wentworth on shore after the action in 1806 to await a commission for a vessel of his own, Austen provides him with the opportunity to visit family in Somerset and thus to meet and fall in love with Anne. By arranging for Anne and Wentworth to separate later the same year, Austen allows for the eight-year gap in their relationship before their story continues in 1814, the year *Persuasion* begins.

Austen also mentions the Battle of Trafalgar (21 October 1805) in relation to the career of Admiral Croft. This most famous fleet action, when the British navy soundly defeated the French and their allies, was common knowledge for her readers. Jane Austen had a personal interest in this battle, as Francis had been part of Nelson's fleet but was greatly disappointed when his vessel, the *Canopus*, and five other warships were directed to go and replenish their water and provisions just before the British went into action. Because he was absent from the offensive, Francis was precluded from having a place among the widely feted and honored officers who, under Nelson's leadership, secured the famous victory. In *Persuasion,* Admiral Croft is luckier than Francis, for Jane Austen makes him a participant at Trafalgar. This is an apt detail in the novel: given the practice of naval promotion by seniority, it makes sense that the then captain Croft had reached the rank of rear admiral of the white by 1814.[18]

Identifying and reflecting on the use of biographical material by Jane Austen provides a way of appreciating her particular brilliance.[19] There is intriguing evidence that her characters, and their ways of life, resonate with the experiences of Charles and Fanny, Francis, and their naval associates.[20] From the actions, opinions, and emotions that Austen associated with Charles and Fanny, she selected some and imaginatively shaped them for her own purposes. The parallels between real naval life and events in *Persuasion* give readers insight into Austen's creation of fictional characters. Wentworth is entirely Austen's creation, but he reflects traces of the personality and career of the charismatic Charles. In addition, Austen's deft use of historical naval facts demonstrates her skill in contextualizing and enlivening the narrative of the novel. Exploration of these ideas offers students a glimpse into the creative genius at work in the writing of *Persuasion*.

APPENDIX
Letters by Charles and Fanny Austen

The appendix offers longer extracts from letters by Charles and Fanny that are mentioned in this essay and suggestions for ways students might explore resemblances between aspects of Charles's and Fanny's lives and Austen's portrayal of naval characters in *Persuasion*.

The letters are all transcribed in Kindred, *Jane Austen's Transatlantic Sister*. Their original spelling and punctuation are retained.

EXTRACT 1

An ecstatic Charles Austen wrote from Bermuda to his sister Cassandra on 25 December 1808.

> "[M]y beloved Fanny was safely deliver'd [of] a fine girl on the 22nd December, and . . . they are both doing remarkibley well. The Baby besides being the finest that ever was seen is really a good looking healthy young Lady of very large dimensions and as fat as butter I mean to call her Cassandra Esten and beg the favour of you to be a Sponsor your Coadjutress will be Mrs. Esten [Fanny's sister] and Captain Hawker of HMS Melampus your other partner. I esteem myself very fortunate in having been allowed to be in port at this criticale moment to support my Fanny. . . .
>
> I wrote to Jane about a Fortnight ago acquainting her with my arrival at this place and of my having captured a little Frenchman which I am truely sorry to add has never reached this port and unless she has run to the West Indies I have lost her and what is the real misfortune the lives of twelve of my people two of them mids [midshipmen], I confess I have but little hopes of ever hearing of her the weather has been so very severe since we captured her. . . . (215–16)

A great part of the duties of a British naval officer on the North American Station was to "cruize" in search of enemy vessels and to stop enemy commerce (J. Austen, *Jane Austen's Letters* 169 [24 Jan. 1809]). This repetitive and sometimes dangerous work was made acceptable by the right of the commander to seize enemy vessels and cargo for judicial condemnation as lawful prizes and to receive a quarter of their value from public sale if the court ruled in the captor's favor; the rest of the crew would also receive a share of the prize money. It was possible to accrue a considerable fortune in prize money, depending on the captain's luck and skill.

Students might be asked if they can detect any resemblances between Charles's writing and Jane Austen's narrative style and mode of thought.

EXTRACT 2

Fanny Austen wrote to her sister Esther from Bermuda on 4 August 1810, expressing her concern that there had been no word from Charles since he left Halifax on 1 July as part of a squadron ordered to deliver British troops to a war zone off the Rock of Lisbon in Portugal. Not only would the squadron have faced the dangers of crossing the North Atlantic, the six hours needed for offloading the troops and their equipment would have made the squadron vessels stationary targets for any hostile warships that might have appeared.

> [I] felt most truly for your anxiety respecting us: it was indeed a most tedious time before you heard of our arrival [in Halifax], however I hope

> you were in some degree compensated, by our letter: I shou'd have written you a much longer one, but Capt. Austen's [Charles's] sudden departure, & the uncertainty about his returning, [completely] upset me, as you will easily imagine: if he is not here by the middle of Sepr. I shall give him up; but I will not allow myself to think of it.—Many thanks for the straw plaits by Capt. Hickey. . . . (60)

Fanny's empathic response to her sister's concern, when Esther awaited news of Fanny's safe arrival in Halifax in May 1810, triggers Fanny's own admission of anxiety that Charles has not yet been heard from.

Students might be asked how important "uncertainty," which Fanny mentions, is in *Persuasion*. What other uncertainties are depicted in the characters' civilian lives?

Students might be asked what echoes can be detected between Fanny's emotional state as described in the letter and Mrs. Croft's during the winter when the then captain Croft is away at sea (J. Austen, *Persuasion* 76–77; vol. 1, ch. 8). They can be asked what Jane Austen achieved by having Mrs. Croft tell this story about herself when she was a young wife, and how the story affects readers' perception of Mrs. Croft as a naval wife.

Extract 3

Fanny's mood had changed by the time she wrote to Esther on 23 September 1810.

> Since writing you last my dear Sister I have been made happy by the return of my beloved Charles, which, after the arrival of the July [Mail] Packet, I quite despaired of—He had a most tedious passage back, which was rendered doubly unpleasant, by his great apprehension, that the Admiral would have left Halifax before he arrived; but he is, thank God, perfectly well, tho' if possible thiner than ever. . . . (68)

In writing about his return, Fanny refers to her husband as "my beloved Charles," although she ordinarily refers to him as "Capt. Austen" in her letters, even those addressed to members of her family (see extracts 2 and 4).

Students might be invited to compare Fanny's response to her husband's return with Jane Austen's presentation of the reunion of Anne and Wentworth.

Extract 4

In a letter dated 4 October 1813, Fanny confides to her brother-in-law, James Esten, in Bermuda, her confused feelings concerning Charles's stalled career. After the family had lived for some years together on board the *Namur*, which was anchored at the Nore, Charles hoped for a more active posting on a frigate, preferably one serving on the North American Station, while Britain was at war with America and prize money might be had.

> I am afraid that three years indulgence have quite spoiled me, & do not know how I shall reconcile myself to Capt. Austens going to Sea again: he is very anxious to be in active service just now & I am of course obliged to acquesce in the propriety of his wishing it but something tells me we that are much happier in our present situation: however that being only a temporary one, it is but right that he should endeavour to be in the way of making a little Money while there is an opporty [opportunity]. I look forward with great pleasure the prospect of again visiting dear little Bermuda for shou'd he be fortunate enough to get a Frigate before the American War is over he will certainly endeavour to get out on that Station & has promised that I shall accompany him. (127)

Students might be asked how far Fanny's predicament resembles the one that Anne may have to face, even in the happiness of her engagement and marriage to Wentworth, at the end of *Persuasion* (274–75; vol. 2, ch. 12).[21]

NOTES

1 The War of 1812, between the United Kingdom and the United States, took place from 1812 to 1815 and overlapped with the Napoleonic wars.

2 The Royal Navy's North American Station extended from the Gulf of Saint Lawrence to Cape Canaveral, Florida, and included the waters north, south, and east of Bermuda. St George's, Bermuda, was the station's southern base; Halifax, Nova Scotia, was its northern base.

3 Another parallel that may be explored is between the historical figure Admiral Sir John Warren and the fictional Admiral Croft. See Kindred, "Influence." See also Southam, *Jane Austen* [2nd ed.] 280.

4 Jane Austen wrote to Francis in 1805 (22, 23, 29 January); in 1809 (26 July); in 1813 (17 February, 3–6 July, 25 September); and in 1814 (21 March). All references to Austen's letters are from J. Austen, *Jane Austen's Letters* (Le Faye, 3rd ed.).

5 Jane Austen lived with her mother and her sister, Cassandra, in Chawton cottage, Chawton, Hampshire from 1809; the family also gathered periodically at Godmersham Park, Kent, home of Jane Austen's brother Edward.

6 See Kindred, "Charles." For a comprehensive analysis of naval prize taking, see Hill. See also Lavery.

7 For Charles's letter about this tragedy, see extract 1 in the appendix. For Jane Austen's reference to the lost prize, see *Jane Austen's Letters* 176 (24 Jan. 1809).

8 Fanny Austen's letters are published in their entirety in Kindred, *Jane Austen's Transatlantic Sister*.

9 Unfortunately, no letters from Francis to Jane have survived, but the clarity and detail of his writing can be judged by his descriptions of his naval activities at the time of the

Battles of Trafalgar and San Domingo in letters written to his fiancée, Mary Gibson. See Hubback and Hubback. See J. Austen, *Jane Austen's Letters* 174–76 (7 Feb. 1806).

[10] See Hubback and Hubback 54.

[11] See Kindred, "Charles Austen's Capture."

[12] See Kindred, *Jane Austen's Transatlantic Sister* 26.

[13] Fanny Austen to Esther Esten, 4 Aug. 1810 (Kindred, *Jane Austen's Transatlantic Sister* 60).

[14] Fanny Austen to Esther Esten, 23 Sept. 1810 (Kindred, *Jane Austen's Transatlantic Sister* 68). Fanny had hoped the packet boat carrying the July mail would bring news about Charles and the squadron, but there was no information to ease her increasing worries.

[15] For further parallels between Fanny and Mrs. Croft, see Kindred, "Influence," and *Jane Austen's Transatlantic Sister* 195–202.

[16] Fanny Austen to Esther Esten, 8 Mar. 1814 (Kindred, *Jane Austen's Transatlantic Sister* 155).

[17] In addition, Anne had previously overheard Wentworth's warm commitment to "assist any brother officer's wife that I could" (75; vol. 1, ch. 8).

[18] Fanny Austen to James Esten, 4 Oct. 1813 (Kindred, *Jane Austen's Transatlantic Sister* 127–28).

[19] Details in *Mansfield Park* are also connected to the real-life experiences of Francis and Charles Austen. In July 1813, Jane wrote to Francis asking if she might mention his vessel the *Canopus* and two or three others in her current novel (*Jane Austen's Letters* 222 [6 July 1813]; see J. Austen, *Mansfield Park* 437; vol. 3, ch. 7). She also used the names of two of Charles's ships, the *Endymion*, where he served as both midshipman and lieutenant, and the *Cleopatra*, his first frigate command, in *Mansfield Park* (439; vol. 3, ch. 7). In addition, the fictional William Price's gift to his sister, Fanny, of a "very pretty amber cross" parallels Charles Austen's use of prize money to purchase topaze crosses with gold chains for his sisters (295; vol. 2. ch. 8). As Jane wrote to Cassandra, "[W]e shall be unbearably fine," protesting in mock horror, "what avail is it to take prizes if he lays out the produce in presents to his sisters" (*Jane Austen's Letters* 95 [27 May 1801]).

[20] In his "Biographical Notice of the Author," Jane Austen's brother Henry observed that Jane's "power of inventing characters seems to have been intuitive, and almost unlimited," adding that "she drew from nature; but, whatever may have been surmised to the contrary, never from individuals" (H. Austen, "Biographical Notice" [*Memoir*] 141). Arguably, Austen's powers of invention were of a subtlety and complexity beyond what Henry ascribes to intuition.

[21] See the essay by Paul Westover in this volume, which addresses the tensions created by warfare as it intersects with domestic life.

"Her Own More Elegant and Cultivated Mind": Anne Elliot and Music

Gillian Dooley

This essay considers the role that music plays in Jane Austen's depiction of Anne Elliot in *Persuasion*. Anne is a unique character set apart from her society not only by her family's contempt for her and the failure of other characters to appreciate her qualities but also by her own refusal to compromise her sense of self. She is presented as a musician of a particular type: she plays the piano expertly but does not sing; she provides music for others to dance to; and she is an appreciative listener. Each of these qualities tells us something about her isolation from and invisibility to most other characters, as well as her fractured connection with Captain Frederick Wentworth, which slowly mends as the novel progresses.

Music making was a common activity in social and domestic life in Austen's time. She uses this familiar feature of her social world not to stereotype her characters but to draw precise and subtle distinctions among them and, often, to advance the narrative and dramatize characters' motivations. Drawing attention to the information Austen provides about what kinds of musicians the various female characters are—how well they perform, what part music plays in their daily lives, and their feelings and attitudes about music—will give students an excellent example of her characteristic technique of using commonplace aspects of her domestic world as elements in the drama of her narratives. Many passages from *Persuasion* could be used for exercises in close reading in the classroom. Passages about music making from Austen's other novels can also be used in classroom exercises, and in an advanced course on Austen's novels, comparisons across them might be fruitful topics of assignments or examination questions.

In addition to considering the place of music in Austen's literary practice, there is ample opportunity to use music as a lens through which to view the social and historical context of the novels: contemporary expectations of women's behavior and education, for example, or the place of musical activities in social life. Marian Wilson Kimber, a musicologist at the University of Iowa, explains various pedagogical approaches to using Austen's novels and musical activities in music history classes, and some of these approaches might be adapted for literature classes. Wilson Kimber points out that her music students could provide "insightful criticism" of literature scholars' discussions of music, and the reverse might also prove an interesting exercise. For example, a literature class might find it instructive to critique Arthur Loesser's chapter "The Piano as a Female Accomplishment" in *Men, Women and Pianos* (267–79), or Patrick Piggott's *The Innocent Diversion*.

Musicianship was one of a range of accomplishments widely discussed in the conduct literature of Austen's time. Authors varied in their opinions of the worth of music in a young woman's education. Many expressed anxiety about the frivolity of an education that, as Mary Wollstonecraft suggests, "in aiming to accomplish them, without cultivating their understandings," takes women "out of their sphere of duties" and makes them "ridiculous and useless when the short-lived bloom of beauty is over" (*Vindication of the Rights of Women* [Todd] 76). In contrast, Maria and Richard Lovell Edgeworth wrote in their 1798 book *Practical Education*, "[E]very art . . . which enlivens and embellishes domestic life, must be advantageous, not only to the female sex, but to society in general" (378–79). However, Juliette Wells points out that "the influence on Austen's novels of the conduct literature's discourse on accomplishments, and of her own experience as a writer and musician, is rarely either straightforward or explicit" (99).

Austen, who was an amateur musician herself, uses musicianship and the appreciation of music in a variety of ways in her novels. In *Sense and Sensibility*, musicality is both an important aspect of Marianne's romantic sensibility and a plot device. In both *Pride and Prejudice* and *Emma*, the social function of music is evident, and accomplishments in genteel young women are explored in a variety of ways: for most of the young female musicians in these novels music making is a pleasant pastime and addition to their attractions, while for Jane Fairfax it is also an uncomfortable measure of her market worth as a governess. In *Mansfield Park*, Mary Crawford's harp playing is part of Mary's dangerous attraction for Edmund, a force that Fanny fears but to which she is herself susceptible, while the musical accomplishments of the Bertram sisters are symptomatic of their superficial education.

In Anne Elliot, Austen presents her readers with a solitary heroine who is emotionally estranged from her father and sister, with whom she nevertheless is expected, as an unmarried woman, to live. Anne may pay extended visits to other family members (such as her married sister Mary) and close family friends (such as Lady Russell), but her home is with Sir Walter and Elizabeth. Even those who are fond of her and wish her well, like Lady Russell and the Musgroves, do not share her artistic and intellectual tastes. In this, she shares some qualities of Austen's earlier characters: Elinor Dashwood (in *Sense and Sensibility*) and Fanny Price (in *Mansfield Park*). Each of these characters has a strong sense of social obligation, coupled with a need to keep a part of herself private, partly because she has a hopeless love she must keep secret not just from its object but from the rest of the world, but also, perhaps, because she knows that she is surrounded by those who would not understand or appreciate the qualities that she most values in herself. The extent of Anne's emotional isolation is made explicit when the narrator writes, "In music she had been always used to feel alone in the world" (50; vol. 1, ch. 6). Anne has inner strength and a sense of self-worth, however. She does not envy the Musgrove sisters: "Anne had always contemplated them as some of the happiest creatures of her acquaintance; but still, saved as we all are by some comfortable feeling of superiority from wishing for the possibility of exchange, she would not have given up her own more elegant and cultivated mind for all their enjoyments" (43; vol. 1, ch. 5).

This passage might prompt students to consider the notion of Anne's "superiority." What does it mean to say that Anne feels superior to the Musgrove sisters? Is it a criticism of Anne or merely a statement of fact on the narrator's part? Is the phrase "saved as we all are" an appeal to readers for understanding of a moral weakness on Anne's part? Students might be encouraged to research the history of the word *superior* so as to appreciate its different shades of meaning in Austen's time and in its modern usage.

There is a distinct generational difference between Anne and the Musgrove girls. The sisters are seven and eight years younger than Anne, respectively, and have recently "brought from a school at Exeter all the usual stock of accomplishments" (43; vol. 1, ch. 5). Anne had spent three years at school in Bath after her mother's death thirteen years earlier (16; vol. 1, ch. 2), and her education did not include learning the harp, an instrument that was more expensive and thus more fashionable than the piano: "She played a great deal better than either of the Miss Musgroves, but having no voice, no knowledge of the harp, and no fond parents, to sit by and fancy themselves delighted, her performance was little thought of, only out of civility, or to refresh the others, as she was well aware" (50; vol. 1, ch. 6).

In addition to being unappreciated, Anne's music making is by its very nature, as Linda Zionkowski and Mimi Hart have pointed out, solitary and self-effacing: "By making Anne a non-singer, Austen heightens readers' awareness of her limitations in expressing her deeply felt emotions" (179). Anne has "no voice" in more ways than one: she has no say in family decisions that affect her. At evening parties at the Musgroves she would play the piano while others would dance:

> The girls were wild for dancing; and the evenings ended, occasionally, in an unpremeditated little ball. . . . Anne, very much preferring the office of musician to a more active post, played country dances to them by the hour together; a kindness which always recommended her musical powers to the notice of Mr and Mrs Musgrove more than anything else, and often drew this compliment;—"Well done, Miss Anne! very well done indeed! Lord bless me! how those little fingers of yours fly about!" (51; vol. 1, ch. 6)

In an important scene, Anne plays the piano so that the younger women can dance with Captain Wentworth: "though her eyes would sometimes fill with tears as she sat at the instrument, she was extremely glad to be employed, and desired nothing in return but to be unobserved" (77; vol. 1, ch. 8). It is significant that she believes that she can be "unobserved." Kathryn Libin, discussing Mrs. Weston's music making in *Emma*, comments that playing the piano to accompany dancing "requires the ability to efface oneself" as well as the ability to play rhythmically, correctly, and audibly (19). The Musgroves "notice" her playing only in the sense of technique: they see her "fingers fly about." When she plays for dancing, it is true that her fingers are "mechanically at work, proceeding for half an hour together, equally without error, and without consciousness" while she is preoccupied with other thoughts (77; vol. 1, ch. 8). The Musgroves compliment her on this mechanical playing but fail to notice the depth of the musicianship that, the novel implies, she displays on other occasions when their daughters are also playing to entertain them. The daughters engross their "fond parents'" attention, and any compliments paid to Anne are, she believes, "only out of civility" (50; vol. 1, ch. 6).

In Austen's world—indeed, until the invention of recording—music was necessarily embodied. There could be no dancing without someone to play an instrument. There was no music in homes or public spaces unless it was provided by live musicians, professional or amateur. In England, professional musicians of this period tended to be seen as artisans rather than artists, and music was viewed as a "feminine art" (Libin 19). In aristocratic homes, professional musicians might have been employed, but in the level of society usually described by Austen, though sometimes a violin-playing servant was recruited to play for dancing, most domestic music was provided by the women of the family.

Playing for others to dance is a good way to escape notice. However, although Anne wishes to be unobserved, she feels that Captain Wentworth is looking at her, "observing her altered features, perhaps, trying to trace in them the ruins of the face which had once charmed him" (78; vol. 1, ch. 8). Anne has already heard from her tactless sister Mary that he thought her "so altered he should not have known [her] again" (65; vol. 1, ch. 7). She hears him ask his partner—presumably Louisa or Henrietta—"whether Miss Elliot never danced?" The response he receives is dismissive and unobservant: "Oh! no, never; she has quite given up dancing. She had rather play. She is never tired of playing" (78; vol. 1 ch. 8). This marks her further as of an older generation than the Musgrove sisters: at twenty-seven she has given up the pleasures of dancing, and along with dancing she has surrendered the expectation of marrying. She has in effect passed from girlhood to the invisibility and usefulness of the older woman.

For an Austen heroine, Anne is indeed unusually invisible when playing music. In most of the other novels, young women attract the attention of eligible men with music. In *Sense and Sensibility*, Colonel Brandon pays Marianne Dashwood "only the compliment of attention" when he first sees her playing the piano (41; vol. 1, ch. 7). Mr. Darcy finds it difficult to ignore Elizabeth Bennet in *Pride and Prejudice* when she plays, while her sister Mary relishes the chance to play in company: "such an opportunity of exhibiting was delightful to her" (112; vol. 1, ch. 18). Mary Crawford uses her harp to attract Edmund Bertram's attention in *Mansfield Park*, and in *Emma* both Emma Woodhouse and Jane Fairfax perform at evening parties, where their performances are observed and discussed by several other characters.

However, Anne does not mind that nobody appreciates her music: "Mr. and Mrs. Musgrove's fond partiality for their own daughters' performance, and total indifference to any other person's, gave her much more pleasure for their sakes, than mortification for her own" (50; vol. 1, ch. 6). Anne has her "comfortable sense of superiority" (43; vol. 1 ch. 5), as well as genuine goodwill toward the Musgrove sisters, to prevent her being offended by the Musgroves' evident indifference. This self-confidence is in stark contrast to the anxiety of poor Mary Bennet in *Pride and Prejudice*, who is desperate to show off her hard-won but deficient musical skills in public. It also shows an interesting difference from Emma, a character who also seems to have a healthy sense of her own worth and her superiority, but who "was not much deceived as to her own skill either as an artist or a musician, or sorry to know her reputation for accomplishment often higher than it deserved" (*Emma* 46; vol. 1, ch. 6). Emma's self-worth depends to a large extent on her social position and, as she later realises, on "being *first* with Mr Knightley" (452; vol. 3, ch. 12). Anne does want to be "*first*" with Captain Wentworth, but until he reappears in her life, she has given up all hope of that.

Music, for Anne, is both a socially useful accomplishment that she can offer to her hosts and apparently a private resource for solitude such as her sisters, Elizabeth and Mary, lack—although unlike many of Austen's other musical heroines, she is never shown playing or practicing the piano when she is alone. The narrator tells us rather than shows us that she is musical: "She knew that when she played she was giving pleasure only to herself; but this was no new sensation. Excepting one short period of her life, she had never, since the age of fourteen, never since the loss of her dear mother, known the happiness of being listened to, or encouraged by any just appreciation or real taste" (50; vol. 1, ch. 6).

This passage could be used in class as a starting point for a discussion of various themes in the book: the characterization of Anne, including the implication in this passage that she alone in her family has "real taste" in music; the mother-daughter relationships, both actual and surrogate, in the novel; and the significance of the "one short period of her life" and how it colors the novel's present. Reading this passage in class could also be a way to begin an exploration of the meaning of aesthetic taste in Enlightenment and Romantic thought.

The appreciation of music is another important aspect of Anne's musicianship. Music helps reunite Anne with her soul mate, the only other character in the novel who listens to music with "any just appreciation or real taste." After Captain Wentworth comes to Bath, and he and Anne have one brief meeting, Anne becomes frustrated when she is not able to see him for some days: "The theatre and the rooms, where he was most likely to be, were not fashionable enough for the Elliots, whose evening amusements were solely in the elegant stupidity of private parties" (195; vol. 2, ch. 7). She, being merely a younger sister, has no say (no "voice") in how she and her family spend their time, and there is no question of her going out alone to a public place. However, there is a concert coming up that the members of her family will attend, not because they appreciate music, but because their aristocratic relative Lady Dalrymple is to be there. For once, family pride and genuine musical taste are not in conflict: "[The concert] was really expected to be a good one, and Captain Wentworth was very fond of music" (195; vol. 2, ch. 7). Anne knows that she will meet him there: at the concert they have a very satisfactory conversation, though she is constrained by politeness and etiquette to sit with her family and Mr. William Elliot, and the evening does not end well. Zionkowski and Hart point out that,

> [a]lthough [Wentworth] dismisses the concert as a waste of time, Wentworth's exasperation finally conveys to Anne the depth of his feeling. This scene, with each lover trying within the boundaries of propriety to impart crucial information to the other, serves as a pivotal point for Anne and Wentworth: music is their metaphorical as well as literal meeting ground, providing them with a vocabulary and opportunities to express their passion for one another privately, while in a public setting. (183)

Anne's "elegant and cultivated mind" has attracted the attention of other men: Charles Musgrove proposed to Anne unsuccessfully before marrying her sister Mary, and she is conscious of Captain Benwick's admiration when they first meet. Mr. Elliot's inconvenient courtship is at first flattering, and the idea of being the mistress of Kellynch Hall is momentarily tempting, but she is sure she "never could accept" Mr. Elliot (174; vol. 2, ch. 5). When the discord caused by Captain Wentworth's misplaced jealousy of Mr. Elliot is finally dispelled, Wentworth and Anne meet with "spirits dancing in private rapture" (261; vol. 2, ch. 11). This expression implies Anne's return to youthfulness, and the emotional and physical pleasures of loving and dancing, shared privately with the only man who shares Anne's pleasure in music.

Persuasion in a Women's Studies Course

Sheryl Craig

The chair of the women's studies program at the university where I teach asked me to develop a Jane Austen course that could be taken for credit by either upper-level undergraduate or graduate students and cross-listed in either English or in women's studies. It was an intriguing offer, especially when I learned that, at the time, the university had no courses that considered women's rights before the 1848 Seneca Falls Convention in the United States, and there were no courses on the British women's rights movement at all. Although the women's studies students had heard of Mary Wollstonecraft, they really did not know who she was, had no context for her, and probably had never been assigned to read *A Vindication of the Rights of Woman*. Obviously, there was a need for my course Jane Austen and the Plight of Women, but before I could teach it, I had to give myself a crash course in the British women's rights movement.

To better inform myself on women's social and legal status in Georgian England, I consulted a colleague in the History Department who taught eighteenth- and nineteenth-century British history. She directed me to the four seminal works of the historian Lawrence Stone. Stone's first book, *The Family, Sex and Marriage: In England, 1500–1800*, follows social and legal changes regarding women and marriage but concludes a decade before Jane Austen began to publish. Chapter 8, "The Companionate Marriage," explains the growing eighteenth-century movement away from marriage as merely a legal and financial contract between two men, the husband and the bride's father. Before the late eighteenth century, the wife was considered to be part of the chattel in the marriage settlement; she was legally the property of her father until she married, and then she became an appendage of her husband, literally like his arm or leg. Harming a married woman was considered to be equivalent to assaulting her husband, as she did not legally exist as a person in her own right. In *Persuasion*, the silly Mrs. Wallis thinks that in his marriage settlement Mr. William Elliot can forbid Sir Walter Elliot to marry Mrs. Clay. While "sensible nurse Rooke sees the absurdity of it" (J. Austen 225; vol. 2, ch. 9), men could and did make such arrangements in divorce settlements and in wills. Marriage was also thought to be a union of two families, and, just as in Sir Walter's Baronetage, the male heirs produced from the marriage were of more importance than the women who gave birth to them (3; vol. 1, ch. 1). Uniting families was such an ingrained concept that people often bolstered their family's fortunes by marrying their cousins, just as Sir Walter and his daughter Elizabeth expect Kellynch's heir apparent to attempt to marry his cousin.

Stone's *Road to Divorce: England, 1530–1987* charts the expansion of women's legal rights under the progressive judge Lord Mansfield, who served as lord chief justice from 1756 to 1788. When Mansfield became the lord chief justice, women could not buy, sell, or own land, their signatures were not legally binding unless a male guardian also signed a document with them, and they could not take a case to court without a man to represent and speak for them. Mansfield first expanded the rights of single women to hold and control portable property in their own names and then extended the same rights to married women, thus acknowledging both spinsters and wives as persons in their own rights. Mansfield also declared slavery to be illegal in Britain in the 1772 landmark case *Somerset v. Stewart*. Although Mansfield's slavery ruling held, reactionary backlash followed Mansfield's precedents for women, as his successor, the "fire and brimstone" evangelical Chief Justice Lord Kenyon, systematically overturned Mansfield's women's rights rulings in what Stone describes as "The Moral Panic of the 1790s" (273). The pursuit of women's rights did not occur as a smooth progression of legal victories but as a series of suddenly granted rights in test cases that were later reversed in appeals or in similar cases. The battle for women's legal rights raged back and forth throughout Jane Austen's lifetime, during which women sometimes gained rights only to have them subsequently challenged and taken away.

The lord chief justice from 1788 to 1802, Kenyon not only reversed Mansfield's rulings that acknowledged a married woman as a person in her own right, he increased a husband's legal authority over his wife. Kenyon even advocated reintroducing pillorying and public whipping for errant wives, as spoofed in James Gillray's 1797 print *Discipline à la Kenyon*. Apparently, Kenyon's zeal did not go down well with the general public, and lower court judges and juries declined to comply with his rulings. It is, however, interesting to note that Fanny Price's father in *Mansfield Park* agrees with Kenyon's punishment for adulterous wives: "I'd give her the rope's end as long as I could stand over her" (J. Austen, *Mansfield Park* 509; vol. 3, ch. 15). The contradictory summations and rulings of Mansfield and Kenyon are vital to understanding the legal and social forces in opposition in Georgian society, including in Parliament, the Church of England, the evangelical movement, the press, and in Jane Austen's novels. Kenyon's crusade against women's rights was at its peak as Austen was writing "Elinor and Marianne" and "First Impressions," her original versions of *Sense and Sensibility* and *Pride and Prejudice*.

As Kenyon methodically deprived women of legal rights they had been granted by Mansfield, the Church of England continued to expand women's rights in their ecclesiastical courts, which were higher than civil courts and had the power to grant wives legal separations and one-third of their husbands' property and incomes. Unhappy couples first had to be granted legal separations in civil courts, which considered a husband's adultery to be immaterial to any case and only considered cruelty to be relevant if it left the wife disfigured or disabled or if the husband had threatened her life. Even then, a wife could sue only for a separation, not a divorce. With few notable exceptions, civil courts generally favored men, but either husband or wife could appeal the case to the ecclesiastical courts, which were thought to favor women, as judges and jury members in those courts, who were Church of England clerics, considered a husband's adultery or cruelty to be relevant and serious offenses for which the husband was held accountable. Ecclesiastical courts nearly always granted wives more generous financial settlements than they had been given by civil courts.

Stone's *Uncertain Unions: Marriage in England, 1660–1753* and *Broken Lives: Separation and Divorce in England, 1660–1857* examine landmark court cases, such as Lovedon v. Lovedon in 1810, Otway v. Otway in 1811, and Westmeath v. Westmeath, the longest separation and divorce case in British legal history, which began in 1812 and finally concluded in 1857. The Westmeath case repeatedly created legal precedents that appeals then reversed, as Mr. and Mrs. Westmeath kept suing and countersuing each other for the custody of their child. No woman had ever previously been granted custody of her child in such cases. Stone's examples demonstrate the relative ease with which a married man could obtain a legal separation or divorce on the grounds of adultery, as local gossip or the testimony of one or, at most, two servants was considered sufficient as valid evidence. The fact that such servants were employed by the husband was not considered relevant.

Parliament was also arguing over women's rights, but strange bedfellows, ultraconservative Tories and radical Whigs in the House of Commons, were united in setting the reactionary agenda. The Divorce Bill was proposed, debated, and defeated four times in the House of Commons from 1800 through 1807. The House of Lords approved the bill all four times, but the House of Commons balked. At one vote, the bill failed to pass by eight votes in a packed house. Had the bill become law, a divorced man would have been able to legally remarry, but his divorced wife would not, as she would remain her ex-husband's perpetual property. The husband would have retained the right to all his wife's marriage settlement, subsequent earnings, and inheritance for the rest of his life, as well as to the money of any subsequent wife or wives. The bill was designed to punish an adulterous wife in every conceivable way, leaving her homeless, in poverty, alone, and unable to have any contact with her own children. Chief Justice Kenyon and the bill's supporters in Parliament believed such harsh punishment would discourage wives from committing adultery and, thus, promote family values. To its credit, the Church of England officially opposed the bill.

For teachers researching the legal history of women's rights in England, it is also helpful to consult a biography of the prince regent, such as *Prince of Pleasure*, by Saul David. When Austen was writing and publishing, the heir apparent to the British throne, who would become George IV, was attempting to divorce his wife, Princess Caroline of Brunswick, for adultery. The prince was a notorious philanderer, but that, of course, gave his wife no legal advantage in a divorce case. The melodrama of the royal couple's troubled marriage played itself out in the national press as the prince regent attempted to rally public support in the newspapers, and Princess Caroline retaliated in print. When the princess circulated a letter to the newspapers, Jane Austen wrote to her friend Martha Lloyd: "I suppose all the World is sitting in Judgement upon the Princess of Wales's Letter. Poor woman. I shall support her as long as I can, because she is a

Woman . . ." (*Jane Austen's Letters* [Le Faye, 4th ed.] 216–17 [16 Feb. 1813]). Understanding the controversy over women's legal rights in Georgian England, and what is at stake for Austen's characters when they consider marriage, opens up a different approach to teaching Austen's novels, and this informed background is the basis for my course.

The course begins with a packet of background readings that I pass out in the first class with the syllabus. This packet includes excerpts from the King James Version of the Bible;[1] Joseph Swetnam's tremendously popular 1615 *The Arraignment of Lewd, Idle, Froward, and Unconstant Women; or, the Vanity of Them* (pages 74–89 are sufficiently representative and insulting); the marriage services from the 1662 *Book of Common Prayer* (311–19), still used in Jane Austen's lifetime; the explanations of women's inferior legal status in William Blackstone's 1765 *Commentaries on the Laws of England* (442–45); and James Fordyce's 1768 *Sermons to Young Women*.[2] In the following class, a lively discussion of the packet material is absolutely guaranteed.

We discuss the readings in chronological order to demonstrate the pervasiveness of female stereotypes and how they had grown over time. Then I pose two questions: Which reading is the most offensive, and which reading probably did the most damage to women? Swetnam the woman hater, as he was nicknamed in his own lifetime, will easily prevail as the most misogynistic author, but, on reflection, students believe the marriage vows were probably the most problematic for women, as they repeatedly reinforced the inferior status of a woman to her husband, presented this inequality as the will of God, and required women to vow to "obey" four times, as well as to "serve" (*Book* 313), "submit," and "be in subjection to" (319) their spouses. Now sufficiently informed, the class proceeds to read Mary Wollstonecraft's 1792 *A Vindication of the Rights of Woman*, followed by a few selected lines from *The Unsex'd Females*, by Richard Polwhele, written in response to *A Vindication*, published in 1798, and reprinted in 1800. An attack on "the alarming eccentricities of Mrs. Wollstonecraft" that makes repeated assertions of the "inferiority of women in the scale of intellect" (21, 19), Polwhele's *Unsex'd Females* demonstrates the immediate and vigorous backlash to the publication of Wollstonecraft's *Vindication*.

Wollstonecraft identifies two major prejudices that society would have to overcome before there could be any possibility of progress for women. The crippling assumptions holding women back were that women were mentally inferior to men, just as they were, in society's general view, physically weaker, and that women were irrational and emotional beings, incapable of caring for themselves and others without the assistance of men, who were, by contrast, more intelligent, rational, and logical and were equipped by nature to take charge of their wives, female relatives, and women in general. As Wollstonecraft points out, the assumption was that "man was made to reason, woman to feel" (*Vindication of the Rights of Woman* [Dover] 63). Wollstonecraft argues that the difference in the mental powers of the sexes was not the fault of nature but of nurture, and that women, if given equal educational and occupational opportunities, would be "rational creatures" who behaved just as logically as men (8). She entirely rejects the notion that physical strength is in any way linked to intellectual powers: "I will allow that bodily strength seems to give man a natural superiority over woman; and this is the only solid basis on which the superiority of the sex can be built" (38).

Wollstonecraft maintains that, no matter how well educated women were, as long as they were unable to be employed and paid wages equal to those of men, there would be no opportunity for them to demonstrate their full potential. British women were still making the same arguments in 1914 when Emmeline Pankhurst wrote *Suffragette*. In Georgian, and in Edwardian, England, women were routinely paid half the wages of men doing the same type of work, so working women could supplement a family's income but were rarely able to financially support themselves, let alone any dependents, on their wages alone. Additionally, a retired man's pension ended when he died. The financial insecurity of women's lives was used as a justification to deprive mothers of the custody of their own children after the deaths of their husbands or in separation or divorce cases. In *Persuasion*, the widow Mrs. Clay's two children from her "unprosperous marriage" are in the legal custody of Mr. Shepherd, their grandfather (J. Austen 17; vol. 1, ch. 2). As a woman, Penelope Clay is not even guaranteed visitation rights to her own children. This may explain why the children are not heard of again when Mrs. Clay moves to Bath.

Persuasion deals with the women's rights talking points that Wollstonecraft considered and forwards the ideal of the companionate marriage. Championed by Jean-Jacques Rousseau in his essays and novels, the companionate marriage assumed that women could enter marriage as equal partners and expect to maintain that status throughout their married lives. The companionate marriage also assumed that this type of union offered the couple their best chance for mutual and lasting happiness. The novel suggests that Anne Elliot and Captain Frederick Wentworth will eventually achieve this ideal marital state, but other married couples in the novel, most notably the "particularly attached and happy" Admiral and Mrs. Croft (69; vol. 1, ch. 8), demonstrate the principle in the book. A "well-spoken, shrewd lady" who is "more conversant with business" than her spouse (25; vol. 1, ch. 3), Mrs. Croft is her husband's equal if not his superior. Anne notices that Mrs. Croft assists her husband when he is driving their carriage, and Anne assumes that Mrs. Croft's management of their gig to be "no bad representation of the general guidance of their affairs" (99; vol. 1, ch. 10). Indeed, "Mrs. Croft seemed to go shares with [her husband] in every thing" (182–83; vol. 2, ch. 6), including embracing her husband's profession as if it were her own. Anne notes that Mrs. Croft looks "as intelligent and keen as any of the officers" (183; vol. 2, ch. 6), and she has been "almost as much at sea as her husband" (52; vol. 1, ch. 6), just as Jane Austen's sister-in-law, Fanny Palmer Austen, lived—and died—in the captain's quarters of her husband's ship. As Mrs. Wentworth, Anne may similarly take on her husband's career: "She gloried in being a sailor's wife, but she must pay the tax of quick alarm for belonging to the profession . . ." (275; vol. 2, ch. 12).

The happily married Harvilles and Charles Musgrove's parents also have companionate marriages where the wives, like Mrs. Croft, share in their husbands' activities. Captain Benwick and Fanny Harville, "a very superior creature" (199; vol. 2, ch. 8), seemed likely to have a promising companionate marriage of intellectual equals, but their engagement was thwarted by Fanny's untimely death. Captain Wentworth demonstrates his own belief in the companionate marriage by approving of Benwick's choice of Fanny Harville and later by expressing his concern about the intellectual inequality of Captain Benwick and his second fiancée, Louisa Musgrove: "there is a disparity, too great a disparity, and in a point no less essential than mind" (199; vol. 2, ch. 8). Louisa, however, promises to be fully supportive of her husband's career when she "burst forth into raptures of admiration and delight on the character of the navy . . . sailors having more worth and warmth than any other set of men in England" (107; vol. 1, ch. 11).

We are also given a contrast to the companionate marriage in the examples of unhappy marriages between unequal partners, such as Sir Walter's marriage to Lady Elliot, Anne's mother; the marriage of Mr. William Elliot, which ended with his wife's death; and the marriage of Mrs. Smith, which ended with her husband's death. In all cases, the wife's happiness and possibly her health have been undermined by the stress of living with her spouse. The constant squabbling of Charles and Mary Musgrove remind Anne and the reader of what daily life is like when two people with nothing in common marry. Lady Russell, Mrs. Smith, and Lady Dalrymple are examples of comparatively liberated women, widows who can manage their own affairs and express no desire to return to married life.

Mrs. Croft asserts to her brother that women are not foolish and helpless but "rational creatures" (75; vol. 1, ch. 8), a term Wollstonecraft repeatedly uses in *A Vindication of the Rights of Woman*, and female characters in the novel continually demonstrate that this assertion is true. When Louisa initially falls from the Cobb and chaos reigns, Anne gives directions to presumably capable and competent men, two sea captains and a gentleman farmer, who immediately recognize her practical common sense and follow her instructions. Mrs. Harville quietly takes charge and "under Mrs. Harville's direction" all the party go "to their house" (120; vol. 1, ch. 12), where Mrs. Harville assumes the role of primary caregiver to the injured Louisa Musgrove. Deciding who should stay to help, Captain Wentworth declares, "[N]o one so proper, so capable as Anne!" (123; vol. 1, ch. 12).

All the sensible characters in the novel admire Anne for "the perfect excellence" of her "collected mind" (263; vol. 2, ch. 11). All these capable female characters disprove the theory of women's intellectual inferiority. Mary Musgrove is perhaps an exception, but it is worth noting that Mary's fits of hysteria are uniformly well-timed, like her bouts of ill health and her rapid recoveries. Mary is no more hysterical or irrational than anyone else, only more manipulative. As Anne shrewdly asserts, when there is no motive Mary "will not be hysterical again" (60; vol 1, ch. 7).

Anne's and Nurse Rooke's skills in administering to the sick and injured suggest that the medical profession could well be further opened to women, as Wollstonecraft argues in *A Vindication*: "Women might certainly study the art of healing, and be physicians as well as nurses" (152). Of course, women already acted as paid nurses and midwives, as does Nurse Rooke, "a shrewd, intelligent, sensible woman" (J. Austen, *Persuasion* 168; vol. 2, ch. 5), but there were also female apothecaries and surgeons practicing medicine, who were trained as their male counterparts were, by working with professional men as apprentices. Widows and orphaned daughters of male apothecaries and surgeons sometimes carried on the family business alone, prescribing drugs, performing minor surgeries, and setting broken bones. Anne assures her sister Mary that "nursing does not belong to a man, it is not his province" (61; vol. 1, ch. 7). Charles Musgrove agrees: "This was quite a female case" (59; vol. 1, ch. 7). In the Georgian era, medical doctors, unlike surgeons or apothecaries, were required to attend colleges or universities, where women were not yet admitted as students, so women could not become medical doctors until higher education was available to them.

Captain Harville's conversation with Anne in Bath is a veritable chess match in which Harville, in jest, presents typical eighteenth-century anti-equality arguments, and Anne rebuts them. It is obvious that Harville, with a highly competent wife and "a very superior" sister (199; vol. 2, ch. 8), cannot seriously believe his talking points to be valid arguments, but he begins "with a smile" and cites them to see how Anne will reply (252; vol. 2, ch. 11). When Harville brings up "a true analogy between our bodily frames and our mental" (253; vol. 2, ch. 11), Anne will not allow that assertion to go unchallenged: "Man is more robust than woman, but he is not longer-lived" (253; vol. 2, ch. 11). This was, of course, also Wollstonecraft's concession, but Anne adds an additional proof of equality in lifespans. When Harville proposes a preponderance of evidence to support the supposition of female instability, "all stories, prose and verse. . . . Songs and proverbs, all talk of woman's fickleness" (254; vol, 2, ch. 11) Anne also nullifies that point: "Men have had every advantage of us in telling their own story. Education has been theirs in so much higher a degree; the pen has been in their hands" (255; vol. 2, ch. 11). Anne continues to have the last word until Harville considers himself to have been outmaneuvered and amiably concedes the argument: "There is no quarrelling with you . . . my tongue is tied" (256; vol. 2, ch. 11). Anne's spirited defense of women to Harville is also overheard by Wentworth, and her prowoman assertions do nothing to diminish Anne in either man's estimation. All of Austen's novels support ideas of women's equality and present women as "rational creatures" rather than overly emotional and hysterical "fine ladies" who must be protected, coddled, and led by the hand (75; vol. 1, ch. 8), but *Persuasion* offers the most obvious and sustained endorsement of Wollstonecraft's arguments in *A Vindication*. Austen also accomplishes this feat without disparaging men, diminishing her male characters, or alienating her male readers.

On the last day of class, I discuss the progress of women's rights in Britain since the death of Jane Austen in 1817, which allows us to end the course on an upbeat note. The 1839 Custody of Infants Act permitted women, in extreme cases, to be awarded custody of their own children. The 1857 Matrimonial Causes Act made it much easier for women to obtain divorces and allowed women to divorce their husbands because of cruelty or adultery. The 1870 Married Women's Property Act gave married women the right to earn, inherit, and control their own money, the same rights as single women, and restored the right to private property that Chief Justice Mansfield had given women nearly a hundred years earlier. The law also allowed women to buy, sell, own, and inherit land in their own names. In 1918, the Representation of the People Act gave women aged thirty and older who owned property the right to vote, although it extended the vote to men aged twenty-one and older who did not own property. In 1919, Nancy Astor, an American heiress who married an English lord and became a naturalized British citizen, became the first woman to hold a seat in Parliament. Had Lady Astor remained in the United States, in 1919 she would not even have been able to vote. The 1920s witnessed a resurgence of interest in the ideal of the companionate marriage, and British women aged twenty-one and older were given the right to vote on the same terms as men in 1928.

NOTES

[1] The excerpts are *Bible*, Gen. 2 and 3, which include the second creation story and the fall of Adam and Eve; Judg. 16, which is about Delilah's deception of Samson; Prov. 31, which describes a virtuous woman; and 1 Cor. 14:34–35, Col. 3:18, and Eph. 5: 21–32, which admonish women to be subservient to men.

[2] Forsythe 106–13 deals with "Profligate" and "Improper Books" (read novels), and 197–99 mansplains women's intellectual inferiority to men.

Persuasion as a Wartime Novel

Paul Westover

Teaching *Persuasion* as a novel of wartime foregrounds its blending of home, battlefield, and sea, as well as Jane Austen's effort to capture the psychological fabric of a home-front experience too often ignored by histories—histories typically written, as the novel's climactic scene reminds us, by men. The approach invites students to perceive wartime—its casualties, its confused temporality, and its distress—even in passages where they might least expect it, empowering them to engage with more than the usual pleasures of the novel-of-manners plot. To be sure, *Persuasion* offers a passionate love story, but it does so against a palpable historical backdrop. Placing the novel in its 1814–15 setting explodes the old myth that Austen somehow ignores national affairs, yet it also highlights the personal stakes for Austen's characters in ways that intensify the story and, in turn, give students new reasons to love the book.[1]

Unless assigned to read a historical introduction, most undergraduates, especially first-time Austen readers, likely won't realize that *Persuasion* was published just after the end of a conflict with France that had lasted, with only brief interruptions, for over two decades—that is, for the novelist's entire adult life and for much of the lives of her book's principal characters. Nor will they likely realize that Austen's knowledge of the navy and naval families was personal.[2] The teacher's task is to help them see how such facts can shape productive reading.

The decision to teach *Persuasion* as a wartime novel means emphasizing the book's portrayal of lived history. None of Austen's other books is so precisely dated as *Persuasion*. It opens in the summer of 1814 and concludes as Anne Elliot and Captain Frederick Wentworth reunite in Bath in February 1815. Later that same month, just beyond the horizon of the novel, Napoleon will escape from the island of Elba, setting the stage for the Hundred Days War and the Battle of Waterloo in June. Furthermore, the novel's composition history is nearly as suggestive as its internal chronology, since Austen began writing the novel on the day newspapers reported Napoleon's departure for his second, permanent exile on Saint Helena, 8 August 1815. Indeed, the setting of *Persuasion* makes it relatively easy to put alongside the historical novels of Walter Scott as a parable of national change as revealed in the life of a protagonist and the people around her.[3]

Persuasion engages students of all levels. I have assigned it most often in sophomore-level surveys, but I have also taught it in upper-division period courses and in senior capstone seminars. The novel fits many syllabi because it is both compelling and short. Its two volumes can be taught in as little as two days, depending on the length of the class periods. Since my readers will have various courses of their own in mind, I focus below on teaching hints that seem portable. My imaginary lesson plan comprises two days—two reading assignments and two seventy-five-minute class meetings—but teachers will have no trouble distributing the material over additional class periods.

I begin by informing students that I have a thesis: I mean to persuade them that *Persuasion* is a war novel. I do this because the claim usually contradicts their expectations. Many students are looking for a romantic plot from Austen, and they are going to get it, but it will come with historical specificity and types of emotional urgency that they do not anticipate.

One favorite launching place for elaborating this thesis is the initial sequence (plus a few seconds) from the outstanding 1995 film adaptation of *Persuasion*, directed by Roger Michell. The excerpt runs from the unusual first shot—white oars and a longboat viewed from under water—to the moment when the credits end and we hear Corin Redgrave's Sir Walter Elliot announce that he dislikes the navy and cannot possibly retrench. Having encouraged the students to take notes on the clip, I ask what particulars they have noticed and why these belong (or not) at the story's beginning. We invariably discuss why the film begins with tired, weather-beaten sailors rowing an officer toward a ship—the flagship of Admiral Croft, we may suppose, though uninitiated viewers will not yet know his name. The entire British fleet is about to be told that Napoleon has abdicated and the war has ended.

Certain facts need highlighting here. One is that Austen and her contemporary readers know that the war is not truly over in 1814—that Napoleon will yet escape and renew hostilities.[4] So, for readers armed with this historical knowledge, suspense—literally a suspension of conflict—hangs over the entire novel. It adds to the plot's tension, which culminates in the final page's reminder that, though gloriously happy at book's end, Anne will have to "pay the tax of quick alarm" for being a sailor's wife (275; vol. 2, ch. 12).

A teacher may not wish to go quite that far on the first day—the ending of the novel is worth saving for day two—but it is crucial to observe that everything in *Persuasion* occurs during the so-called false peace.[5] Naval officers must come ashore to set the plot in motion. The crosscutting of the film's beginning, which suggests that the actions depicted happen simultaneously and relate to one another, lets viewers understand that interactions between the naval world and domestic life will define the story. What do Sir Walter's financial woes, class snobbery, and impending relocation have to do with the fortunes of Admiral Croft and other men at sea? Much, as it turns out.

I move from this clip to a digital slide titled "Austen's Opening," which features a facsimile title page from Arthur Collins's *The Baronetage of England* and a painting of a gentleman reading in his library.[6] We have already discussed the logic of the filmmakers' opening strategy; now we observe that this was not Jane Austen's strategy. Several questions follow: Why does Austen begin as she does? What issues does *her* opening scene establish? (Here all sorts of topics emerge, from family dynamics to inheritance law.) My next slide poses the inevitable follow-up question: How are the two openings related? Many students will focus their responses on the attitudes of Sir Walter. Why doesn't he approve of the navy? What values does it represent, and how do those values compare with his? How are the two worlds bound to collide? Opportunities will arise at this point for reading passages closely and elucidating details.

By now, students will usually buy the idea that we are dealing with wartime fiction, even as we are also engaging with an analysis of social class, a love story, and so forth. I now explain some reasons why I feel my thesis is important, offering a brief reception history that goes something like this: "A number of readers over the years have said that Austen was provincial in her concerns, that she seemed uninterested in politics or the great conflicts of her time. Reading *Persuasion* should convince us that she was hardly avoiding the issues. Nonetheless, rather than depict the drama of politics or battle, Austen gives us fine-grained social experience. Why?" Students will often make astute observations here, but the instructor can stress a few points as needed. Austen addresses several important, neglected questions: How does war pervade everyday life? How does it affect the noncombatants, especially the women, left behind? How does it shape the character of the warriors who return? How does it put stress on personal and family relationships? How does it transform the social and economic structure of society?

With this backdrop for discussion, the teacher can turn to other passages. The excitement comes in showing how the war and the domestic story interpenetrate. Below I discuss a few favorite moments, but you can see the patterns I describe in many other places.

Volume 1 reaches a crescendo with the distressing scene at the Cobb in Lyme Regis.[7] I like to turn there early and provoke students: "Is this a battle scene?" At first, the suggestion seems mildly absurd, but when you ask students to discuss the section in small groups, they perceive things—the shocking injury, the frantic pace ("all done in rapid moments" [119; vol. 1, ch. 12]), the desperate call for a surgeon, the disorientation. Students may realize that it's as if the characters are on board ship. But then it turns out that Anne is the only one who remains cool under fire. She takes command on the deck, so to speak. It is often useful to discuss this role reversal, where naval officers, who presumably are used to having enemy vessels pull alongside and open fire, don't know what to do in this crisis. Anne, meanwhile, shows fortitude and presence of mind that reveal her afresh as the equal of Captain Wentworth.[8] Wentworth sees this and acknowledges it, so the incident proves key to his dawning self-knowledge and his revised evaluation of Anne's character.

Note that Louisa Musgrove suffers a head injury, a concussion incident to her "severe contusion" (121; vol. 1, ch. 12). Falls, the teacher might observe, were a typical risk on warships—and then, think of "concussion" (137; vol. 2, ch. 1) in terms of violent shock from guns or explosions. Moreover, the narrator makes sure that Louisa's accident looks like a fatal incident. Louisa is "taken up lifeless," her "face . . . like death" (118; vol. 1, ch. 12). Mary screams, "She is dead!" while local boatmen and workers gather around "to enjoy the sight of a dead young lady," or rather of two, since Henrietta has fainted (120; vol. 1, ch. 12).

During this part of our discussion, some of my students have noted the setting's possible significance. Lyme is a liminal space, literally at the edge of the land and the sea. The Cobb juts out into the water, as if to bring home the fact that this is the place where land and sea intermingle. A young person goes there for a holiday but comes away injured. Readers may sense that the overseas war front and the home front may not be so distant from each other—that the distinction between them has become unstable.

With the Cobb scene in mind, earlier details of the novel can be revisited. For instance, the teacher might remind students about the fall of little Charles Musgrove, which foreshadows the accident of his aunt Louisa at the Cobb (57; vol. 1, ch. 7). Like the scene at the Cobb, that episode brings home the insight that casualties can happen anywhere (and that Anne handles them better than most). If, as Deidre Shauna Lynch notes in her introduction to the novel, the actual violence of war happens offstage, the novel's "discretion about wartime carnage is offset, all the same, by the fact that security of life and limb is a precarious thing even under the peace that has brought the surviving sailors home" (Introduction xiv). Even characters who avoid physical harm cannot avoid alarm distress, and shock—words that Austen frequently repeats, along with others like them.

The falls of young Charles and Louisa remind us that the poor Musgroves face more than their fair share of calamity. Indeed, teachers may want to highlight passages in the first volume, chapters 6–8, where readers learn of the lost Musgrove son, Richard (or Dick), who died two years before and was a midshipman on Captain Wentworth's *Laconia*.[9] Richard Musgrove may have been "thick-headed" and "unprofitable" (54; vol. 1, ch. 6), but he nonetheless occupies his mother's thoughts. Richard's recurrence in the narrative is easy for first-time readers to miss, but notice how insistently Mrs. Musgrove's "fat sighings" for him (73; vol. 1, ch. 8), however exaggerated, capture the psychology of a mother's loss (see 54–55, 56; vol. 1, ch. 6; and 69, 72–73; vol. 1, ch. 8). Mrs. Musgrove frequently needs to relieve her feelings by speaking of him. Hearing Captain Wentworth's name triggers in her "one of those extraordinary bursts of mind which do sometimes occur" (55; vol. 1, ch. 6), and meeting Wentworth in person prompts her to reflect on what the young Richard might have become if his life had not been cut short (69; vol. 1, ch. 8). The mourning of the Musgroves hastens their intimacy with Wentworth, who seems to have "felt all the motive of their attention," that is, their gratitude for his treatment of Richard, "just as he ought!" (58; vol. 1, ch. 7). His compassion "for all that was real and unabsurd in the parent's feelings" (73; vol. 1, ch. 8) brings him quickly into the Uppercross circle, part of the dynamic that leads him unintentionally to oblige himself toward Louisa. In this way and others, Richard casts a shadow that deepens the novel's emotional insight and psychological complexity (73; vol. 1, ch. 8).

Resonant in the light of Louisa's accident is her earlier exchange with Captain Wentworth about the moral necessity of a firm head. During the long walk of chapter 10, Wentworth playfully compares Louisa to a nut, an emblem of "decision and firmness" (94; vol. 1, ch. 10). Regrettably, this exchange leaves Louisa "armed" (an interesting word choice) "with the idea of merit in maintaining her own way" (101; vol. 1, ch. 11) and leads directly to her obstinacy at the Cobb.

She *will* jump—and so her nut gets cracked. This is grim humor, and from it spring any number of references, both serious and comic, to head injuries, starting when the surgeon at Lyme determines that Louisa's fall has not produced the harm that it might have to her limbs: "There was no injury but to the head" (121; vol. 1, ch. 12). John Wiltshire aptly describes *Persuasion* as a story of "broken bones, broken heads and broken hearts" (*Jane Austen* 165). In wartime, these kinds of physical and emotional damage overlap.

The melancholy history of Fanny Harville and Captain Benwick, soon to be intertwined with Louisa's story, further underscores the dangers of everyday life and the ubiquity of wartime loss. When Benwick goes to sea, the natural worry is that he will not live to be married, but ironically, it is his fiancée, Fanny, who dies, becoming a war casualty in her own way. Again, land and sea change places with disturbing facility.

Attentive readers will notice other instances of war permeating life on the home front. The first reading matter mentioned in connection with the bookish Anne is not poetry, though the war-inflected poems mentioned in *Persuasion* are well worth exploring, but "navy lists and newspapers" (32; vol. 1, ch. 4). Anne has been something like the reader depicted in Anna Barbauld's *Eighteen-Hundred and Eleven*: "Oft o'er the daily page some soft-one bends / To learn the fate of husbands, brother, friends" (162).[10] Teachers familiar with Benedict Anderson's *Imagined Communities* will perhaps wish to point out the language of national belonging that Anne's reading allows her to employ: "The navy . . . who have done so much for *us*" (J. Austen, *Persuasion* 21; vol. 1, ch. 3; emphasis added). They may also wish to emphasize the cost of that identification. Arguably, it took a global conflict with mass mobilizations, extensive losses, and a constant flow of war news, collectively absorbed, to create this sense of national identity.[11]

On the second day of teaching *Persuasion*, focused mainly on the novel's second volume, I begin with the climactic penultimate chapter set at the White Hart Inn in Bath. This may be the most powerful scene in all of Austen, and it has still greater impact when read through the wartime lens. It illustrates how essential strands of the novel's tapestry—war and home, love and loss, and men's experience and women's experience—weave together. Let me address just three points that the chapter drives home:

First, when Anne and Captain Harville compare the natures of men and women, they do so explicitly from the wartime standpoint. Anne observes, "You have difficulties, and privations, and dangers enough to struggle with. You are always laboring and toiling, exposed to every risk and hardship. Your home, country, friends, all quitted. Neither time, nor health, to be called your own" (253; vol. 2, ch. 11). This is not simply a man's life that she describes; it is an officer's life. It is Wentworth's life as well as Harville's, and Wentworth certainly understands her words that way as he listens. Teachers might pose two simple questions: What kind of man's life is this? What kind of woman's life is this? The second question points to other passages that are as poignant as the one just cited—for instance, Anne's words about remaining "at home, confined," where "feelings prey upon us" (253; vol. 2, ch. 11).[12]

Second, this crucial chapter recalls yet again the shadow plot of Fanny Harville. Even more than Richard Musgrove, Fanny recurs in the novel like a ghost. Benwick's miniature portrait, first made for Fanny and now reset for Louisa, becomes the occasion for Anne's discussion with Captain Harville, Fanny's brother. Readers at this point in the novel feel almost sure that Anne's love story will work itself out, but this resolution will be all the more moving because things might have gone otherwise. The possibility of Anne and Wentworth's marriage, like that of Fanny and Benwick, might easily have been erased. Wentworth might, for instance, have been caught in the storm that hit Plymouth Sound just after his battle-damaged sloop made it to safety, and he could easily have been "only . . . a gallant Captain Wentworth, in a small paragraph at one corner of the newspapers" (71; vol. 1, ch. 8). Anne has every reason to shudder when she contemplates this possibility. Not all of the dangers that Lady Russell pointed out eight years earlier, when persuading Anne to break off her engagement with Wentworth, were imaginary.

Third, this chapter, perhaps more than any other, makes explicit the novel's feminist argument. Harville appeals to literature—"all" histories, stories, poems, songs, and proverbs—to support his claim about men's superior constancy (254; vol. 2, ch. 11). Anne "will not allow books to prove any thing" since "the pen has been in [men's] hands" (255; vol. 2, ch. 11). And note that, just before this exchange, Anne's passionate words on women's feelings are enough to make Wentworth (serving as a representative man?) drop his pen. *Persuasion* itself is precisely the result of a pen taken up by an acute, thoughtful woman; Austen offers readers the story of wartime that literature has too often overlooked—the tale of what happens in the hearts of the people, especially the women, who must wait at home, even "when existence or when hope is gone" (256; vol. 2, ch. 11).

The scene at the White Hart sets up the novel's happy closure. Students now understand that the navy has done for Captain Wentworth precisely what Sir Walter feared: it has brought a person "of obscure birth into . . . distinction" (21; vol. 1, ch. 3). "[N]o longer nobody," Wentworth has come home with a fortune of £25,000, which makes him a millionaire in today's terms and "worthy to address the daughter of a foolish, spendthrift baronet" (270; vol. 2, ch. 12).[13] Both lovers bring moral, intellectual, social, and financial capital to the match, though at present Sir Walter can give Anne only "a small part of the share of ten thousand pounds which must be hers hereafter" (270; vol. 2, ch. 12). Consequently, the novel's ending presents us with a picture of equitable partnership—a marriage more like the Crofts' than any other we have seen, an exemplary merger of naval values with domestic life.

After discussing the novel's final chapter, I use whatever time remains to supplement key discussions from day 1, first by observing that volume 2 discusses the effects of the Cobb's "frightful hour" in terms of battlefield trauma (198; vol. 2, ch. 8). Wentworth can hardly speak of the accident without flinching, "pass[ing] his hand across his eyes, as if the remembrance were still too painful" (198; vol. 2, ch. 8). Charles Musgrove, reporting on Louisa's recovery, says that his sister is "quite altered": "if one happens only to shut the door a little hard, she starts and wriggles" (237; vol. 2, ch. 10). This account of Louisa starting at loud noises may strike modern readers like a description of post-traumatic stress disorder.[14] Perhaps there was no established medical term for post-traumatic stress as yet, but surely this world war, with its cannons and mass casualties, produced its share of traumatic brain injuries and shaken veterans, their "nerves susceptible to the highest extreme of tenderness" (140; vol. 2, ch. 2).

One of the main lessons of *Persuasion* is that war isn't over when it's over—and in fact that trauma of all sorts may last and return. Mrs. Musgrove exemplifies one aspect of this argument, not only because of her mourning for Richard, but also because of her peculiar long-term worry about head injuries. When Anne shows herself stunned by Wentworth's letter of disclosure, Mrs. Musgrove must "[assure] herself, with some anxiety, that there had been no fall in the case; that Anne had not, at any time lately, slipped down, and got a blow on her head" (259; vol. 2, ch. 11). Mrs. Musgrove can think "only of one sort of illness" now, and maybe the same should go for readers, since literal and figurative head problems have been pervasive (259; vol. 2, ch. 11). But clearly references to heads are merely one vehicle for showing that "to retentive feelings . . . years may be little more than nothing" (65; vol. 1, ch. 7).

Underscoring the tendency of war to saturate everyday spaces, *Persuasion* explicitly blurs the distinction between warships and homes. This theme, already present in the first volume, emerges even more strongly in volume 2, so it pays to discuss it with students on the second day.

Mrs. Croft is the first to raise the subject, teasing her brother about his reluctance to take women on his ships as passengers: "Women may be as comfortable on board, as in the best house in England. I believe I have lived as much on board as most women, and I know nothing superior to the accommodations of a man of war" (74; vol. 1, ch. 8). Admiral Croft, later on, describes Kellynch Hall as if it is his latest command: one of its chimneys smokes a little, but "only when the wind is due north and blows hard, which may not happen three times a winter" (138; vol. 2, ch. 1). Later, he mentions his and Mrs. Croft's liking for their new lodgings in Bath, explaining that "[t]he wind blows through one of the cupboards just as it did in the lodging [they] first had at North Yarmouth" (185; vol. 2, ch. 6). Students don't normally notice his habitual attention to the winds, and they are often amused when I compare him to Admiral Boom in *Mary Poppins*: "Banks, shouldn't wonder if you weren't steering into a nasty piece of weather!"

Teachers may wish to underline these examples with an examination of the Harvilles' lodgings at Lyme, a location with features that may remind one of quarters in a ship—ingenious weatherproofing, fishing nets, souvenirs from distant deployments, and so forth. When the injured Louisa and her friends come to stay, the Harvilles offer to "[swing] up a cot somewhere" (122; vol. 1, ch. 12). But more significant than the furniture is the sociality the Harvilles' home embodies. Its warm naval atmosphere appeals so strongly that Anne finds herself depressed, reflecting, "These would have been all my friends" (105; vol. 1, ch. 11). Louisa comes away from her first visit "burst[ing] forth into raptures of admiration and delight on the character of the navy—their friendliness, their brotherliness, their openness, their uprightness; protesting that they only knew how to live, and they only deserved to be respected and loved" (106–07; vol. 1, ch. 11). However over-the-top Louisa's effusions may be, Austen, along with her heroine, seems to sympathize with them, and she ends her novel with a memorable encomium on "that profession which is, if possible, more distinguished in its domestic virtues, than in its national importance" (275; vol. 2, ch. 12).

This isn't to say that domestic life in *Persuasion*, whether on shore or at sea, is consistently depicted as comfortable or happy. Those in charge may be tyrannical or indifferent. Daily routines may cause weariness, sickness, or injury. *Persuasion* never depicts harsh naval discipline or the gruesome details of battle, but it does capture, by absorption or redirection, various difficulties of shipboard existence, including living in close quarters and amid troubling sounds. Particularly in moments of stress, Anne often finds rooms "full—full of persons and voices" (64; vol. 1, ch. 7). The novel's descriptions of "the domestic hurricane" (146; vol. 2, ch. 2), including of noises and crowded bodies, repays attention. Forced togetherness may promote friendship, but it may also be hard on those who often crave solitude, like this novel's introverted heroine.

Still, home in this book is more than a physical space; it is also a state of mind, feeling, and companionship. This fact matters a good deal for Anne, who is literally homeless for most of the novel. The admirable experience of Mrs. Croft offers hope. It illustrates that one consequence of war—uprooting people, making them constant travelers (76; vol. 1, ch. 8)—potentially leads to another, a conviction that even the most distant places can become a home: "While we were together, you know, there was nothing to be feared" (76; vol. 1, ch. 8).

Discussions of ships as homes could conclude with a review of the closing scene of the 1995 *Persuasion* film.[15] We first see Anne (portrayed by Amanda Root) seated at a writing desk, presumably composing a letter, next to an open window with a breeze and sunlight pouring through. This seems to be a typical domestic scene. However, Anne soon stands and leaves the room, and we quickly realize, as the film cuts to a new perspective, that she is emerging from the captain's cabin onto the quarterdeck of a ship.[16] Her uniformed husband (Ciarán Hinds) stands on the poop deck above, looking ahead with a spyglass, and she steps up to stand beside him. They glance at each other, smile, and gaze forward, as if to the future together. The film's parting images are longer shots of the ship sailing peacefully as the sun sets. Austen never gives us such pictures as these—in fact, she gives us no reason to expect that Anne will ever go to sea—but do students approve of this visual interpretation of the novel's ending? Posing this question provides a fitting bookend to the first day's discussion comparing the novel's beginning with the film's.

As time permits, teachers may also want to observe that *Persuasion*'s merger of the naval, the domestic, and the national occurs on the level of language as well as setting. There may be no "rears and vices" jokes in *Persuasion* as in

Mansfield Park (71; vol. 1, ch. 6), but there are plenty of instances when we may suspect Austen of a pun. At least, she employs words that work on multiple levels. One of my students recently noticed *Persuasion*'s interest in the phrase "a long engagement" (251; vol. 2, ch. 11), which suggested to her a possible double meaning. Clearly, the primary sense of "engagement" is betrothal, but it also has its military use: "The state of being engaged in fight; a battle, conflict, encounter" ("Engagement, *N.* 8").[17] Everyone in this book has been involved in a "long engagement" in one way or another.

At the White Hart, Mrs. Musgrove and Mrs. Croft agree that long engagements are undesirable, and Mrs. Croft adds that worse still is "an uncertain engagement; an engagement which may be long," a situation she regards as both "unsafe and unwise" (J. Austen, *Persuasion* 251; vol. 2, ch. 11). Here she describes more or less the situation of Benwick and Fanny Harville,[18] but also of other couples who might better "settle on a small income at once, and have to struggle with a few difficulties together" (251; vol. 2, ch. 11). Uncertainty is a key term here; it defines wartime, that "uncertain engagement" that may end soon or may not. If one could know that it would be over (with all concerned safe) "in six months, or even in twelve," people could plan, but its nature is to keep hearts and minds on the stretch (251; vol. 2, ch. 11).

Earlier in the novel, Admiral Croft observes that "sailors can't afford to make long courtships in time of war" (98–99; vol. 1, ch. 10). Anne and Captain Wentworth come to agree. But in a sense, the novel's point is that their "engagement" has stretched out painfully since "the year six" (68; vol. 1, ch. 8). I ask students to watch the novel's uses of "engaged," "disengaged," and their variants, and to see if they agree that Austen is sometimes up to something. I also ask them to look for other words that have military overtones as well as everyday ones. One shouldn't press this exercise too far—an ingenious student may be too clever by half—but it is nonetheless fruitful to observe how a reader preoccupied with war may perceive semantic slippage, the crossing of linguistic domains.

Usually, the novel's wartime idiom is less a question of multiple meanings than of register. Characters shift into naval language, either playfully or from force of habit. Even Sir Walter does this, referring to Kellynch as a "prize" for a tenant (19; vol. 1, ch. 3). The naval officers do it frequently, such as when Admiral Croft observes that Wentworth should "spread a little more canvas" and decide on a wife (99; vol. 1, ch. 10), or when Harville assures Wentworth that he does not need to rush his letter: "There is no hurry on my side. I am only ready whenever you are.—I am in very good anchorage here, . . . well supplied and want for nothing.—No hurry for a signal at all" (254; vol. 2, ch. 11). Students will be able to identify additional examples.

Let me note in closing that the wartime approach links easily and obviously to other important issues raised by *Persuasion*: questions related to physical, social, and economic mobility; competing values of inherited privilege and meritocracy; themes of memory and mourning; the switching of gender codes; Anne's painful introversion and thwarted efforts to promote family peace; and even formal techniques for representing characters' interior lives. Lynch, echoing other appreciative readers, writes of the novel's "language of psychological tumult," its "energetic, agitated prose" (Introduction vii). These stylistic features reflect the societal upheaval the novel depicts, but surely they also embody the emotional turmoil of wartime, which induces mixed longing, hope, and fatigue and tests the limits of the expressible. Wartime intensifies most of the key tensions and possibilities that structure *Persuasion*. Demonstrating this to students energizes and defamiliarizes the novel, just when many of them think they know what to expect of Jane Austen.

NOTES

[1] Recent scholarship offers excellent resources for thinking about Austen's conversations with contemporary events and models of history, not to mention Austen's representations of wartime specifically. In particular, Mary Favret's *War at a Distance* has thoroughly influenced my reading of *Persuasion*, to the point that I feel my whole teaching of it now is little more than a gloss on what Favret has done, with bits of Deidre Shauna Lynch (Introduction) and Brian Southam (*Jane Austen* [2nd ed.]) thrown in. Thus, I have no pretensions to originality in this essay. I merely endorse the application of good scholarship in the classroom and invite others to join me in the pedagogy of theft (privateering?).

[2] Since *Persuasion* draws on the experiences of Austen's two youngest brothers, Francis and Charles, naval officers who saw action in important theaters of the Napoleonic wars, and of various family members and friends connected with them, teachers may want to offer some brief Austen family history as they frame the text. They will almost certainly want to sketch out a thumbnail history of the wars between Britain and France, which lasted from 1793 to 1815, and mention signal naval victories at the Battle of the Nile in 1798 and the Battle of Trafalgar in 1805, emphasizing the importance of naval supremacy for British identity and pride. This history can be rehearsed with a quick, lively lecture or provided in a preliminary handout. Teachers may also consult the essays in this volume by Monica F. Cohen and Sheila Johnson Kindred.

[3] Evan Gottlieb and Ian Duncan offer helpful ideas for teaching Austen alongside Scott in *Approaches to Teaching Scott's Waverley Novels*.

[4] In truth, the war *was* basically over for the navy, which did not need to be remobilized, though it did help transport troops and supplies to the Continent. Nonetheless, nobody knew for sure how things would turn out.

[5] The peace—the interval between the May 1814 signing of the Treaty of Paris and Napoleon's return in March 1815—will be outlined in the apparatus of most teaching editions of *Persuasion*, but teachers can easily explain this history if students are using mass-market or electronic texts without such guidance.

[6] The point of this slide is to show what sort of thing Sir Walter is reading. Teachers can get the same effect by using a facsimile of a title page from any edition of *The Baronetage*.

[7] Volume 1 ends after chapter 12, which is to say, just after the accident at Lyme. Some editions mark this volume division, while others simply number chapters sequentially. This is a natural dividing spot for reading assignments.

[8] Anne displays what the novel elsewhere calls her "right of seniority of mind" (108; vol. 1, ch. 11). The *Oxford English Dictionary* offers this definition for "seniority," one of the various meanings activated by Austen here: "Priority or precedence in office or service; esp. *Military*."

[9] The details of Richard's death are never reported. Favret aptly remarks, "I imagine that Dick's death involved some sort of fall, because falls—to boys and young women—just happen throughout this novel" (*War* 169).

[10] Barbauld's poem works well in a Romanticism course and may be worth inserting earlier in the syllabus as a prelude to *Persuasion* and its wartime atmospherics. Also interesting in terms of wartime news is Thomas De Quincey's "The English Mail-Coach" which some readers of *Persuasion* might recall during the discussion of how "the news [is] to be conveyed" after Louisa's accident (122; vol. 1, ch. 12).

[11] See also Favret, *War at a Distance*, on the effects of mediated war, and Linda Colley on the feeling of national belonging that developed as Britons rallied "against the major threats their nation faced from without" (1). This cluster of insights provides an additional link to Scott for teachers interested in exploring it. In *The Historical Novel*, Georg Lukács famously describes a new sense of living in history that was occasioned by the Napoleonic wars and that was captured by Scott. Several of Lukács's observations on Scott's fictions apply also to *Persuasion*.

[12] Compare Mrs. Croft on the painful winter she spent alone, at Deal, while her husband was on the North Sea (76–77; vol. 1, ch. 8). Southam notes that Jane Austen models this experience on that of her sister-in-law, Mary Austen, wife of Jane's brother Francis (*Jane Austen* [2nd ed.] 302). See the essay in this volume by Sheila Johnson Kindred on the experience of Austen's sister-in-law Fanny Palmer Austen as well.

[13] Most introductions to the novel will outline the navy's system of awarding prize money. If teachers do not assign such background material, they will want to explain the basics. The government rewarded the crew of a naval ship for capturing an enemy vessel and its cargo. The ship's captain received a three-eighths share or, after 1808, a one-quarter share.

[14] Meanwhile, Louisa and Benwick fall in love through what looks like the Florence Nightingale effect. Nursing is another theme in the novel that takes on extra edge through the wartime perspective. See the essay in this volume by Sylvia A. Pamboukian, "Nursing in *Persuasion*."

[15] It is just possible that one other land structure morphs briefly into a ship. We learn of it when Charles Musgrove reports on his improved opinion of Benwick: "His reading has done him no harm, for he has fought as well as read. . . . We had a famous set-to at rat-hunting all the morning, in my father's great barns; and he played his part so well, that I have liked him the better ever since" (J. Austen, *Persuasion* 237; vol. 2, ch. 10). Sailors faced constant belowdecks struggles with rats, and I suppose that Austen would have heard stories about rat hunts aimed at protecting food supplies. Perhaps Benwick revives his naval experience in this moment, transferring it from one enclosed, timbered space to another.

[16] Fittingly, this scene was shot on Lord Nelson's HMS *Victory*.

[17] This meaning of the word *engagement* has been available since at least the seventeenth century. Samuel Johnson's 1755 *Dictionary* has "Fight; conflict; battle" ("Engagement, 5").

[18] Benwick and Fanny Harville "had been a year or two waiting for fortune and promotion"; these "came at *last*; but Fanny did not live to know it" (104; vol. 1, ch. 11).

Baronets and the Baronetage: Close Reading the Opening Chapters of *Persuasion*

Margaret Case

One challenge in teaching *Persuasion* is conveying to students the cultural and narrative complexity of its brilliant opening chapters. These chapters provide important thematic foundations for the rest of the novel; however, some students have difficulty understanding Sir Walter Elliot's relation to the book, the Baronetage. The highly stylized genealogical phrasing (which is integral to the point) in the passage of the Baronetage read by Sir Walter in the novel's opening chapter can impede novice readers. Other students take issue with the scene for making fun of Sir Walter's pride in his family. They feel that Jane Austen pronounces too harsh a judgment when she writes that "[v]anity was the beginning and the end of Sir Walter Elliot's character" (4; vol. 1, ch. 1). These are understandable traps for readers who have been misled, as Sir Walter certainly is, by the formal syntax of the Baronetage.

Rather than trying to correct misinterpretations after the fact, I target problem areas well before students know that they will be reading *Persuasion*. On the first day of the term, for example, I hand out bookmark-sized slips of paper, which quote from the beginning of *Persuasion* without identifying the source:

> Fill in the blank in the opening sentence of this nineteenth-century novel:
>
> > [He] never took up any book but the B_____; there he found occupation for an idle hour, and consolation in a distressed one; there his faculties were roused into admiration and respect. . . .

Hints:

1. This same character records family deaths and marriages in the B_____.
2. Later in this chapter the narrator refers to the B_____ as "the book of books."

Although of course *Persuasion* fills in the blank with "Baronetage," none of my students has ever filled in the blank with that word. Instead, they usually guess "Bible." Not only does *Persuasion* deliberately invite that answer, but most of my (primarily American) students have never heard of the Baronetage. If they google the term, they might or might not find the information they need, but by then they have completely missed the ironic allusions to the Bible in this passage. However, once the word "Baronetage" has been removed, my students become quite adept at catching the point. For example, they have pointed out that the Bible

starts with *B*
could be referred to as the "book of books"
is known for its ability to provide "consolation" in "distress"
is where many families used to keep genealogical records
can create feelings of "admiration and respect"
advocates avoiding an "idle hour"[1]
was often the only book that families owned in the eighteenth and nineteenth centuries
might be the only book one would read if one was very religious (or only owned one book)

As we discuss their reasons for guessing the Bible, I ask students to record all this persuasive evidence (and their names) on their bookmarks. I then collect the bookmarks and pass them back right before they begin reading *Persuasion* (so that when they come to that passage, they will be able to refer back to their bookmarks).

The point of Austen's allusions to the Bible emerges once students have read the opening chapters. Sir Walter turns to the Baronetage, not his Bible, for consolation in distress in much the same way that he prioritizes his "dignity" as a baronet over the ethical dignity "due to the character of an honest man" (14; vol. 1, ch. 2). Since he himself is the "constant object of his warmest respect and devotion" (4; vol. 1, ch. 1), it makes sense that he would neglect his Bible (just as he neglects paying his bills).

However, although this opening exercise allows students to enjoy *Persuasion*'s first sardonic joke, it still leaves the elephant in the room. No matter how excellent the annotations, students need further coaching in order to understand how and why Austen hitches *Persuasion*'s opening paragraphs to the barge of the Baronetage. This early passage is a case in point: "[T]here his faculties were roused into admiration and respect, by contemplating the limited remnant of the earliest patents; there any unwelcome sensations, arising from domestic affairs, changed naturally into pity and contempt, as he turned over the almost endless creations of the last century . . ." (3; vol. 1, ch. 1). Sir Walter's admiration for something called the "limited remnant of the earliest patents" is richly parodic, but only if one understands these terms. Likewise, his "pity and contempt" for the "almost endless creations of the last century" reward decoding. Since these passages depend on the stylized genealogical language of the Baronetage, as well as specialized background history, it is no wonder that so many first-time readers of *Persuasion* either give up or respond negatively after reading only a paragraph or two.

I turn this problem to advantage by bringing the elephant into the classroom. Because Jane Austen herself very likely had personal access to *The New Baronetage of England*, I try to borrow a copy or two through an interlibrary loan.[2] I also lug to class an interlibrary loan edition of William Betham's impressive folio-sized, five-volume *The Baronetage of England; or, The History of the English Baronets*.

Recent editions of *The Peerage* and *The Baronetage* provide a nice contrast to the older editions, while emphasizing that the peerage and baronetage are still a living aspect of modern British culture.[3] Such books are in print and are important to those who enjoy tracing genealogical lineages. Indeed, both older editions and newer editions that arrive through interlibrary loan sometimes contain interlined genealogical information, illustrating the types of additions that Sir Walter makes in his copy.

The first time I brought in a print copy of *The Baronetage*, my students' intense interest caught me by surprise.[4] They eagerly perused the large volumes, trying to make sense of them, and exercised far more attention than I have ever seen them give to digital facsimiles. Students wanted more time than I had originally allotted to peruse the pages, and they generated excellent questions that allowed me to feed them the background information that *Persuasion* assumes they already know. With this in mind, I now borrow enough print editions of *The Baronetage* to have one for every pair of students, and I allow at least a full class period for them to examine the work. Several versions are also available electronically, which is handy for projecting specific pages when I want the entire class to look at the same passage from a particular edition.

I guide students with prepared questions and prompts, but I also leave ample time for them to generate and explore their own questions. For example, I ask selected groups to read aloud from family histories that mention service in "the office of High Sheriff" (J. Austen, *Persuasion* 4; vol. 1, ch. 1) or the seventeenth-century antiquary William Dugdale, who cataloged authentic titles for the nobility and the baronetage. Hearing the syntax and vocabulary used in *The Baronetage* allows students to notice how well Austen's text imitates it. I make sure students understand that it is a mark of prestige to be "mentioned in

Dugdale" (*Persuasion* 4). I also ask students to find actual mentions of Dugdale in their editions of *The Baronetage*. (There are plenty of these.)

During the session, I also guide students to important background information, most of which Austen's original readers would not have needed, but which is important for understanding the novel. For example, some students already understand that in Regency England, titles such as knight or baronet would have been granted by the monarch. Others, however, have sometimes assumed that Austen's novels contain *only* titled characters. Time spent discussing class distinctions and some of the details of entitlement is perhaps more important in *Persuasion* than in Austen's other novels, which contain very few main characters with titles. To make sure everyone has the same foundation, I start with the basics.

Some of my students assume that all titles are inheritable, and do not realize that inherited titles carry more social prestige than noninherited titles. I mention that in *Pride and Prejudice*, after William Lucas is knighted at court, he becomes Sir William Lucas. Sir William Lucas's first son could not inherit his father's title, since the title of knight is not hereditary. In contrast, the title of baronet is always hereditary. If Sir Walter Elliot's son had survived, he would have become the next Sir Walter. Since Sir Walter had no surviving sons, however, upon his death his title would pass to Mr. William Walter Elliot, the next closest male kin.

Austen's contemporaries would have understood the ranking system that allows Sir Walter to be so impressed with his own title. On *Persuasion*'s first page, readers learn that the title (the "dignity of baronet") was first granted to the Elliot family in "the first year of Charles II" (i.e., 1660, the year of the Restoration of the British monarchy). Sir Walter relishes the fact that the Elliot patent—the document conferring the grant of the title—was issued relatively soon after the order of baronets had been founded, in 1611.

Asking these types of questions invites students to actually use *The Baronetage*. It also acclimates them to specific genealogical terminology (e.g., title, patent, baronet) that suffuses the opening paragraphs of *Persuasion*, which are entrenched in the language, history, and cultural attitudes surrounding hereditary titles. I have noticed that students especially enjoy studying the family trees in these volumes, so I ask them to hunt for a family tree that shows a title that does not pass from father to son. If students try to find the Elliot family tree, I ask them where it might have appeared in any of the volumes of the editions we have in class. That question allows them to work together to establish the organizational pattern of *The Baronetage*. I also ask why there are no families named Elliot who received the title of baronet in any of their editions. This question reminds them both that the Elliots in *Persuasion* are a fictional family and that there are obvious reasons why Austen would have chosen a fictional family name.

In order to explain the confusing phrase "limited remnant," I briefly recap the history of the Restoration, including the toll it took on many of the families who had received the title of baronet. By Sir Walter's day, many of these families had died out: some through military service, others because they had failed to produce male heirs, and so forth. Sir Walter's admiration and respect for those precious "limited remnants" (i.e., the few remaining families still passing down the earliest patents) is directly correlated with his contempt for those who have more recently been made baronets. The phrase "endless creations" reveals Sir Walter's frustration with the relatively large number of baronets created in the eighteenth century.

In addition to its age, a title's status is also increased by its rarity. Sir Walter is upset by the "endless" number of new creations not only because such new patents strain the title's social prestige but also because, as the preface to Betham's 1801 edition of *The Baronetage* delicately phrases the situation, the "greatly augmented" number of baronets created during the previous century were not all from the landed gentry or yeoman class but included some who did not own land or who were from the merchant class (xiii).

What Sir Walter fails to realize (perhaps because he primarily reads only his own entry in the Baronetage) is that his own title was granted during a similar bumper crop of baronets. King Charles II created just over four hundred baronets, almost doubling the number of baronets created by all earlier monarchs. The 1660 creation, therefore, was itself part of an original batch of "endless" creations.

If one considers the baronetage in relation to the even older peerage, Sir Walter's contempt looks even more ridiculous. As Katherine S. Van Eerde explains in "The Creation of the Baronetage in England," the earliest patents themselves were created under conditions of financial exigency, and even those earliest patents that Sir Walter so admires "embraced a far wider section of society than [their] founders had proposed" (322).

Regency readers might not have known this history in detail; however, that information is available in the preface to Betham's widely circulated edition. And educated Regency readers would have known that baronets do not belong to the peerage. Baronets are subject to the laws for commoners in the British legal system, and, unlike nobility, they cannot serve in the House of Lords.[5] The peerage includes dukes, marquesses, earls, viscounts, and barons.[6] This distinction is noted clearly in forms of address: although baronets and knights have titles, they are technically commoners and are addressed as "sir," in contrast to peers of the realm, who are addressed as "lord."

Sir Walter's contempt for the bumper crop of baronets created only a few decades after he received his title should have been qualified by his knowledge that the order of baronets was established several centuries after the orders that constitute the peerage. Some dukes and earls, among others, could trace their patents back to the twelfth century or earlier, whereas the baronetage was not established until the seventeenth century.[7] Sir Walter's contempt for "new creations," therefore, ignores the humbling fact that the baronetage itself is a relatively "new creation" (82; vol. 1, ch. 9).[8]

All these ideas lend force to the parody that is *Persuasion*'s opening, which itself sets the foundation for an alternative ranking system that emerges later in the novel with the introduction of Captain Frederick Wentworth and his naval comrades. Initially, however, readers familiar with the cultural context of the peerage will understand that Sir Walter's delight with "the place he held in society" is analogous to the delight of "the valet of any new made lord" (J. Austen 4; vol. 1, ch. 1).

Vanity has made Sir Walter oblivious to the concept of service and to "exertions of loyalty" (e.g., serving as "High Sheriff," serving in Parliament, or serving one's liege in wartime). In contrast to his word-for-word reading of the paragraph in the Baronetage that mentions him specifically, the text suggests that Sir Walter skims over the rise of the Elliot family, "in the usual terms," just as he skims over "all the Marys and Elizabeths [his ancestors] had married" (4; vol. 1, ch. 1). The exertions that earn entitlement do not seem to interest Sir Walter. He accepts no responsibility, even for paying his bills to merchants. Nor does he bother to say goodbye to his tenants when he relocates to Bath. He instead relegates that duty to his daughter Anne.

After Sir Walter departs for Bath, Anne quietly observes to herself that her father actually did not "deserve" to stay at Kellynch Hall: "Kellynch-hall had passed into better hands than its owners" (136; vol. 2, ch. 1). Having relocated to Bath, Sir Walter and Elizabeth assume they are "deeply regretted in their old neighbourhood," but Anne is unable to corroborate that assumption (148; vol. 2, ch. 3). Once Admiral Croft and his wife move into Kellynch Hall, Anne notes ruefully that the Crofts will perform Sir Walter's duties better than he did himself. They will ensure "the poor of the best attention and relief" (136; vol. 2, ch. 1). The tradesmen, too, will no doubt be relieved to be paid liberally by the Crofts for their goods and services, in contrast to their treatment by Sir Walter, who did not even pay his creditors.

The same inability to link the honor of a title to exertions of loyalty is apparent when Sir Walter mocks naval officers who have risked their lives during the Napoleonic wars. Sir Walter at first hesitates at the thought of renting Kellynch Hall to a naval officer. When Anne observes that the navy "who have done so much for us, have at least an equal claim with any other set of men, for all the comforts and all the privileges which any home can give," Sir Walter objects to the entire profession because it threatens his two favorite prepossessions: "the blessing of beauty" and "the blessing of a baronetcy" (4; vol. 1, ch. 1). He sneers at naval officers with weather-beaten complexions. He objects to sailors "of obscure birth" being raised "into undue distinction" and finds it offensive that the profession "cuts up a man's youth and vigour most horribly" (21; vol. 1, ch. 3).

Persuasion's parody of Sir Walter's vanity may participate in what Mr. Elliot calls the "unfeudal tone of the present day" (150; vol. 2, ch. 3). The idea that a title might catalyze a more intense desire for achievement was a hotly debated topic in the late eighteenth century. Benjamin Franklin, for example, invited a contrast between those who have received titles for services rendered (ascending titles) and those who have inherited their titles (descending titles) to argue that an inherited title was likely to have a debilitating effect on "[p]osterity, since it is apt to make them proud, disdaining to be employ'd in useful Arts, and thence falling into Poverty" (Franklin 163).

Persuasion illustrates this contrast by pitting the proud, enervated, and financially distressed Sir Walter against vigorously active, treasure-laden naval officers such as Wentworth. One real-life Regency example of such an officer is Horatio Nelson, who was born a commoner. Nelson's admission to the peerage was so famously controversial that it would almost certainly have come to the minds of Regency readers when Sir Walter contemptuously dubs naval service "offensive" because it is a "means of bringing persons of obscure birth into undue distinction" (J. Austen 21; vol. 1, ch. 3). Calling such titles "undue" contradicts the established historical justification for the granting of titles, which were given to reward exertions of loyalty.

Regency readers would also probably have thought of Lord Nelson when Sir Walter references naval men whose youth and vigor are most horribly "cut up." Nelson famously suffered the loss of vision in one eye during the 1794 invasion of Corsica, and most of one arm in the Battle of Santa Cruz de Tenerife in 1797. The head wound he suffered during the Battle of the Nile in 1798 required two years of recuperation. He later lost his life in Britain's great naval victory against Napoleon's fleet at Trafalgar in 1805.

Consistently dismissive of the correlation between sacrifice and nobility, Sir Walter has "not been very much tempted" to give up anything (5; vol. 1, ch. 1). Unlike Lady Russell and Anne, Sir Walter cannot even be convinced by the argument that a "person who has contracted debts must pay them" (13–14; vol. 1, ch. 2). Instead of being inspired by his forefathers' exertions of loyalty to be good and brave, Sir Walter is a "foolish, spendthrift baronet, who had not had principle or sense enough to maintain himself in the situation in which Providence had placed him" (270; vol. 2, ch. 12). Although Mary Musgrove reflects near the end of the novel that Wentworth might one day earn the title of baronet (272), *Persuasion*'s argument for social value clearly does not depend on his entitlement. Instead, *Persuasion* sides with Franklin in favoring tangible merit over inherited honors.

In short, from its opening sentence, *Persuasion* channels the language and syntax of the Baronetage ostensibly to legitimize Sir Walter's point of view, while in fact exploring the lack of correlation between entitled dignity and earned dignity. By subtly yet relentlessly exposing Sir Walter's self-importance, the first chapter invites readers to contrast Sir Walter's descending entitlement with Wentworth's ascendancy. Since most students have no difficulty reading *Persuasion* for its romance, Wentworth's value is usually obvious to them. However, they might miss the way Wentworth's social value stands in direct competition with Sir Walter's love of the baronetage and with Mr. Elliot, who gradually learns "to pin his happiness upon the consequence he is heir to" (223; vol. 2, ch. 9).

I ask students to track which characters are able to successfully evaluate character. Lady Russell is unable to ascertain actual value. Her assessment that Wentworth "had nothing but himself to recommend him" is strikingly close to Sir Walter's assessment that Edward Wentworth is "nobody" (26; vol. 1, ch. 3), a term that Sir Walter also applies to his own daughter Anne (6; vol. 1, ch. 1). As the novel continues, these assessments are gradually overturned by more discerning characters, none of whom confuse titles with actual dignity.

To help students understand their roles as active close readers in these early chapters, it is useful to draw their attention to Austen's use of indirect free discourse in the passage mentioned above, where Anne is first introduced. This passage begins squarely from Sir Walter's point of view, but it soon shifts:

> [Sir Walter's] two other children were of very inferior value. Mary had acquired a little artificial importance, by becoming Mrs. Charles Musgrove; but Anne, with an elegance of mind and sweetness of character, which must have placed her high with any people of real understanding, was nobody with either father or sister; her word had no weight; her convenience was always to give way;—she was only Anne. (6; vol. 1, ch. 1)

When I teach this passage, I project it on a screen and ask students to identify phrases that are clearly from Sir Walter's point of view (e.g., "nobody," "inferior value," "artificial importance," and "only Anne"). I then ask my students to identify phrases or ideas that are not from Sir Walter's point of view (e.g., "any people of real understanding" and "her elegance of mind"). I then ask them why this paragraph moves from one point of view to another—and then back again.

We then return to the opening sentences of chapter 1 to see whose point of view the novel is channeling through the diction of the Baronetage (the answer is, Sir Walter's). As students recognize these and other moments in which Austen plays with point of view, they begin to learn why one must read a Jane Austen novel nimbly. It is easy, but dangerous, to align the narrator's own point of view with a particular character's or with a cultural viewpoint that the novel is exploring. This exercise also prepares students to watch for the growing ascendency of Anne's point of view as the novel progresses.

I also ask students how Mr. Shepherd's brilliant rhetorical manipulation convinces Sir Walter to let Kellynch Hall. Mr. Shepherd bides his time until the aggrieved Sir Walter complains that "he would sooner quit Kellynch-hall at once" (14; vol. 1, ch. 2) than remain in it without the luxuries that Lady Russell has suggested he eliminate. Mr. Shepherd pounces:

> "Quit Kellynch-hall." The hint was immediately taken up by Mr. Shepherd, who . . . was perfectly persuaded that nothing would be done without a change of abode.—"Since the idea had been started in the very quarter which ought to dictate, he had no scruple," he said, "in confessing his judgment to be entirely on that side. It did not appear to him that Sir Walter could materially alter his style of living in a house which had such a character of hospitality and ancient dignity to support.—In any other place, Sir Walter might judge for himself; and would be looked up to, as regulating the modes of life, in whatever way he might choose to model his household." (14–15; vol. 1, ch. 2)

Since Sir Walter has not, in fact, proposed quitting Kellynch Hall, Mr. Shepherd must torture both truth and syntax to make the suggestion appear as if it has come from Sir Walter. He oils the attempt with liberal appeals to Sir Walter's vanity. His rhetorical manipulation works swiftly. The next paragraph begins, "Sir Walter would quit Kellynch-hall." Mr. Shepherd succeeds where Lady Russell had failed because "the art of pleasing . . . at Kellynch-hall" requires pandering to vanity (17; vol. 1, ch. 2).

After anchoring in the opening chapters of *Persuasion*, students are ready to sail through the rest of the novel. And indeed, my students generally do realize how the opening chapters chart the course for the entire novel. Alerted to the importance of point of view and to Sir Walter's dangerous vanity and reminded by my constant references back to the opening chapters, several students have noticed on their own that the final chapter of this novel constitutes a full revolution. Instead of dismissing Anne and Wentworth as "nobody" (6; vol. 1, ch. 1), Sir Walter prepares "his pen with a very good grace for the insertion of the marriage in the volume of honour" (271; vol. 2, ch. 12).

The marriage that occurs is Anne's, not Elizabeth's, the one Sir Walter had been expecting (6; vol. 1, ch. 1). These are just two of many reversals in the final chapter. Perhaps the single greatest reversal is the final line's emphasis on the importance of the navy as a profession that is "distinguished" for both its domestic virtues and its national importance. Instead of channeling one character's narcissistic entrenchment within culturally sanctioned systems of entitlement, the final lines float free from any one character's point of view. Captain Wentworth's profession was "all that could ever make [Anne's] friends wish [her] tenderness less; the dread of a future war all that could dim her sunshine. She gloried in being a sailor's wife, but she must pay the tax of quick alarm for belonging to that profession which is, if possible, more distinguished in its domestic virtues than in its national importance" (275; vol. 2, ch. 12). Here, Anne and Wentworth's friends worry about her as she worries about her husband, who is acting on behalf of his country in the Napoleonic wars. Instead of reveling in pity and contempt, the voice in these lines expresses community concern. Despite dwelling on the past with contentment, it dreads the possible loss of life in a future war even as it values both tenderness and military service. Regency readers of this novel in 1818 were in a position to know just how devastating these losses would be and how close the world would come to being overtaken by a self-styled emperor.[9] In marrying the daughter of a "nobody" who descends from an entitled family to a "nobody" who ascends to wealth and property, *Persuasion* thus radically ennobles domestic virtue.

NOTES

1 Once in a while, a student will cite the quotation "idle hands are the devil's workshop" from Proverbs 16.27 (*Holy Bible*). If no one in the class knows it, I supply it.

[2] Any handsome duodecimo edition will do.

[3] Any recent print editions would do: for instance, Kidd et al. and Mosley. One benefit to bringing in a separate edition of *The Peerage* is that it provides a physical demarcation between the baronetage and the peerage to help students realize that they are not the same thing. (I use a small rolling piece of luggage to bring these books to class—which piques students' interest.)

[4] Bringing any eighteenth- or nineteenth-century edition of *The Baronetage* to class will have the same effect.

[5] The composition of the House of Lords changed in 1958 with the Life Peerages Act, which altered the system for granting hereditary titles, allowing, for example, women to sit in the House of Lords.

[6] See Smith's diagram of class structure (72–73).

[7] There were a few earlier baronets, but the baronetage itself was not established until 1611.

[8] The phrases "new creation" and "new creations" appear later in the text and are uttered by Mary Musgrove. "'Upon my word it would,' replied Mary. 'Dear me! If he should rise to any very great honours! If he should ever be made a baronet! "Lady Wentworth" sounds very well. That would be a noble thing, indeed, for Henrietta! She would take place of me then, and Henrietta would not dislike that. Sir Frederick and Lady Wentworth! It would be but a new creation, however, and I never think much of your new creations'" (81–82; vol. 1, ch. 9). Here Mary exhibits the same Elliot snobbery toward new creations that is evident in Sir Walter's thoughts in the first paragraph of the novel, where Sir Walter feels "pity and contempt" for the "endless creations of the last century" (3; vol. 1, ch. 1). In both cases, the Elliots are privileging older titles over newly created titles.

[9] For a comprehensive treatment of the Napoleonic wars in Austen's novels, see Southam, *Jane Austen* (2nd ed.).

Writing the Life of Feeling in *Persuasion*

Timothy Peltason

Attending to the life of feeling in *Persuasion*—both to the value that Jane Austen assigns to feeling and to her particular genius for representing it—students can find a way through the novel that touches on many of its most important topics and follows its central line of action and thought. For beginning students, this exercise in attention offers training in the skills of close reading and bears witness to its value; for advanced students it opens an approach to the study of narrative technique and, in particular, of Austen's advances—both on earlier novelists and in the course of her career—in the representation of inwardness.

Although this essay glances at other characters, it spends most of its time, as does Austen's narrator, in the company of Anne Elliot. Austen represents and admires both Anne's powers of rational thought and her moral judgment. But the novel comes most fully to life in representing Anne's capacity for something less categorical and harder to describe, for an intelligent fullness of feeling, a sympathetic alertness to experience and to other persons that is unmatched by any other character in the novel and that Anne shares with her creator. This power of feeling is clearly connected with intelligence, but it is distinct from it. Our richest experiences of Anne's capacities occur in those passages in which the rush of her feelings outpaces and even overwhelms rational thought and requires from Austen new and protomodernist techniques of notation.

Students will readily take up the invitation of the opening chapters to follow the fortunes of the undervalued daughter of Kellynch Hall—"she was only Anne"—and will recognize this familiar plot structure from many other Cinderella-like narratives. Looking more closely at the opening chapters of *Persuasion*, they can readily discern a distinctive further feature of Austen's narrative—that Sir Walter Elliot and his daughter Elizabeth are not just less worthy than Anne, but less substantial in every way. It's not merely that the novel will attend less to these characters, but that they have so much less character to attend to. Sir Walter's outrageous vanity and Elizabeth's coldness are signs not just of moral failure but of cognitive limitation, an inner emptiness that prepares the coming contrast with the richness of inward experience that we will find in Anne when the narrative settles into its intimacy with her in a few chapters.

That process begins with the last sentence of chapter 3, as Anne reacts privately to the news that Admiral and Mrs. Croft will be the new tenants of Kellynch Hall.

> Mr. Shepherd was completely empowered to act; and no sooner had such an end been reached, than Anne, who had been a most attentive listener to the whole, left the room, to seek the comfort of cool air for her flushed cheeks; and as she walked along a favourite grove, said, with a gentle sigh, "a few months more and *he*, perhaps, may be walking here."
>
> (27; vol. 1, ch. 3)

The attentive listening, the flushed cheeks, and the italicized "*he*" all signal a quiet intensity of feeling that we find in nobody else in this circle, not even the sympathetic Lady Russell. As if prompted by Anne, the next chapter begins with her breathless pronoun—"*He* was not Mr. Wentworth, the former curate of Monkford, however suspicious appearances may be, but a captain Frederick Wentworth, his brother"—and goes on to tell the story of Anne's canceled engagement to the young captain, who was "full of life and ardour," a match to Anne's own capacities for feeling.

From this point forward, the narrative rarely leaves Anne's company, passing subtly in and out of her consciousness. When the novel first tells us of Sir Walter's falling into debt, it offers a first, brief course in this Austenian narrative technique:

> While Lady Elliot lived, there had been method, moderation, and economy, which had just kept him within his income; but with her had died all such right-mindedness, and from that period he had been constantly exceeding it. It had not been possible for him to spend less; he had done nothing but what Sir Walter Elliot was imperiously called on to do; but blameless as he was, he was not only growing dreadfully in debt, but was hearing of it so often, that it became vain to attempt concealing it longer, even partially, from his daughter. (9–10; vol. 1, ch. 1)

Asked to say whether the novel really holds Sir Walter "blameless," students will readily see that the forthrightly evaluative narrator who assigns "all . . . right-mindedness" to his wife cannot think so. Instead, this assignment of blamelessness must be Sir Walter's own, efficiently establishing not just his improvidence but his comically complete self-approval. Borrowing in this way the inward voices of the characters, Austen's narrative stations itself at once inside and outside their minds, making possible a complex perspectivism of judgment and experience.[1] The perspective of Sir Walter is not so complex though, since his experience of the world is depthless and unvarying, and the narrative judges him with sharp irony.

But with Anne this strategy of representation produces extraordinary results, permitting us to enter into the fullness of her experience of the world and at the same time to see her as she does not always see herself, with an irony that is never less than affectionate but that comprehends a range of feeling and understanding even larger than Anne's own. Here is a first, great set piece, when Anne's sister Mary suddenly announces that Wentworth is about to pay them a visit:

> Mary, very much gratified by this attention, was delighted to receive him; while a thousand feelings rushed on Anne, of which this was the most consoling, that it would soon be over. And it was soon over. In two minutes after Charles's preparation, the others appeared; they were in the

> drawing-room. Her eye half met Captain Wentworth's; a bow, a curtsey passed; she heard his voice—he talked to Mary, said all that was right; said something to the Miss Musgroves, enough to mark an easy footing: the room seemed full—full of persons and voices—but a few minutes ended it. Charles shewed himself at the window, all was ready, their visitor had bowed and was gone; the Miss Musgroves were gone too, suddenly resolving to walk to the end of the village with the sportsmen: the room was cleared, and Anne might finish her breakfast as she could.
>
> "It is over! it is over!" she repeated to herself again, and again, in nervous gratitude. "The worst is over!"
>
> Mary talked, but she could not attend. She had seen him. They had met. They had been once more in the same room! (64; vol. 1, ch. 7)

It's both a narrative joke and a simply asserted truth that Anne has a thousand feelings to Mary's one. Working together through this passage, students can learn a great deal both about Anne and about Austen's way of bringing her to us. What, do we suppose, are some of those thousand feelings that course through Anne at the anticipation of Wentworth's appearance? Why—with what effect—does Austen throw out this comically large number? When the meeting itself comes, what happens to the narrator's sentences? How do they mimic the rapidity and disorder of Anne's thoughts? What do we infer from Anne's ability in the midst of this rapidity and disorder to attend admiringly to Wentworth's manners (he "said all that was right") and to discern in them that he's already familiar with Louisa and Henrietta Musgrove? To whom do the exclamation marks in those last paragraphs belong, and does it make a difference that the last three sentences are not in quotation marks even though the thoughts are surely Anne's?

I'm engaged in a kind of comic excess myself—a thousand questions rush upon me—but I want to supply enough such questions to discharge my own responsibilities, while deferring to the different questions that will readily occur to teachers as they open the passage with their students. A few points do insist upon themselves. As intelligent and well-judging as Anne is—and there is no heroine in Austen whose judgment is less often second-guessed by the narrator—what this passage offers is not ratiocination, but a buzz and flood of feeling. The power of Anne's mind first registers itself here not as a sequence of thoughts or judgments but in its absolute capacity for feeling and in its ability, even while overwhelmed, to engage in small but significant acts of discernment and recognition. As the passage continues, Anne both rises and falls into the mode of rational consideration, but not without considerable resistance and backsliding.

> Soon, however, she began to reason with herself and try to be feeling less. Eight years, almost eight years had passed, since all had been given

> up. How absurd to be resuming the agitation which such an interval had banished into distance and indistinctness! What might not eight years do? Events of every description, changes, alienations, removals,—all, all must be comprised in it; and oblivion of the past—how natural, how certain too! It included nearly a third of her own life.
>
> Alas! With all her reasonings, she found, that to retentive feelings eight years may be little more than nothing. (64–65; vol. 1, ch. 7)

And then Anne quickly sets to the business at hand—"Now, how were his sentiments to be read? Was this like wishing to avoid her?"—only to be interrupted again by sobered reflection. "And the next moment she was hating herself for the folly which asked the question." So much for "feeling less." And so much for any analytic ambition—either Anne's or ours—to disentangle feeling from "reasonings" and to place one in authority over the other. As the rest of the novel demonstrates forcibly, and as any alert reader will know already, there's nothing "absurd" about "resuming the agitation" of the life of feeling, a life that can be banished into indistinctness only by those whose feelings are as shallow as those of Sir Walter and Elizabeth, or as unreal as those of Mary Musgrove.

A few chapters later, Austen discovers another occasion of surging feeling in a moment that is less obviously significant than a first encounter, a moment when Wentworth finds himself awkwardly in company with Anne, who is engrossed in attending to her injured nephew, Charles, on a sofa. Henrietta Musgrove's suitor, Charles Hayter, enters the room, followed quickly by the two-year-old Walter Musgrove, who promptly fastens himself to Anne's back so that she is unable to extricate herself from one child to care for the other.

> In another moment, however, she found herself in the state of being released from him; some one was taking him from her, though he had bent down her head so much, that his little sturdy hands were unfastened from around her neck, and he was resolutely borne away, before she knew that Captain Wentworth had done it.
>
> Her sensations on the discovery made her perfectly speechless. She could not even thank him. She could only hang over little Charles, with most disordered feelings. His kindness in stepping forward to her relief—the manner—the silence in which it had passed—the little particulars of the circumstance—with the conviction soon forced on her by the noise he was studiously making with the child, that he meant to avoid hearing her thanks, and rather sought to testify that her conversation was the last of his wants, produced such a confusion of varying, but very painful agitation, as she could not recover from, till enabled by the entrance of Mary and the Miss Musgroves to make over her little patient to their cares. She could not stay. (86–87; vol. 1, ch. 9)

Sensation precedes knowledge here as Anne finds herself "in the state of being released"—odd phrasing—before she knows how she got there. Overwhelmed as she is, Anne closely tracks the flow of feelings in the room—Wentworth's quick withdrawal and its possible meaning, the bustling interest of the women who have entered, Charles Hayter's resentment of Wentworth, who has stepped forward to help as Hayter ought to have done. "But neither Charles Hayter's feelings, nor any body's feelings, could interest her, till she had a little better arranged her own." As in the account of Anne's first meeting with Wentworth, Austen breaks the narration briefly into fragments to capture Anne's disorientation, the rush of noticings and feelings, one following another too quickly to be processed into the orderliness of the understood. This is apprehension, stalled and receptive, on its way to comprehension.

Such passages differ notably from those that represent the effortful self-understandings of earlier Austen heroines, such as the one in *Pride and Prejudice* in which Elizabeth Bennet sorts out her feelings at chapter length as she reads and rereads Darcy's letter after she has refused his proposal (227–32; vol. 2, ch. 13); or, in *Emma*, the great sequence of paragraphs, a tour de force of represented consciousness, in which Emma Woodhouse must confront the evidence of Mr. Elton's proposal that she has misread her world disastrously (145–49; vol. 1, ch. 16). These are extraordinary passages, especially the second of them, which is dense with turns of phrase and feeling that characterize Emma's mind and its movement. But they are also passages of relative clarity and deliberateness, appropriate for representing the inner lives of young women who are accustomed to the self-possession of social mastery.

In *Persuasion*, and in the representation of Anne Elliot, Austen has set herself a different task and discovered different resources. In the passages that we've examined thus far, and in many others, Anne proves her exceptional strength and worth not with displays of wit or achieved understanding, but by demonstrating repeatedly an enlarged capacity for feeling as it passes in and out of reflective thought.

Elsewhere in the early narrative of Anne's reacquaintance with Wentworth, the narrator presents us with further instances of Anne's capacities for attention and response. There are moments of concentrated feeling like the passages above, as when Wentworth assists Anne into Admiral and Mrs. Croft's carriage because he sees that she is tired: "Yes,—he had done it. She was in the carriage, and felt that he had placed her there, that his will and his hands had done it, that she owed it to his perception of her fatigue, and his resolution to give her rest" (98; vol. 1, ch. 10). But there are other moments, less intense moments, in which the narrator expands our understanding of Anne with a different mixture of exposition and dramatization. This is partly a matter of Anne's alertness to the feelings of others—especially Wentworth—as well as to her own feelings. Finding herself frequently in company with him, she is alive to his moods and responses and reads his feelings confidently across the social space between them. Hearing him mention other events of the year in which they first met, Anne knows what he must be thinking:

> [A]nd though his voice did not falter, and though she had no reason to suppose his eye wandering towards her while he spoke, Anne felt the utter impossibility, from her knowledge of his mind, that he could be unvisited by remembrance any more than herself. There must be the same immediate association of thought, though she was very far from conceiving it to be of equal pain.
>
> They had no conversation together, no intercourse but what the commonest civility required. Once so much to each other! Now nothing! There had been a time, when of all the large party now filling the drawing-room at Uppercross, they would have found it most difficult to cease to speak to one another. (68–69; vol. 1, ch. 8)

The passage opens outward in many directions. Once again, the narrative thinks and feels with Anne, this time as she feels and thinks with Wentworth, and her "knowledge of his mind," neither confirmed nor questioned by the narrator, leads her to repeated intensities of inward exclamation. Does the narrator know anything that Anne doesn't here? Is there any room for ironic discrepancy between Anne's understanding—either of Wentworth or of herself—and our own? What can we infer about Anne's mind from her inferences about Wentworth's—about the "utter impossibility" that one memory will not trigger another? What can we infer about Anne's values and the novel's from this thumbnail definition of intimacy, that it is especially a matter of "finding it difficult to cease to speak to one another"? This passage and many others in its vicinity dramatize the sequence of Anne's thoughts and feelings, advancing at once our knowledge of Anne, our presumptive knowledge of Wentworth, and a family of implied propositions about what it is that constitutes a rich inwardness. As controlled as Anne's behavior is—and she is a model of thoughtful conduct throughout—feeling itself is anarchic, its authenticity demonstrated at least partially by its irrepressibility.

This anarchy of feeling takes a variety of forms in the passages that follow. When Mrs. Musgrove grows tearful about her dead son—the "thick-headed, unfeeling, unprofitable Dick Musgrove," who served briefly on one of Wentworth's ships (54; vol. 1, ch. 6)—Anne knows from "a momentary expression . . . a certain glance of his bright eye," a sign "too transient . . . to be detected by any who understood him less than herself," that Wentworth hardly regretted the loss of Dick (73; vol. 1, ch. 8). Again, the narrative lets us infer the accuracy of Anne's perceptions and seems to confirm them as it slides from Anne's consciousness into the most notorious instance in Austen's fiction of what D. W. Harding memorably refers to as "regulated hatred."[2] It's Anne and Austen together who register for us Wentworth's "sympathy and natural grace," his kind consideration for "all that was real and unabsurd" in Mrs. Musgrove's feelings. But in a sentence that looks from without on "Anne's slender form, and pensive face," it seems to be the narrator who then allows Wentworth "some credit for the self-command with which he attended to [Mrs. Musgrove's] large fat sighings over the destiny of a son, whom alive nobody had cared for" (73; vol. 1, ch. 8).

This is an extraordinary and disturbing passage, the discussion of which can lead in a variety of directions. Readers who are repelled by this passage—as many students are in my experience—will have strong arguments to offer, particularly ones that relate to our still underdeveloped consciousness of the ubiquity of prejudice against fatness. But it will be salutary to complicate their responses and our own by considering, first, the mercilessly satiric moments on television or at the movies that we might have laughed at (students will be able to offer their own fair number of these); and second, the observation that this satiric perception is located entirely in the privacy of feeling.

Austen herself insists on the forgivability of such feelings in an additional paragraph in which she acknowledges that, although "a large bulky figure has as good a right to be in deep affliction, as the most graceful set of limbs in the world," and whether it's "fair or not fair," there are appearances and circumstances "which ridicule will seize." Again, irrepressibility is at issue, and we should hear an emphasis in this phrase on the word "will." Ridicule has a mind of its own. No attentive reader of the novel can suppose that Anne, or Wentworth, would behave cruelly, and it seems likely that the narrator has left them behind in a passage whose satiric sharpness is notably unregulated, something that we encounter occasionally in Austen's letters but nowhere else in her fiction. What has led the narrative here—and what the narrator does share with Anne, indeed, confers upon her—is a freedom of thought and feeling that will include moments both of surprising sharpness and of unapologetic self-concern.

The novel dramatizes elsewhere this right to self-concern as a part of the free life of feeling. When Louisa falls disastrously at Lyme, it is Anne who responds most quickly and usefully—"with all the strength and zeal, and thought, which instinct supplied"—without Mary's self-indulgent hysterics or Henrietta's somewhat more justifiable fainting fit (119; vol. 1, ch. 12). It is Anne whose power of mind shows itself in alert responsiveness in several directions. And it is also Anne, when Wentworth advises the others to heed her—"no one so proper, so capable as Anne!"—who "paused a moment to recover from the emotion of hearing herself so spoken of" and to note that Wentworth speaks to her "with a glow, and yet a gentleness, which seemed almost restoring the past" (123; vol. 1, ch. 12). The narrative forgives Anne readily for her moment of self-regard and even allows her, a few pages later, the tough-minded thought that Wentworth may now think less of the willfulness that he earlier admired in Louisa. When the news of the accident spreads to the other people on the Cobb, they crowd in to be useful, but also "to enjoy the sight of a dead young lady, nay two dead young ladies, for it proved twice as fine as the first report" (120; vol. 1, ch. 12). Austen is hardly outraged at what she understands so well, this spectatorial interest in what does not touch us directly. If life is a tragedy to those who feel and a comedy to those who think, it is something odder and fuller to those who do both, like Anne and her creator.

Once we are alerted to the theme of pardonable self-regard, we notice small signs everywhere of Anne's gratified responsiveness to the attentions of others, of Wentworth primarily, but also of Mr. William Elliot, Captain Benwick, and Admiral and Mrs. Croft, who "always met her with a kindness which gave her the pleasure of fancying herself a favourite" (136; vol. 2, ch. 1). Unlike *Emma*, whose protagonist indulges to excess in this naturally pleasurable sensation, *Persuasion* allows us to enjoy unreservedly a good fortune that comes late to Anne Elliot and that neither spoils nor deceives her.

Anne's clear-eyed judgments of Mr. Elliot are of special interest. With the speed and sureness granted by her own intelligence, Anne determines when she meets him that "[t]here could be no doubt of his being a sensible man. Ten minutes were enough to certify that. His tone, his expressions, his choice of subject, his knowing where to stop,—it was all the operation of a sensible, discerning mind" (155; vol. 2, ch. 3). In observing his "knowing where to stop," Anne anticipates the praise of discretion that Lady Russell offers a few pages later in a narrative paragraph that channels her entirely affirming judgment of Mr. Elliot: "He was steady, observant, moderate, candid; never run away with by spirits or by selfishness, which fancied itself strong feeling" (159; vol. 2, ch. 4).

For Lady Russell, who "could not seriously picture to herself a more agreeable or estimable man," this praise of reserve is offered unreservedly. Anne, however, has known for years now "that she and her excellent friend could sometimes think differently" (158; vol. 2, ch. 4). Though she does not it say, even to herself, the narrative makes clear that she is larger-minded than Lady Russell in every way, able to picture more in Mr. Elliot than Lady Russell sees, and able to picture larger and other virtues than those that Mr. Elliot seems to display. The traits that Lady Russell admires in Mr. Elliot distinguish him from the shallow and unimaginative Sir Walter and Elizabeth, as from the selfish Mary Musgrove. But it's an impoverishing weakness in this novel to be "never run away with by spirits." When Anne measures Mr. Elliot directly against Captain Wentworth in a later passage—and this is before the melodramatic revelations of Mr. Elliot's scheming wickedness—she and the novel offer an explicit declaration on behalf of strength of feeling.

> Mr. Elliot was rational, discreet, polished,—but he was not open. There was never any burst of feeling, any warmth of indignation or delight, at the evil or good of others. This, to Anne, was a decided imperfection. Her early impressions were incurable. She prized the frank, the open-hearted, the eager character beyond all others. Warmth and enthusiasm did captivate her still. (175; vol. 2, ch. 5)

The novel testifies most effectively to the values of "[w]armth and enthusiasm" in those exhilarating passages in the second volume that invite us to share, again and more pleasurably than ever, in the enlarging exercise of Anne's own feelings. As Anne enters her second spring of attraction in the second volume of the novel, she matures in healthy self-love and approaches the final happiness of her reunion with Wentworth through a sequence of further episodes in her life of feeling. Deliberately protracting and diffusing Anne's discovery of this happiness, Austen indulges herself and the reader by writing a series of scenes in which Anne both knows and doesn't know that Wentworth loves her, scenes that make the wonderful conclusion of the novel less a climax than the last in an extended sequence of gratifications.

A full third of the novel remains when Anne hears the news of Benwick's engagement to Louisa: "She had never in her life been more astonished. Captain Benwick and Louisa Musgrove! It was almost too wonderful for belief; and it was with the greatest effort that she could remain in the room, preserve an air of calmness, and answer the common questions of the moment. Happily for her they were not many" (179–80; vol. 2, ch. 6). Students will by now recognize this mind-melding narrative technique, in which we both watch Anne's response and feel it with her, trying to take in this new wonder, trying to manage feeling into ordered thought. With the help of the *Oxford English Dictionary* students can ponder the various meanings of both "astonished" and "wonderful." And they can then watch Anne, as she works her way into a tentative understanding of the match, only to surrender again to unmanaged feeling:

> The conclusion of the whole was, that if the woman who had been sensible of Captain Wentworth's merits could be allowed to prefer another man, there was nothing in the engagement to excite lasting wonder; and if Captain Wentworth lost no friend by it, certainly nothing to be regretted. No, it was not regret which made Anne's heart beat in spite of herself, and brought the colour into her cheeks when she thought of Captain Wentworth unshackled and free. She had some feelings which she was ashamed to investigate. They were too much like joy, senseless joy!
>
> (182; vol. 2, ch. 6)

Students will be able to notice for themselves the color in Anne's cheeks and the beating of her heart, also the components of the emphatic finish—the repetition, the exclamation point, the force and rightness of "senseless." With help and prompting they can see how the paragraph moves forward in both substance and style from distanced reflection—Is the match suitable? Will Captain Wentworth's friendship with Benwick be damaged by it?—to the happy abandonment of senseless joy. And other questions present themselves. Where is the narrator in these reflections? Should Anne be "ashamed" to investigate these feelings? What might be revealed if she does? Perhaps Anne will discover that she is precipitate in thinking that Captain Wentworth's freedom will bring Wentworth to her, or perhaps that she is not yet ready to acknowledge to herself how ardently she longs for such a culmination.

Whatever the result of such investigations, the novel makes clear soon enough that Anne cannot and need not suppress this new round of surging feeling. We can complete our survey with two last passages, one from each of the two next chapters. There are many more passages and observations, both before and after this point in the novel, that teachers and their students might pause over to fill out this discussion and to touch on the many important discussions that are adjacent to it. But these last two set pieces are especially rich, as they echo and extend the presentation of Anne's inner life that we have been following.

When Anne first spies Wentworth in Bath, just the day after she receives the news that Louisa is out of the way, she and the narrative give themselves completely to a rush of feeling that echoes her first encounter with him at Uppercross. But now she is ready to acknowledge his continuing importance to her, having been brought along by the passage of time and also by her own new standing in the world, as demonstrated by the attentions of Mr. Elliot.

> Her start was perceptible only to herself; but she instantly felt that she was the greatest simpleton in the world, the most unaccountable and absurd! For a few minutes she saw nothing before her. It was all confusion. She was lost; and when she had scolded back her senses, she found the others still waiting for the carriage, and Mr. Elliot (always obliging) just setting off for Union-street on a commission of Mrs. Clay's.
>
> She now felt a great inclination to go to the outer door; she wanted to see if it rained. Why was she to suspect herself of another motive? Captain Wentworth must be out of sight. She left her seat, she would go, one half of her should not be always so much wiser than the other half, or always suspecting the other of being worse than it was. She would see if it rained. She was sent back, however, in a moment by the entrance of Captain Wentworth himself, among a party of gentlemen and ladies, evidently his acquaintance, and whom he must have joined a little below Milsom-street. He was more obviously struck and confused by the sight of her, than she had ever observed before; he looked quite red. For the first time, since their renewed acquaintance, she felt that she was betraying the least sensibility of the two. She had all the advantage of him, in the preparation of the last few moments. All the overpowering, blinding, bewildering, first effects of strong surprise were over with her. Still, however, she had enough to feel! It was agitation, pain, pleasure, a something between delight and misery. (190–91; vol. 2, ch. 7)

Is it Anne or the narrator who rushes so quickly through the closing lists of adjectives and nouns, struggling to name and tame this welter of feelings? What does it show us about Anne that she engages in such an exercise of self-understanding or about Austen that she brings these resources to bear on representing such an exercise? How does this passage compare to the earlier one at

Uppercross? Does it make use of the same techniques? Does it show Anne in a new light or a new position? Students can notice as the scene unfolds that Anne no longer tries to resist her own impulses, though both she and Wentworth control their behavior well enough to engage in the necessary civilities with each other and with all of those present.

In just the next chapter—and with a quarter of the novel still remaining—Wentworth finds a way to make those feelings clear to Anne in an evening scene that brings to fruition so much of what has come before. Over a spread of several pages, Austen introduces and sustains an experience of delighted discovery and confirmation in Anne of what Anne has sensed for so long about her unity of feeling with Wentworth. They are together at an evening concert, and they fall awkwardly into conversation about the engagement between Benwick and Louisa. Although we experience the event, as always, with Anne, the narrative confirms through dialogue and observation that she and Wentworth are both vibrating with emotion. At one point, as Wentworth is speaking: "[h]e stopped. A sudden recollection seemed to occur, and to give him some taste of the emotion which was reddening Anne's cheeks and fixing her eyes on the ground." He goes on to describe Benwick's loss of Fanny Harville in language that inescapably recalls his own earlier loss of Anne. "Fanny Harville was a very superior creature; and his attachment to her was indeed attachment. A man does not recover from such a devotion of the heart to such a woman!—He ought not—he does not." Austen continues:

> Either from the consciousness, however, that his friend had recovered, or from some other consciousness, he went no farther; and Anne, who, in spite of the agitated voice in which the latter part had been uttered, and in spite of all the various noises of the room, the almost ceaseless slam of the door, and ceaseless buzz of persons walking through, had distinguished every word, was struck, gratified, confused, and beginning to breathe very quick, and feel an hundred things in a moment. It was impossible for her to enter on such a subject; and yet, after a pause, feeling the necessity of speaking, and having not the smallest wish for a total change, she only deviated so far as to say,
>
> 'You were a good while at Lyme, I think?' (199; vol. 2, ch. 8)

It's an extraordinary moment and an extraordinary passage. The hundred things that Anne feels in a moment recall the thousand that rushed upon her when Wentworth was about to enter the room for their first meeting in the novel. Here, however, Anne's new strength—the result of a gradual process of which Wentworth's implicit disclosures to her here are the culmination—permits her and us to experience this pile-up of sensations as a form of mental power. As much as Anne is feeling here, her mind is operating at full strength, "distinguish[ing] every word" in a busy public room that instantiates the obstructive social world through which Anne and Wentworth must find their ways to each other. Readers of *Sense and Sensibility* will recall the oppressively hot, packed evening room in which Marianne Dashwood spies John Willoughby only to be coldly repelled by him, her cry of genuine feeling setting her painfully apart from the social artifice of the occasion. Here it is hearteningly different; Anne combines Marianne's strength of feeling with Elinor Dashwood's virtues of conduct and restraint; the two lovers, Anne and Wentworth, are alone *together* in the midst of company, psychically connected as Anne could only imagine that they were in those earlier parties at Uppercross. Feeling the social necessities of the occasion, Anne can speak as she must, keeping herself open to new signals from Wentworth, but otherwise deferring until she can speak to him as unmistakably (if obliquely) as he has just spoken to her. That won't happen until the end of the novel when she has a chance to tell Captain Harville in Wentworth's hearing—poor Fanny Harville again performing an important service to this new love affair—that women's feelings are at least as enduring as men's. For now, both social and aesthetic decorum prevent Anne from breaking down and pressing herself into Wentworth's arms, as Marianne would have done. Instead she vindicates the life of strong feeling by affirming its consistency with the requirements of both social form and moral obligation.

Her continued conversation with Wentworth enacts a further dance of decorous revelation—students will readily sense the vibrations of something deeper in their exchange of views about Lyme and about what they experienced together there. But they are interrupted, as they have been constrained, by the demands of civility:

> The others joined them, and it was a group in which Anne found herself also necessarily included. She was divided from Captain Wentworth. Their interesting, almost too interesting conversation must be broken up for a time; but slight was the penance compared with the happiness which brought it on! She had learnt, in the last ten minutes, more of his feeling towards Louisa, more of all his feelings, than she dared to think of! And she gave herself up to the demands of the party, to the needful civilities of the moment, with exquisite, though agitated sensations. She was in good humour with all. She had received ideas which disposed her to be courteous and kind to all, and to pity every one, as being less happy than herself. (200–01; vol. 2, ch. 8)

When she looks back again,

> [h]e was gone—he had disappeared: she felt a moment's regret. But "they should meet again. He would look for her—he would find her out long before the evening were over—and at present, perhaps, it was as well to be asunder. She was in need of a little interval for recollection."
> (201; vol. 2, ch. 8)

This passage is noteworthy for the inner quotation marks, as if the last words are a transcription not just of thought but of thought passing into inner speech. It's intriguing to speculate with students about the distinction Austen might be asking us to make, though I would hesitate to rest large conclusions on such slender evidence. What is unmistakable, however, is that Anne and the novel have reached a new state of confidence and security. In another page, she draws the clear and marvelous conclusion from what she has experienced in the course of the evening: "He must love her."

Asking students what the novel gains from such an early and inward declaration can lead discussion in several directions. That this revelation comes so early calls attention to the pleasure and meaning that Austen derives from watching the lovers find each other out through the obstructive medium of meetings in company and then through the mediation of overheard conversation and of letters. There are dozens of places, in the passage above and elsewhere, in which Austen stresses the demands of civility, a stress that has the force not of lessening the prestige of feeling in the novel but of dramatizing its ability to find strength and form in social constraints. By locating these passages and considering these issues, advanced students can extend the comparisons above with *Sense and Sensibility* or can look back on Emma Woodhouse's struggle to keep her free life of feeling from overflowing into social transgressions, at Box Hill and elsewhere.

That the revelation in *Persuasion* is inward—that the declaration of Wentworth's love happens in Anne's mind before it happens in his letter to her—confirms yet again the centrality to the novel of representations of enhanced consciousness. When the two lovers finally declare their love for each other openly in the penultimate chapter, the narrative insists on privacy of at least two kinds—on Wentworth's and Anne's privacy, as Austen characteristically declines to write for them the actual language of their spoken declarations, and on the privacy that they must maintain even after they have understood each other but before their love can be acknowledged. They are not the only lovers in Austen's novels who cherish their understanding secretly in this way, but the cherishing has a new force here because of the long education the novel has given us in the quality of Anne's inner life. Returning home after she and Wentworth have declared themselves, "Anne was at home again and happier than any one in that house could have conceived" (266; vol. 2, ch. 11). This tells us not just that Sir Walter and Elizabeth and Mrs. Clay did not imagine Anne's happiness but that they *could* not imagine it and thus could not experience anything like it, that Anne Elliot has capacities for feeling that place her far beyond their reach, capacities that the novel has dramatized for us with unexampled resourcefulness.

NOTES

I first developed some of the arguments of this essay, and make them at greater length and with different emphases, in Peltason.

[1] This distinctive Austenian technique also goes by the name of free indirect discourse in contemporary discussions of narratology. For further discussion of free indirect discourse, see Wood 8–38. See also the introduction to this volume and the essay by Peter J. Capuano.

[2] D. W. Harding's "Regulated Hatred: An Aspect of the Work of Jane Austen" was originally published in *Scrutiny* in 1940 and is collected in Harding (5–26).

Thinking with Austen: Literature, Philosophy, and Anne Elliot's Inner World

Magdalena Ostas

Through the form of the novel, Austen thinks in insightful and expansive ways about knowledge, truth, morality, community, subjectivity, identity, and many other concepts whose explication has traditionally belonged to philosophers. When I teach *Persuasion* in courses situated at the intersection of literature and philosophy, I ask students to attend to the ways Austen can help us approach classic concepts like these from a uniquely literary perspective. I suggest that *Persuasion* can help us think from a point of view that reflects the difficulties inhabiting the definitions of such concepts, one that is guided by a willingness to probe and explore rather than fix. Philosophers have always had theories—about people, language, understanding, and fiction—that we can draw on to illuminate literary texts. In my courses on philosophical approaches to literature, I stress a different philosophical avenue into *Persuasion*, and I focus, contrastingly, on Austen as a writer whose novels suspend the traditional priority of philosophical argument over literary insight. My engagement with *Persuasion* in this context differs from my approach to teaching Austen's novels in courses focused on British literary history, Romanticism, or nineteenth-century literature. In the course Literature and Philosophy and the course Art and Ideas, I foreground how *Persuasion* takes up, talks back to, tarries with, and throws light on classic philosophical questions about morality, identity, and the self's inner life. These are questions that were alive for Austen's contemporaries, and my students find that they also resonate forcefully with contemporary debates about identity and ethics.

The breadth of considerations that such an approach opens means that everything is on the table: historical context, social background, class, gender, marriage, love, memory, regret, narrative form, sentence structure, and style. This has the effect of letting students think by means of the novel, because they are asked to enter its world as a whole and to continually consider foundational questions: What is important for Austen in understanding how her characters live? What does she make vivid about their interactions, the connections among them, and their relation to themselves? What aspects or parts of the world are especially significant for her moral explorations? What does a sketch of the coordinates and horizons of Austen's moral interests include? The gap between my students' world and the world of *Persuasion* begins to dissipate as the class works to understand Austen's literary moves as perspectives that have the power to bring aspects of Anne's world into view. I tell my students that narrative can be similar to photography or painting in this regard: like images, novels are bounded by a frame, one that contains things within it but that excludes innumerable other things. If *Persuasion* were a picture, I ask, what is it a picture of—what is its subject? I encourage the class, then, to conceive of the novel's literary thinking as an open field bounded by horizons that prompt our looking and probing in particular directions. Our philosophical approach thus never yields a distinct moral message or an essential argument, and it never entails distilling Austen's stance about an issue or idea. Instead, the approach encourages students to read with a greater attentiveness to the resonances of Austen's meanings within their context.

Accessing Austen's explorations of human identity in *Persuasion* depends on understanding the novel's protagonist. No character in Austen's novels is as silently intelligent, quietly reflective, and absorbed in her own inner life as Anne Elliot, and as students enter the novel, they slowly register that *Persuasion*'s perspectival frame centers on Anne's solitary consciousness and that the story will not entail any sensational happenings. The families will travel, Louisa Musgrove will fall from steps on the Cobb, and Captain Frederick Wentworth's pen will slip during a conversation so that Anne hears it drop—but nothing more dramatic than that will happen. Rarely had so much happened only on the inside in fiction, at least before the Romantic period, and the observation that *Persuasion* is a drama that initially unfolds only in an inner world steers students' sense of the novel's subject.

Our engagement with the novel as a whole extends from a directed classroom activity that I introduce after students have read four chapters, when I give them the straightforward task of collectively sketching a lucid and detailed characterization of Anne. The activity often elicits enthusiasm and full participation because it calls for a range of answers expressed in each student's own words, and I gather responses and passages on the board. As our portrayal deepens, some responses amend and build on others, and the answers add up to a satisfying and uniquely filled-out portrait visible to the entire class. Suddenly the reserved and vaguely interesting Anne receives complete attention. Characterizing Anne is much more demanding than it might appear, and even advanced students find this activity an appropriately challenging entryway into the novel, as they slowly find that Anne's character carries few outward or definitive signs in the first four chapters. The activity thus forces students to become articulate about and more interested in a character who is unseen to those around her within her fictional world: Anne is passive, isolated, excluded, slighted, and often silent. I push students to get past the too-easy idioms: wallflower, introvert, pushover, and so on. As the class patiently stays with Anne and considers her disposition with attention, we uncover her depth, complexity, and internal range together.

What can emerge from this directed but informal brainstorming is a carefully formed contour of someone living entirely for others and in exile from her own life. Students are eager to cite passages in which Anne allows herself to be serviceable, accommodating herself to others in the roles of nurse, babysitter, caregiver, or quiet confessor. Anne is unacknowledged by others, yet students note that she responds to others' cares and concerns constantly. The class quickly sees the weakness in Anne's cooperativeness and sympathy, and they often conclude that she is self-effacing and tragically cocooned within her own unassertiveness.

As emblematic of Anne's fundamental estrangement—and the unclear, vexed perspective of the narrative voice on her condition of inner exile—students often point to her geographic displacement: "She disliked Bath, and did not think it agreed with her—and Bath was to be her home" (15; vol. 1, ch. 2). Yet students also see that Anne becomes a uniquely perceptive interpreter of the world from such a position. Like a novelist, she stands aside and looks out with calm intelligence, honest emotion, and patient vision at the world around her, registering things with a third-person-like capaciousness. Since Anne lacks an active function in the world, she lives buried within her own contemplative and emotional responsiveness. Students who have read *Pride and Prejudice* (or have seen one of the film adaptations) frequently point out the contrast in this regard between the introspective Anne and the bold and sparkling Elizabeth Bennet, who shares with Anne the fate of being stuck in a silly family from which she requires an escape. Unlike Elizabeth, Anne has a rich inner life that is rarely penetrated by other characters, but for her the world is a place that offers little possibility of fulfillment. To confirm the class's sense of Anne's character in volume 1, I often conclude with Virginia Woolf's comments about *Persuasion*. Woolf writes that Austen sees life in this novel "through the eyes of a woman who, unhappy herself, has a special sympathy for the happiness and unhappiness of others, which, until the very end, she is forced to comment upon in silence" (144).

Equipped with this rich portrait of Anne from *Persuasion*'s early chapters, the class is then prepared to leap conceptually to *Persuasion*'s second volume, where we witness Anne's slow emergence out of the quiet discontent of her inner world. We discuss moments in the novel during which Anne is pressed into action and is thereby rendered visible, particularly the scenes surrounding Anne's reaction to Louisa's falling unconscious from an overhasty jump (J. Austen 118–21; vol. 1, ch. 12). With the shift between volumes as a demarcation line, The class charts Anne's change in a second characterization activity that considers how Anne changes between volumes 1 and 2. For many students, *Persuasion*'s central concern turns out to be Anne's emergence as a character who comes to be known in the world, and students emphasize that the novel dramatizes this process of her coming to be a character outside the rich life of her interiority. In advanced courses I often assign or read aloud in class excerpts from secondary criticism that is similarly attuned to Austen's preoccupation with inner life and its outward or social forms of expression.[1] As Anne's inside comes to make contact with the outside, she takes on the role of a "proper" and "capable" subject (123; vol. 1, ch. 12)—and a proper heroine too. In the end, Anne is acknowledged—by Wentworth, to be sure, by the friends around her, and by her family, but she is also acknowledged by the novel itself, which in its beginnings seems to struggle with the undertaking of rendering this particular heroine visible. Austen, in thinking about human identity, utilizes the novel, a temporal form, to progressively turn her character inside out.

To turn Anne increasingly outward in this way and to give her inner life expressive force, Austen needs the freedom of moving in and out of her character's thoughts and feelings. For example, we know that in the end Anne glories in her destiny as a sailor's wife, but we register how earnest and complete her contentment is ("happier than any one . . . could have conceived" [266; vol. 2, ch. 11]) only because we have glimpsed firsthand her deepest desires for her life and witnessed her sharpest internal struggles throughout the novel. The novel's moral explorations of identity pivot on Austen's ability to dwell on the experience of being Anne from the inside as much as on Austen's ability to convey Anne's circumstances and actions. I introduce the narrative techniques and structures whereby Austen affords us access to Anne's inner world and thereby "lyricizes the novel" (Tuite 7), giving priority to happenings within her character's internal landscape rather than to events or occurrences: Austen's methods are more than simple narrative devices. I ask the class to entertain the idea that the details of Austen's narrative building in *Persuasion* are expressions of the author's moral imagination. We investigate free indirect discourse as a kind of perspectival mirror that captures points of view whose convergence adds up to meaningful moral exploration. To be carried along by the modulations of free indirect discourse as one reads is to imaginatively involve oneself in the variances of perspective that constitute the moral dimensions of living. Our examination of free indirect discourse, then, focuses on the ways this technique in Austen's storytelling delineates the world and communicates an understanding of it through the shaping and manipulation of prose sentences.

When students near the conclusion of *Persuasion*, I ask them to prepare a brief presentation for the class that explicates an instance of free indirect discourse and that focuses on the broader significance of the technique for the moment they have chosen: What does free indirect discourse allow Austen to convey about the character and situation in this instance? What aspects of character and situation more broadly does this narrative approach allow her to reveal and to consider? To prepare students for the assignment, we practice together with a handful of key passages, and we begin with Austen's emblematic fragment "she was only Anne" (6; vol. 1, ch. 1). A simple question about the fragment often draws out answers that concisely highlight the power of Austen's technique to embed varied points of view. As I ask whose perspective "only Anne" captures, we begin to catalog the phrase's possible issuers: she is "only Anne" from the point of view of her family, all of whom undervalue her; or perhaps from the point of view of just her father, who is even more uncaring and neglects her; or from her own perspective, which results from her having internalized her family's disregard; or perhaps loosely from the narrative point of view, which is momentarily ironic here and thereby doubts the judgment that Anne is supposedly ordinary. Sometimes students discover "only Anne"—her singleness and singularity—echoed in Wentworth's final letter, wherein he has loved "none but" her and her "alone" (258; vol. 2, ch. 11), a statement that transforms Anne's condition of onlyness entirely.

When we move through such passages, students begin to see the moral resonances of Austen's technique, which is essential to the way Austen weaves narrative, as the class addresses the differences between free indirect discourse and omniscient storytelling, the latter of which can appear to transcend perspectives rather than follow their shifting variations. The task, for students, of presenting an interpretive reading to the class demands that they explore the intersection of narrative detail and abstract ideas in the text, finding how the novel's philosophical resonances dwell within the particulars of form and content. The most successful and illuminating student presentations remain tied closely to the modulations of perspective within Austen's sentences.

Students find that sometimes the oscillations in Austen's free indirect discourse suggest the perspectives of actual characters in the novel, and the activity of naming these perspectives can be amusing and engrossing for students, as when Lady Russell seems momentarily to haunt the narrative voice when it suddenly declares, without quotations marks, "Anne Elliot, with all her claims of birth, beauty, and mind, to throw herself away at nineteen; involve herself at nineteen in an engagement with a young man, who had nothing but himself to recommend him . . ." (29; vol. 1, ch. 4). Students also uncover important instances in the novel when the objective or apparently realist narrative voice can be easily intonated with sharp satire and criticism—and when a clear decision about Austen's tonal register is impossible: "The Mr. Musgroves had their own game to guard, and to destroy; their own horses, dogs, and newspapers to engage them; and the females were fully occupied in all the other common subjects of house-keeping, neighbours, dress, dancing, and music" (46; vol. 1, ch. 6). Finally, students are especially eager to trace the rhythms of inner debate and struggle as they emerge into narrative language and, strangely, at times become indistinguishable from third-person commentary. The simple sentence in chapter 7 that relates Wentworth's hard feelings, "[Wentworth] had not forgiven Anne Elliot" (66; vol. 1, ch. 7), certainly might be read as a factual claim about his lingering resentment, but students also perceive Austen's use of the severe "Anne Elliot" as evidence of Anne's cruel self-reproach as she momentarily regards herself through Wentworth's eyes and sees the decision she made seven years ago in the harshest light, now grasping its repercussions. Additionally, this assignment often pushes students to recognize that Austen's allegiance to the details of ordinary life—walks, dinners, conversations, and looks—reflects Austen's moral imagination more broadly. The unextraordinary world Austen portrays is not provincial or limited, in fact, but actually saturated at each step with ethical significance. The ethical charge of the ordinary and trivial in Austen's novels often exceeds that of the supposed dramas of heroism, adventure, politics, and war—and romance as well.

One of the most satisfying aspects of teaching *Persuasion* at the intersection of literature and philosophy stems from Austen's experiments with the genre of romance, her refusal in this novel to indulge the plot of new and spontaneous love. In *Persuasion* Austen shapes a narrative that places the ardent first meeting offstage and within memory. She reshuffles time in *Persuasion* so that the past comes to overlay the present like a transparency. Discussing Austen's decision to deny her reader the satisfaction of an unabridged account of the first encounter between Anne and Wentworth helps students see that *Persuasion*'s plot is much more complex than easy clichés about reviving hope or the triumph of true love would suggest. In fact, the satisfaction of teaching *Persuasion* as a novel deeply engaged with our conceptions of identity and morality and our lives with others stems from students' startling recognition that Austen is occupied with the topic of love precisely because it is not at all a "little," trivial, or indulgent concern (Newman). Marriage is consequential—one might say completely determinative—for the women whose lives Austen sketches in her novels, especially for those who endeavor to find acknowledgment and independence within marriage, an institution that can (as Austen also shows) threaten to swallow or eclipse them instead. To give context to our discussions of marriage, we read from the conversation about the lives of women and men in love at the conclusion of the novel, especially from Anne's public but personal assertions (*Persuasion* 253–56; vol. 2, ch. 11). It can be a revelation for some students that a plot centered on romance can absorb and convey reflections on identity and moral development that have such philosophical weight. Sometimes it is an achievement for students just to have discovered this point. *Persuasion* thus often appears in my courses on literature and philosophy among other works by writers who similarly help us think in complex ways about our identities, our relationships with others, and our inner lives: Mary Wollstonecraft, Emily Dickinson, Henrik Ibsen, and Virginia Woolf. All of them, additionally, recognize that literature can communicate truths that cannot be grasped without the exploratory ground novels, plays, and poems offer us and from which philosophy too can learn.

NOTE

[1] In upper-division seminars I assign critical commentary on the topics of social life, inner life, and representation, drawing most often from these sources: Brown, *Jane Austen's Novels* 1–37, 127–50; Cohn, *Transparent Minds* 107–15; Lynch, *Economy* 207–49; and Wiltshire, *Jane Austen* 155–96 and *Hidden Jane Austen* 1–11, 147–68.

Teaching about Persuasion in *Persuasion*

Julie Ann Melnyk

What is the moral status of persuasion? Should you try to persuade others to change their minds about central life decisions? Should you bow to such persuasion in your own life? Jane Austen's novel *Persuasion* is ideally suited to teaching from a humanistic perspective that treats the novel as a form of moral deliberation. By providing a wealth of social and psychological detail, novels such as Austen's stress the inherently contextual nature of ethical thought. Moreover, the dialogism of the novel incorporates many viewpoints, even if in Austen the subtle, ever-present perspective of the narrator guides the reader's deliberations. Thus, the novel helps destabilize simplistic moral categories of right and wrong and leads to deeper discussions of moral issues and responsibilities.

The Central Persuasion

In discussing *Persuasion*, students will immediately want to examine the act that determines much of the action of the novel: Lady Russell's persuading Anne Elliot to break off her engagement with Captain Frederick Wentworth. Many college-age students, just the age of Anne when she makes the decision, will condemn Lady Russell's interference in Anne's romantic life and Anne's weakness of will in giving in to persuasion. But Austen does not make the decision clear-cut. Anne is just nineteen; she has known Captain Wentworth only "a few months"; Wentworth is her first love. Austen's narrator reveals, using free indirect discourse, Lady Russell's prejudices in favor of class and wealth and against enthusiasm, but the narrator also makes clear that Lady Russell believes herself to be acting in Anne's best interests and to have a position as mother substitute to justify persuasion:

> Anne Elliot, with all her claims of birth, beauty, and mind, to throw herself away at nineteen; involve herself at nineteen in an engagement with a young man, who had nothing but himself to recommend him, and no hopes of attaining affluence, but in the chances of a most uncertain profession, and no connexions to secure even his farther rise in that profession; would be, indeed, a throwing away, which she grieved to think of! Anne Elliot, so young; known to so few, to be snatched off by a stranger without alliance or fortune; or rather sunk by him into a state of most wearing, anxious, youth-killing dependance! It must not be, if by any fair interference of friendship, any representations from one who had almost a mother's love, and mother's rights, it would be prevented. (29; vol. 1, ch. 4)

The diction of the narrator is here influenced by the emotions of Lady Russell, even where her presence is not explicitly noted: "throw herself away," "snatched off by a stranger," "youth-killing dependance," and all tell against the marriage.

Should Anne let herself be persuaded? She is able to withstand other social forces, represented by her father and sister, but is weakened by Lady Russell's opposition. Note, however, that her fundamental reason for breaking off the engagement is Captain Wentworth's welfare: "But it was not a merely selfish caution, under which she acted, in putting an end to it. Had she not imagined herself consulting his good, even more than her own, she could hardly have given him up.—The belief of being prudent, and self-denying principally for *his* advantage, was her chief consolation, under the misery of a parting—a final parting . . ." (30; vol. 1, ch. 4). The narrator does not immediately evaluate these moral choices—Lady Russell's to persuade and Anne's to be persuaded—leaving readers here to their own judgments, but we do get Anne's evaluation at the end of the novel:

> I have been thinking over the past, and trying impartially to judge of the right and wrong, I mean with regard to myself; and I must believe that I was right, much as I suffered from it, that I was perfectly right in being guided by the friend whom you will love better than you do now. To me, she was in the place of a parent. Do not mistake me, however. I am not saying that she did not err in her advice. It was, perhaps, one of those cases in which advice is good or bad only as the event decides; and for myself, I certainly never should, in any circumstance of tolerable similarity, give such advice. But I mean, that I was right in submitting to her. . . . (267–68; vol. 2, ch. 11)

First, note that this evaluation resists consequentialism: negative consequences of the action don't mean that it was wrong. Anne, whose values closely align with the narrator's by this point in the novel, decides that she would not have given such advice in the same situation—the advice was wrong—but that at nineteen and in her situation, she was right to follow it. Many students will be tempted to stop here, with a complex understanding of this one moral act and a happy ending, but Austen is still more deeply engaged with ideas of persuasion, moral decision-making, and happiness.

Other Persuasions

The central act of persuasion in the novel is far from the only act of persuasion, and looking at these lesser acts complicates and illuminates the novel's meaning. To examine these acts, students can be assigned (or at least encouraged) to download a free e-book of *Persuasion* and search for uses of "persuade," "persuasion," "persuading," "dissuade," and so forth, and then to discuss what they find. Some of the analysis is interesting from a distant reading perspective: who persuades whom about what? How often do people persuade themselves of something? Other passages will warrant more attention, leading students to combine digital humanities methods with more traditional close reading methods.

Students will find that Anne is often called upon to be the persuader: to persuade her father to retrench or her sister Mary to change her behavior toward her children. In these cases, persuasion, if it could be accomplished, would clearly be a good thing. We connect Louisa Musgrove's boastful refusal to be persuaded to her serious injury: "What!—would I be turned back from doing a thing that I had determined to do, and that I knew to be right, by the airs and interference of such a person?—or, of any person I may say. No,—I have no idea of being so easily persuaded. When I have made up my mind, I have made it" (93–94; vol. 1, ch. 10). It is sometimes wrong not to be persuaded by good advice, and examples multiply. But is it ever wrong to refrain from persuading others to change their minds? Austen gives us a situation analogous to Lady Russell's interference against Wentworth: Mrs. Smith's noninterference in what she thinks are Anne's plans to marry Mr. William Elliot.

Mrs. Smith believes that Mr. Elliot is a bad man. In fact, she condemns him in the harshest terms used in any of Austen's novels:

> Mr. Elliot is a man without heart or conscience; a designing, wary, cold-blooded being, who thinks only of himself; who, for his own interest or ease, would be guilty of any cruelty, or any treachery, that could be perpetrated without risk of his general character. He has no feeling for others. Those whom he has been the chief cause of leading into ruin, he can neglect and desert without the smallest compunction. He is totally beyond the reach of any sentiment of justice or compassion. Oh! he is black at heart, hollow and black! (215; vol. 2, ch. 9)

None of the villains in Austen's other novels merits this sort of language—not General Tilney, John Willoughby, George Wickham, or Henry or Mary Crawford. Yet Mrs. Smith, believing that Anne is planning to marry Mr. Elliot, at first stands by, apparently willing to let her do it. When she is finally convinced that Anne is not planning to marry him, her excuses for withholding information seem questionable:

> "I beg your pardon, my dear Miss Elliot," she cried in her natural tone of cordiality, "I beg your pardon for the short answers I have been giving you, but I have been uncertain what I ought to do. I have been doubting and considering as to what I ought to tell you. There were many things to be taken into the account. One hates to be officious, to be giving bad impressions, making mischief. Even the smooth surface of family-union seems worth preserving, though there may be nothing durable beneath.

> However, I have determined; I think I am right; I think you ought to be made acquainted with Mr. Elliot's real character." (215; vol. 2, ch. 9)

> "My dear," was Mrs. Smith's reply, "there was nothing else to be done. I considered your marrying him as certain, though he might not yet have made the offer, and I could no more speak the truth of him, than if he had been your husband. My heart bled for you, as I talked of happiness; and yet he is sensible, he is agreeable, and with such a woman as you, it was not absolutely hopeless." (228)

Could considerations of politeness, noninterference, or a public show of family unity justify letting Anne marry without having all the facts about her future husband? Is persuasion not only morally permissible but in some cases morally mandatory?

Anne Elliot and Ancient Ethics

Anne's moral decision-making in the novel links her with two ideas derived from ancient philosophy, both of which concern virtue and happiness. Some critics have analyzed her behavior in terms of Christian stoicism. Originating in the Hellenistic period, Stoicism is a school of philosophy associated first with Zeno of Citium, then with Epictetus, Seneca, and the Roman emperor Marcus Aurelius. Stoics point out that we have no control over what happens to us in our lives—we may be rich, respected, and famous, or we may suffer terrible illness, lose loved ones, and struggle with poverty. What we do have control over is our emotional reaction to these events. So Stoicism recommends that we moderate our emotions, never getting too attached to anything that can be taken away from us. That way, we will be able to be virtuous and happy whatever our external circumstances. Stoics work to remain calm and unruffled.

One otherwise puzzling passage clearly links Anne with this tradition. Mary has just returned from talking to Captain Wentworth, who told Henrietta that Anne was "so altered that he should not have known [her] again." "'So altered that he should not have known her again!' These were words which could not but dwell with her. Yet she soon began to rejoice that she had heard them. They were of sobering tendency; they allayed agitation; they composed, and consequently must make her happier" (65; vol. 1, ch. 7). For a Stoic, there is no contradiction here: moderating her emotions gives Anne victory over circumstances and in the long run makes her happier. As the ancients believed, virtue leads to happiness. Some classroom discussion of Anne's resulting stoic calm can also help circumvent false ideas about Anne being shy or unassertive or a people pleaser.

The other ancient philosophical idea that Anne comes to express is the idea of the golden mean. As Aristotle explains in his *Nicomachean Ethics*, virtuous behavior is the middle between two extremes. Behaving virtuously is like aiming for the middle of a target with a bow and arrow: you can miss by shooting too high or too low, meaning that you have too much or too little of a trait. For instance, when dealing with money, you can be too stingy (a vice) or too profligate (a vice): to be properly generous means balancing the two extremes. Aristotle designates courage as a virtue (29–30), and he would say that you can have too much or too little feeling of fear in the face of danger, or too much or too little action in the face of danger. These extremes can produce the vices of rashness (too little fear and too much action) or of cowardice (too much fear and too little action). But neither extreme represents courage, which is a virtue and therefore occupies a middle ground. One can't have too much virtue. After Louisa's fall, we see Anne endorsing the golden mean with respect to persuasion as well:

> Anne wondered whether it ever occurred to [Captain Wentworth] now, to question the justness of his own previous opinion as to the universal felicity and advantage of firmness of character; and whether it might not strike him, that, like all other qualities of the mind, it should have its proportions and limits. She thought it could scarcely escape him to feel that a persuadable temper might sometimes be as much in favour of happiness as a very resolute character. (J. Austen, *Persuasion* 126; vol. 1, ch. 12)

Students might want to argue that Henrietta is too persuadable, that Louisa is not persuadable enough, and that Anne has the perfect balance. The eighteenth century also valued these classical ideals, as Peter Knox-Shaw has shown in *Jane Austen and the Enlightenment*. *Persuasion* is an excellent novel in which to analyze Austen's moral thinking. Moral deliberation—in the novel and in the classroom—becomes a social act, and the effort to act virtuously is inextricably linked with happiness.

LITERARY CONTEXT

Teaching *Persuasion* in a Transient World

Julia Prewitt Brown

Persuasion, Jane Austen's last completed novel, differs from her earlier work in striking ways. It is the most precisely dated of all the novels, it makes more extensive use of free indirect discourse, its heroine is older than earlier heroines and her moral education has taken place before the novel opens, and, last but not least, *Persuasion* is saturated with themes of memory and forgetting. These are a few of the novel's unique elements, and their implications—aesthetic, psychological, historical, and philosophical—have always fascinated me. I've found that when I teach a single-author course on Austen, elaborating on these elements in class discussion is a fairly straightforward task, given that the students taking the course are usually English majors and already well-versed in Austen's works. More often than not, however, I teach *Persuasion* in other courses alongside works by other artists, including memoirists and filmmakers as well as novelists, to a more diverse group of students. Teaching *Persuasion* in such settings requires integrating discussion of the novel's particular achievements as a work of fiction into a larger thematic or historical design.

Moreover, in recent years I have taught *Persuasion* to an increasingly international and transient student body. One course I devised called Home and World regularly draws students majoring in international relations who have come to the university from around the globe. Most of the literature majors who take the course have also lived in more than one place in their lives. In the fall of 2005, the students enrolled in Home and World included a woman who had transferred from Tulane University for one semester because of the damage caused by Hurricane Katrina in New Orleans, two students who had relocated from Ukraine for political reasons, and several Asian students with student visas, among others—a readership nicely suited to *Persuasion*. At the beginning of the novel the heroine, Anne Elliot, is forced to leave her ancestral home. She moves from place to place until, upon marriage to a navy man, she embarks on a new life, possibly on board a naval ship. Anne is like some of my students in being uncertain about whether to look forward or backward, in wanting to resist nostalgia but being prey to it, in often having to find her way as a guest in another's home, and in feeling unsure about how to remain centered psychologically when she no longer has a center geographically. All of these concerns are a consequence of the experience of leaving home, whether that experience occurs in Jane Austen's fictional world or in our own.

The aim of the course Home and World is to consider the deep psychological significance of home together with the more worldly problems that have historically affected one's ability to establish a home. How do writers imagine the home in relation to self, gender, family, race, class, nation, and the world? Throughout the term we consider a range of sources from other disciplines, including psychology, history, painting, and film, but our main emphasis is on fiction and memoir. We begin with Daniel Defoe's *Robinson Crusoe* and end with W. G. Sebald's collection of stories *The Emigrants*. The assigned texts in between include *Persuasion*, Emily Brontë's *Wuthering Heights*, Joseph Conrad's *Heart of Darkness*, E. M. Forster's *Howards End*, and Walter Benjamin's *Berlin Childhood around 1900*.

Readers familiar with these works will immediately recognize, I think, that each one might be considered seminal to a course that takes as its subject the relations between the home and the larger world. Each marks a crucially important phase in the Western individual's changing relations to home, and of course Austen lived during one of the most decisive of these phases: the first stage of the industrial revolution. When she was a child, England was not entirely preindustrial, and in the last years of her life, England was not entirely industrialized, but in the course of her short life she had the benefit of experiencing the radical contrast between a traditional, rural way of life and a more modern, urban one. In teaching *Persuasion*, I refer students to Park Honan's biography and ask them to draw up a factual comparison between the place of Austen's birth and the place of her death so as to illuminate this contrast.

Austen spent her childhood in Steventon, a rural village of about thirty-five families, where the economy was home-centered, whether in the form of a cottage industry or farming. The largest gathering in this village would likely have numbered fifty or sixty people at the small medieval church on Sundays, where Austen's father was rector. Austen died in Winchester, a city of thousands where she would have had access to a newspaper, and where the economy depended on the trade cycle rather than the seasons. The change in the scale of life from when she was a child to when she died; the growth of an anonymous, urban population; the wider access to information about public affairs; and the decline in commonly held religious beliefs and social habits occupied Austen's attention in the years leading up to the writing of *Persuasion* and are implied or represented in different ways in the earlier novels (Brown, *Bourgeois Interior* 40–42). For most of her life Austen inhabited the rural houses owned by her family, but after the death of her father in 1805 she moved with her sister and mother to a rented house in Southampton.[1] Austen spent the last eight years of her life at Chawton in a rural house owned by her brother Edward, but she had lived in Bath from 1801 to 1804, was familiar with London, and eventually died in rented rooms in Winchester, where she was staying with her sister Cassandra to be near her physician. Her living circumstances at the time of her death were similar to those of Mrs. Smith in *Persuasion*: "Her accommodations were limited to a noisy parlour, and a dark bed-room behind, with no possibility of moving from one to the other without assistance" (167; vol. 2, ch. 5). Beyond her illness, Mrs. Smith is isolated by her circumstances as a city dweller living without strong connections to family or home, a situation that would have been increasingly familiar to Austen's readers (Brown, *Bourgeois Interior* 42).

The broad transition from a rural society of families who live in houses to an urban society of individuals who occupy rooms can be traced in the plot of *Persuasion*: Sir Walter Elliot moves from his rural estate, Kellynch Hall, to rented lodgings in Bath, a change that marks the decline in Sir Walter's position from a member of the landed gentry to a member of the upper bourgeois (Brown, *Bourgeois Interior* 43). England's social and economic shift away from an agrarian society to a more urban, industrialized one, from estate to real estate, is marked in the sheer number of rented spaces in the novel, a number that far exceeds that in any earlier work by Austen. When I recommend that students do a short analysis of the different types of dwellings in *Persuasion*, Austen's emphasis on the transient character of her society becomes evident. Included on the list of rented spaces are Kellynch Hall (rented to the Crofts), Captain Harville's lodgings, the White Hart Inn at Lyme Regis, Sir Walter's rented rooms at Bath, Mrs. Smith's lodgings, and other temporary dwellings at Bath occupied by the Musgroves, the Harvilles, and even Lady Russell and the Dalrymples.

In her sympathetic description of Captain Harville's lodgings, Austen communicates both the strength and the vulnerability of a life of transience. In class I ask students to look closely at the passage in chapter 11 describing the Harvilles' interior:

> On quitting the Cobb, they all went indoors with their new friends, and found rooms so small as none but those who invite from the heart could think capable of accommodating so many. Anne had a moment's astonishment on the subject herself; but it was soon lost in the pleasanter feelings which sprang from the sight of all the ingenious contrivances and nice arrangements of Captain Harville, to turn the actual space to the best possible advantage, to supply the deficiencies of lodging-house furniture and defend the windows and doors against the winter storms to be expected. The varieties of the fitting-up of the rooms, where the common necessaries provided by the owner, in the common indifferent plight, were

> contrasted with some few articles of a rare species of wood, excellently worked up, and with something curious and valuable from all the distant countries Captain Harville had visited, were more than amusing to Anne: connected as it all was with his profession, the fruits of its labours, the effect of its influence on his habits, the picture of repose and domestic happiness it presented made it to her a something more, or less, than gratification.
>
> Captain Harville was no reader, but he had contrived excellent accommodations, and fashioned very pretty shelves, for a tolerable collection of well-bound volumes, the property of Captain Benwick. His lameness prevented him from taking much exercise; but a mind of usefulness and ingenuity seemed to furnish him with constant enjoyment within. He drew, he varnished, he carpentered, he glued; he made toys for the children, he fashioned new netting-needles and pins with improvements; and if everything else was done, sat down to his large fishing-net at one corner of the room. (106; vol. 1, ch. 11)

Harville's resourcefulness, industry, and inventiveness, even down to the building of shelves, echo scenes in *Robinson Crusoe* in which Crusoe constructs his dwelling on the island, but the differences between the two characters point to a subtle critique of Crusoe, the capitalist adventurer. As I have noted elsewhere,

> unlike Crusoe, Harville does not claim ownership of his little spot on the planet, and the passage subtly acknowledges the transitory nature of all possession in the reference to "the winter storms to be expected." Even in this temporary dwelling, with an inhabitant who is "no reader" himself, a special place is fashioned for books or for the cultural past; the objects collected are not merely useful but beautiful; and Harville's activities consider the next generation ("he made toys for the children"). The entire passage pivots in a series of contrasts: small rooms vs. large hearts; deficiencies vs. contrivances; necessity vs. beauty; nearness vs. distance (common objects vs. those collected from afar); reading books vs. building bookshelves; disability vs. activity. Last but not least in this profound and playful dialectic, Austen presents us with a feminine image of a soldier who has fought honorably in a war. He is placed in a scene of "domestic happiness" as he sits down to sew his "large fishing-net" [*Persuasion* 106; vol. 1, ch. 11], engaging in an activity normally associated with women.

In making this middle-class domestic interior a space for human affection, ingenuity, and literacy, Austen offers an arresting image of middle-class endurance in a transient world (Brown, *Bourgeois Interior* 45–46).

In addition to witnessing a great population shift from the country to the city, the period in which the novel is set was further destabilized by war. As the Czech novelist and essayist Milan Kundera writes, the Napoleonic wars "made it clear to every European that the world around him was subject to perpetual change that interferes with his life, transforming it and keeping it in motion" (238). And change engenders forgetfulness, as Kundera so often suggests in his essays and novels. Memory is contingent on place: to change locale is to risk forgetting because memory attaches itself to visible objects. As Anne travels from Kellynch Hall to Uppercross to Lyme to Lady Russell's house and finally to Bath, she takes note of the "total change of conversation, opinion, and idea" at each location and is conscious of the need "to clothe her . . . memory" in as much of each locale as possible (J. Austen, *Persuasion* 45, 46; vol. 1, ch. 6). Living in a world of forgetfulness, only Anne is mindful of the past.

To help students contemplate this theme, it's useful to begin by asking them to search for examples of forgetfulness among the characters in the novel. Anne's family seems to have forgotten that Anne and Captain Frederick Wentworth were once engaged. Sir Walter has forgotten the sacrifices made by naval officers during the war. The Musgroves forget the weak character of their dead son, Richard. Sir Walter and his daughter Elizabeth manage to forget their debt and their obligations when they move to Bath. Captain Benwick forgets Fanny Harville when he becomes engaged to Louisa. The question for students then becomes, what does it signify that the heroine is the only character who remembers deeply? Anne is herself a symbol of memory, and she is often forgotten by others.

Anne's unhappiness is directly related to the forgetfulness of those around her. No one acknowledges that she has suffered in the past; even Lady Russell, who is largely responsible for Anne's misery, can only vaguely recall, with a kind of sublime obliviousness, the reasons for Anne's dislike of Bath: "And with regard to Anne's dislike of Bath, she considered it as a prejudice and a mistake, arising . . . from her happening to be not in perfectly good spirits the only winter which she had afterwards spent there with herself" (16; vol. 1, ch. 2). Nor does anyone consider how much the loss of her country home unsettles Anne. When she arrives in Bath, she notes her father's pleasure in his new dwelling and is dismayed that he "should see nothing to regret in the duties and dignity of a resident land-holder" (149; vol. 2, ch. 3). She herself misses country life and dreads the "imprisonment" before her (148). When I ask the students to elaborate on Austen's use of the word "imprisonment," they point to its external and internal meanings: urban rooms are smaller than those of a country house, Anne dislikes Bath and will be unable to walk in the countryside, she has no say in where she lives, and, most important, her father's and sister's shallow forgetfulness—of their old way of life and her own existence—is profoundly alienating.

Because of the coldness of her family and the absence of love in her life, Anne is of course a deeply sympathetic character. *Persuasion*'s increased use of free indirect discourse, in which Anne's point of view dominates, can give students the impression that the narrator is entirely uncritical of the heroine—unlike, for example, the narrator of *Emma*, who often enters into the consciousness of Emma Woodhouse but is more persistent in directing irony against her. Moreover, the lack of control Anne has over her life and the subordinate position she holds in the family as an unmarried woman lead students to see all her problems as caused by external forces. As a result, students often overlook the few moments when the narrator adopts a more objective view of her character. I always draw attention to these moments in class, not only to illustrate the complexity of Anne's character, but as a way of making students aware of the pervasiveness of Austen's use of free indirect discourse, and the subtlety of Austen's departures from it.

One such moment occurs in chapter 10 during the walk to Charles Hayter's farm. Anne is miserable because she can see the romance between Wentworth and Louisa Musgrove developing, and even before overhearing a dialogue between them, she tries to avoid sinking into gloom, remembering poems that are "fraught with the apt analogy of the declining year, with declining happiness, and the images of youth and hope, and spring, all gone together. . . ." Soon after, however, the narrator shifts out of free indirect discourse and draws the reader's attention to evidence of a nearby farmer at work, who "counteract[s] the sweets of poetical despondence, and mean[s] to have spring again," and who, by implication, understands, unlike Anne, that renewal requires effort (91; vol. 1, ch. 10). In our own more feminist age, students are quick to notice that Anne begins to assert herself in later encounters with Wentworth, but they are much less likely to want to think about the nostalgia and despair that Anne is prey to in the first part of the novel. I will return to this point later.

When teaching *Persuasion*, I draw attention to the profound impact that the social and economic changes of Austen's time had on the form of the novel. Kundera writes of how the scene became the basic element of the novel's composition, "the locus of the novelist's virtuosity," at the beginning of the nineteenth century, for historical reasons. This use of the scene was the novelist's way of resisting "the loss of the fleeting reality of the present" in a world of perpetual change (129). Kundera suggests that in novels written earlier, capturing the concreteness of the present moment is not the issue, and he remarks that "the historical moment is specified only very approximately" (238). For such earlier novels, telling the story is more the issue than imagining a concrete scene that plays out in a specific place at a precisely dated moment in time.

Persuasion is Austen's most precisely dated novel: it opens with a family history and the birth dates of the heroine and her siblings. Near the end of chapter 1, we are told that the events taking place occur in the summer of 1814 (9; vol. 1, ch. 1), which places the action of the novel during the false peace leading up to the Battle of Waterloo. The first fully developed scene takes place in chapter 3 and can usefully be compared to one in *Robinson Crusoe*, as a way of illustrating the development of the scene from the early eighteenth to the early nineteenth century.

In a memorable scene at the beginning of *Robinson Crusoe*, Crusoe's father tries to persuade Crusoe of the virtues of middle-class life. Defoe gives us little more than dialogue—or, to be more precise, a paternal lecture. We don't know where the conversation takes place or when, what objects surround the characters, how the characters gesture or move in the course of their talk, or their psychology as it might be clarified through narrative commentary. The scene in chapter 3 of *Persuasion* is also made up largely of dialogue but is dense in detail and possesses dramatic complexity. The scene is set at Kellynch Hall on a late summer morning. We already know the year is 1814, and Mr. Shepherd, who is holding a newspaper, announces that the "peace" will be turning navy officers ashore soon (J. Austen 19; vol. 1, ch. 3). A conversation ensues that involves five characters—Sir Walter, Mr. Shepherd, his daughter Mrs. Clay, and Anne and Elizabeth Elliott—and, at the end of the scene, Anne's silent thoughts are given. The scene is important to developing the psychological and social complexity of the main plot, which will involve Anne leaving the social milieu she is part of now and joining the naval community that her father ridicules. Psychology is expressed through voice, gesture, and narrative commentary, and encounters take place in the dialogue that bring out conflicts of interest and subtle emotions. In addition to these more psychological elements, quotidian and seemingly random details—such as the fact that Mrs. Clay was driven over to Kellynch by her father—register the ordinary nature of everyday life at a country estate in this period.

This exercise in close reading shows how a formal development in the realist novel may be related to historical change, and it can inspire students to study later, more complex scenes in *Persuasion*, such as the masterful scene at Lyme, in which Austen stretches the moment of Louisa's fall by describing the reactions of those who stand by. The plenitude and concreteness of individual moments are increasingly evoked as the novel progresses, such as in the concert scene at Bath, in which Anne feels "an hundred things in a moment" while hearing Wentworth's startling reflections about the engagement of Captain Benwick, at the same time that she takes in "the various noises of the room, the almost ceaseless slam of the door, and the ceaseless buzz of persons walking through" (199; vol. 2, ch. 8).

Anne's vitality is expressed in her increasing responsiveness to the present. Being alive to the present, conscious of what is going on around you, is of course a trait of heroines and heroes generally. The bildungsroman plots of Austen's earlier novels follow their heroines from different states of uncertainty, self-deception, or unconsciousness to ones of acute awareness and self-knowledge. But Anne is different. She is older than earlier heroines, and her moral education took place eight years before the novel opens. Since her present condition is rooted in a seemingly irreparable mistake of the past, she lacks the confidence to adopt Elizabeth Bennet's so-called philosophy (one that, to be sure, Elizabeth professes only after she has wrestled with her past mistakes): "Think only of the past as its remembrance gives you pleasure," says Elizabeth to Mr. Darcy (J. Austen, *Pride* 409; vol. 3, ch. 16). Elizabeth's optimism, focus on the present, and, above all, insistence on her right to think of her own happiness and not to live for others, as she openly declares when confronted by Lady Catherine, establish her as a progressive heroine, a defender of democratic individualism.

Anne has a more traditional personality and is surely the most cultivated of Austen's heroines in her refinement, gentleness, and learning. (She contemplates the more bourgeois Musgrove sisters "as some of the happiest creatures of her acquaintance; but still, saved as we are by some comfortable feeling of superiority from wishing for the possibility of exchange, she would not have given up her own more elegant and cultivated mind for all their enjoyments" [J. Austen, *Persuasion* 43; vol. 1, ch. 5].) Whereas the Bennet daughters' intellectual and artistic education has been neglected in *Pride and Prejudice*, Anne has had an upper-class woman's education: she is accomplished at the piano and possesses knowledge of literature and a foreign language. Her cultivated sensibility establishes her as the best that her class has to offer, just as her father and sister are the worst. And while it's true that Anne shows her independence of her father's snobbish and dishonorable attitudes early in the novel and later distances herself from her social milieu by marrying Wentworth, a navy man who has risen from a lower class, she respects the past, even to the point where she insists, on the grounds of duty, that she was right to take Lady Russell's advice and break off the original engagement with Wentworth. When Anne contemplates her father's departure from Kellynch Hall, she thinks of it as a failure of duty on his part, the duty of a great landowner to maintain his position in life and to fulfill its obligations. When she reads Mr. Elliot's letter ridiculing her father, it "puts her in a glow." The reader is most likely to be amused when the conceited Sir Walter is written off as a "fool" (*Persuasion* 220; vol. 2, ch. 9), but Anne's reaction to Mr. Elliot's disrespectfulness is telling: "Anne could not immediately get over the shock and mortification of finding such words applied to her father" (221). Drawing the class's attention to these details makes students more aware of what is perhaps the novel's most complex theme. *Persuasion* is clearly on the side of social mobility and democratic change, but in creating a heroine with a strong sense of the past and a respect for tradition, Austen also makes the case against forgetfulness. Anne, the symbol of memory who is herself forgotten, lives in the past as much as in the present and, in doing so, risks being condemned to a continual state of silent mourning, in which she bears the weight of a past that those around her refuse to acknowledge. The novel saves Anne by returning Wentworth's love to her and giving her a new life, but it offers no solution to the problem of retaining the past in a world of perpetual change.

NOTE

[1] Here, like the Harvilles in *Persuasion*, they set about fitting up the rooms, Austen's brother Frank making "a very nice fringe for the Drawingroom Curtains," and the women fashioning furniture left in the house to meet their needs, as described in Austen's letter of 21 February 1807 (*Jane Austen's Letters* [Le Faye, 3rd ed.] 123).

The "Unfeudal Tone" in Context: Teaching *Persuasion* through Mary Wollstonecraft

Magdalena Nerio

Undergraduate English majors at the large regional university where I teach will most likely encounter Austen's *Persuasion* in one of the following courses: an upper-division single-author special topics course covering the six major novels by Jane Austen, or in a survey course that introduces British women's writing. I normally teach *Persuasion* in the survey format in an upper-division majors' seminar titled Women and Literature, whose topic is broad enough to attract many students who have previous exposure to Austen's novels and many who have not read them. Because my department does not permit me to change the title of the course, I subtitle it Jane Austen and Her Predecessors in order to restrict its focus and to provide a frame for the investigation of Austen's novels. The course on Austen is designed to acquaint students with English women's literary history of the late eighteenth and early nineteenth centuries and to illustrate Austen's debts to her feminist foremothers, Mary Wollstonecraft and Elizabeth Inchbald.

Persuasion and its discerning heroine tend to win over undergraduate readers who dislike the novel *Emma*'s snobbish, meddlesome protagonist, Emma Woodhouse, and the contained world of Highbury, which some students find remote and limited. My challenge, then, is to seize on students' enthusiasm for the widening of landscape and vision that *Persuasion* represents, while pointing to the novel's many surprising affinities with the feminism of Mary Wollstonecraft. A polemicist whose unmistakable voice belongs not to the largely indoor environments in which women in *Persuasion* spend much of their time but to the combative, overwhelmingly masculine world of eighteenth-century pamphlet literature, Wollstonecraft tends to be a favorite with undergraduate readers reluctant to take an Austen course.

Once I sense that my students approve of *Persuasion* as a departure from what they find difficult or don't like about *Emma*, then I can urge them to begin thinking about the novel in terms of women's literary history and in terms of its dialogue with Wollstonecraft's repudiation of traditional values. The palpably "unfeudal tone of the present day" against which *Persuasion* is set (150; vol. 2, ch. 3), and which the character Mr. William Elliot disapproves of, comes into sharper focus for students in my course who have already been exposed to Wollstonecraft's political prose, chiefly *A Vindication of the Rights of Men* and the more famous *A Vindication of the Rights of Woman*. The phrase "[t]he unfeudal tone of the present day" does not indicate that the landed gentry have lost their position in society, but rather that they cannot be trusted (by the heroine or anyone else) to discharge their social and moral duties responsibly. Certain prominent representatives of the social class to which the heroine belongs have become self-serving and self-satisfied at the expense of the larger social good. To be clear, my course does not insist that Austen is as radical as her predecessor Wollstonecraft. However, I do think that carefully prepared close reading exercises that focus on rereading the two authors side by side, either during the class discussion in conjunction with lecture slides or in a comparison essay assignment, can show students how the novel engages with complex contemporary cultural and social issues.

This approach encourages students to see that here are relevant and intriguing dialogues between thinkers from an earlier era. Once confronted with Austen's intricate textual dialogue with her radical predecessor, Wollstonecraft, undergraduates tend to abandon simple assumptions about Austen in favor of a more expansive view of the past. The late eighteenth century becomes, then, a century of revolutions in which Wollstonecraft's clarion call for radical social change in England followed America's and France's bolder political experiments. The recognition by students of the full range of Austen's social commentary, culminating in *Persuasion*, is greatly enhanced by their familiarity with Wollstonecraft's political prose. Wollstonecraft's political writings not only introduce students to contemporary discourses on English women's education, which are taken up again in Austen's novels, but also invite readers who are attentive to the language and subdued intertextuality of *Persuasion* to approach the novel as a series of complex and measured responses to Wollstonecraft's forthright prose. *Persuasion*'s various shades of Wollstonecraft, then, invite readers to study the novel in the light of its historical time period, to see its author not as the product of an earlier eighteenth-century literary culture alone but as a commentator equally attuned to the political discourses of Romanticism. In emphasizing Austen's ties to Wollstonecraft, this approach to teaching *Persuasion* stresses the Romantic features of the text: the championing of romance over prudence, the exploration of memory, the focus on the individual, the aversion to stasis and hierarchy, and the turn, if not to revolutionary Wollstonecraftean feminism, then to paradigms of female stoicism embodied by Anne, a heroine for a new era.

Most of the novel's bite lies in an indictment of baseless or exaggerated claims to importance made by those who have inherited titles, an indictment that invites comparison, if not with the style, then with the terms and overall thrust of Wollstonecraftean polemic, and in this respect, the novel reflects a revolution in attitudes. To guide novice readers through one key context for *Persuasion*, I present in class a brief biographical sketch of Wollstonecraft, whose feminism has its roots in unhappy early domestic circumstances (the fault, primarily, of her reckless and tyrannical father, Edward Wollstonecraft), important female friendships (especially with the cultivated Fanny Blood), and her claim, in a 7 November 1787 letter to her sister Everina, that she would make herself, by her pen, "the first of a new genus" (Wollstonecraft, *Collected Letters* 139). I distribute pertinent excerpts from this letter (138–40) either on a PowerPoint slide or in the form of a handout, since the letter reveals Wollstonecraft's keen sense of vocation: "Providence has been very kind to me—and when I reflect on past mercies with respect to the future I am not without hope—And freedom, even uncertain freedom—is dear. . . . You know I am not born to tread in the beaten track—the peculiar bent of my nature pushes me on" (140). My students, for the most part, tend to know about Wollstonecraft not as a significant social philosopher in her own right but as a curious historical footnote—the mother of the author of *Frankenstein*. The emphasis on Wollstonecraft's biography, however, turns the mother into an equally appealing heroine for undergraduate students who admire her resolve and candor.

Wollstonecraft's wonderfully short *A Vindication of the Rights of Men* is an accessible introduction to her political theory, highlighting, as it does, the analysis of moral character that is common to both her work and Austen's. Reading *A Vindication of the Rights of Men* also underscores for students unmistakable differences between the rational feminist, who wrote mainly nonfiction prose, and the satirical novelist, whose political opinions remain a matter of scholarly debate and speculation, and can generate a lively class discussion. Students may even wonder if I have lost all sense of perspective in encouraging them to read *Persuasion* as a companion piece or reply to Wollstonecraft's revolutionary writings. Whether students choose to read *Persuasion* as a reactionary text or as a Romantic one matters less to me than their ability to describe Austen's novel in terms of the bracing literary context that produced it.

Even more important, *A Vindication of the Rights of Men* equips students with the political vocabulary—a rhetoric of inclusivity and natural rights available to people of both genders—for assessing the traditional values, hierarchical relationships, and familial arrangements that *Persuasion* criticizes, if less stridently, as illogical and morally dubious. Moreover, Wollstonecraft's emphasis on human rights and individual freedom—rather than on a more restricted delineation of women's history of oppression under patriarchy—opens up a welcoming space for male students brave enough to take a women's studies course. Composed under pressure of a strict deadline, Wollstonecraft's essay is a reply to Edmund Burke's *Reflections on the Revolution in France* that underlines the conflicting interpretations of property on which the quarrel between the two authors is based. The distribution and social function of property were central concerns for both radicals and reactionaries writing in response to the French Revolution. For Burke, hereditary property fosters a necessary inequality predicated on the role of the landholding classes as careful stewards of their local communities, tasked with maintaining the general social welfare. Burke argues that this ancient system of hereditary property is essential to the preservation of civil society. He would have considered the narcissism and incompetence of Sir Walter in *Persuasion* as undermining the nation itself. In Jocelyn Harris's words, "Burke's belief that the security of the state grew organically out of continuities in families, bloodlines, and property makes Sir Walter's extravagancies look like threats to civil order" (131).

Further, Burke claims that the unequal distribution of property is not morally wrong, since it effects moral improvement on a grand scale: "It makes our weakness subservient to our virtue; it grafts benevolence even upon avarice. The possessors of family wealth, and of the distinction which attends hereditary possession (as most concerned in it) are the national securities for this transmission" (E. Burke, *Reflections* 51). For Burke, the assault on hereditary property perpetrated by French insurrectionaries represents the triumph of the middling, commercial classes and hence, the destruction of civil society: Burke's critique of the French Revolution is also an attempt to shape the political vision of his English readership. His pointed economic metaphors portend modern Europe's enslavement to a petty, rapacious mercantile class. With the future uncertain, Burke reconstructs a more glorious past, stabilized by the presence of an affective culture that he ties to aristocratic families on both sides of the Channel.

Aligning her unadorned and combative style with a concern for the "rights of humanity" (*Vindication of the Rights of Men* 5), Wollstonecraft seizes the opportunity to give offense wherever she can, aiming not to ingratiate herself with her readership but to expose the irrationality of her political opponents, chiefly Burke. In keeping with the discourse of rights invoked by contemporary radicals such as Thomas Paine and William Godwin, Wollstonecraft vilifies inherited property because of its encroachment on those rights, and for its hand in justifying aristocratic tyranny. Burke, in pointed contrast, rejects the theory of rights invoked by radicals—against which there can be "no prescription," "no agreement," "no temperament, and no compromise"—on the grounds that such philosophical abstractions have little to offer in the way of pragmatic political recommendations (58).

In countering Burke, Wollstonecraft extends his reliance on custom to its immoral extreme for the sake of argument:

> Allowing [Burke's] servile reverence for antiquity, and prudent attention to self-interest, to have the force which he insists on, the slave trade ought never to be abolished; and, because our ignorant forefathers, not understanding the native dignity of man, sanctioned a traffic that outrages every suggestion of reason and religion, we are to submit to the inhuman custom, and term an atrocious insult to humanity the love of our country, and proper submission to the laws by which our property is secured.
>
> (*Vindication of the Rights of Men* 13)

Wollstonecraft undercuts the logic of Burke's *Reflections on the Revolution in France* by conflating the recourse to tradition with a lack of integrity and by reminding her readers that chattel slavery is a reprehensible form of inherited property. Her insistence, throughout both *A Vindication of the Rights of Men* and *A Vindication of the Rights of Women*, that the paternalistic sentiments venerated by Burke serve only to stifle individual initiative gives students a way to situate *Persuasion*'s major characters and the competing values they represent in relation to either traditional class values or the new meritocracy of the naval officers. According to the terms of Wollstonecraft's polemic, individuals are only heroic—or "truly sublime"—to the extent that they are radically determined by the intelligence of the emotions (*Vindication of the Rights of Men* 6). To what degree, I ask my students, do any of the characters in *Persuasion* express their allegiance to emotional truth even at the expense of family loyalty? Is this the kind of credo to which the heroine herself subscribes?

The equally bracing discourse on human or natural rights presented in Wollstonecraft's *A Vindication of the Rights of Woman* also models the type of character analysis that Austen's novel demands. When *A Vindication of the Rights of Woman* is assessed on its own terms and according to the Enlightenment political principles that it articulates with such fervor, it becomes clear that this work makes visible Wollstonecraft's commitment to female solidarity, and when it is read alongside *Persuasion*, it puts into relief Austen's parallel critique of women's education in the period. Most significantly, Wollstonecraft identifies how girls are placed at a disadvantage in their formative years:

> Taught from their infancy that beauty is woman's sceptre, the mind shapes itself to the body, and, roaming round in its gilt cage, only seeks to adorn its prison. Men have various employments and pursuits which engage their attention, and give a character to the opening mind; but women, confined to one, and having their thoughts constantly directed to the most insignificant part of themselves, seldom extend their views beyond the triumph of the hour. (*Vindication of the Rights of Woman* [Vindication] 112)

Such early training leads inevitably to a shabby form of domestic tragedy characterized by arrested development and feminine incapacity. Emphatically, Wollstonecraft urges her female readers to assume a stoic, masculine devotion to regular activity and intellectual formation to compensate for the momentary craze for vacuous women espoused by Rousseau, among others. Close attention to Wollstonecraft's vindications of the rights of men and of women helps students see how Austen's novel explores the separation of public and domestic spheres in similar detail, since it reflects a response to and qualification of Wollstonecraft's warnings. If the exceptionally resilient Anne Elliot is, according to Mr. Elliot, "a model of female excellence" (*Persuasion* 172; vol. 2, ch. 5), then the novel's catalog of silly women with very little to do and much to complain about reinforces Wollstonecraft's prescriptions.

In practice, this emphasis on *Persuasion*'s intertextuality asks students to look for patterns and sift through issues broached with equal frequency by both authors. I worry less about how quickly my students manage to finish the novel and more about their immediate grasp of the new set of values it endorses. If my aim is to equip students to read *Persuasion* with a deeper sense of history, then I am also asking students to read the novel less for its romance plot and more through its representation of "the unfeudal tone of the present day" (150; vol. 2, ch. 3). I do not ask students to study the Napoleonic wars or the history of the British navy in any detail, but I do encourage them to see how the tone of the novel opens onto a changing cultural landscape. The style of the novel—the mode of narration and the various studies of character it presents—outweighs considerations of plot in this analysis of the text. For a commentary on the dangers that attend an outmoded reverence for rank, I ask students to consider the narrator's devastating portrait of Sir Walter Elliot in chapter 1:

> Vanity was the beginning and the end of Sir Walter Elliot's character; vanity of person and of situation. He had been remarkably handsome in his youth; and, at fifty-four, was still a very fine man. Few women could think more of their personal appearance than he did; nor could the valet of any new made lord be more delighted with the place he held in society. He considered the blessing of beauty as inferior only to the blessing of a baronetcy; and the Sir Walter Elliot, who united these gifts, was the constant object of his warmest respect and devotion. (4; vol. 1, ch. 1)

The narrator's cool assessment of Sir Walter's moral failings, punctuated and intensified by brisk statements of fact and unflattering comparisons, is a useful starting place for any investigation of *Persuasion*'s "unfeudal tone" (150; vol. 2, ch. 3), which through comic irony and understatement provides a brilliant send-up of the narcissistic baronet. With this character sketch, Sir Walter's "vanity of person and of situation" is introduced as a focal point of the novel's satiric ire—directed, as in this instance, at certain morally dubious and ineffectual figures. And as the class begins to engage carefully with this passage, I point to the cutting irony attached to the notion of Sir Walter's "gifts" (4; vol. 1, ch. 1)—mere accidents of birth rather than talents actively striven for—and demonstrate that *Persuasion* is deeply critical of the unwarranted self-love dissected here.

Reading the novel sensitively, I tell my students, also involves identifying with particular characters and assenting to the heroine's moral choices. Accordingly, I encourage them to tell me how exactly we can be sure that the novel aligns itself with the virtues of characters such as the Crofts, the Harvilles, and Captain Frederick Wentworth. In mourning the seemingly permanent loss of Captain Wentworth's admiration and affection, Anne grieves not only for the man himself but also for the company he keeps. Thus, the visit to Lyme Regis and the introduction of the Harvilles and Captain Benwick is instructive for students intrigued by the novel's rendering of Anne's consciousness. That Anne must resist the looming depression brought on by the thought that Captain Wentworth's sincere and gracious associates "would all have been my friends" is consistent with a significant feature of the novel's tone: its melancholy air, especially in volume 1 (105; vol. 1, ch. 11). Moreover, the scene underscores for students the stoicism and sound judgment of a heroine whose values they tend readily to accept. As Anne develops a preference for warmth over cautious reserve, what my students make of her determines to a large extent where they will land on this question of the novel's tone. What is more, once students can point to key passages or narrative strategies that make the novel's tone easier to grasp, then they are well on their way to proposing interesting readings of the text that advance the class discussion beyond a simple enthusiasm for the novel and its more endearing characters (although I welcome these kinds of remarks as well).

What I would like my students to notice and admire is how the novel embeds certain Wollstonecraftean values within its finely delineated studies of character to signal a preference for the unaffected manners, ingenuity, and energy of the naval officers and their wives. Admiral and Mrs. Croft represent the ideal companionate marriage characterized by easygoing manners, which Anne finds infinitely superior to the haughty coldness of her father and her sister Elizabeth. Mrs. Croft goes so far as to scold Wentworth, her brother, for exhibiting a falsely exaggerated sense of propriety with respect to the opposite sex. His insistence that women and children have no business joining their husbands and fathers at sea prompts his stalwart sister to declare, "I hate to hear you talking so, like a fine gentleman, and as if women were all fine ladies, instead of rational creatures. We none of us expect to be in smooth water all our days" (75; vol. 1, ch. 8). In laying claim to Wollstonecraft's notion of women as "rational" rather than as delicate and feeble, Mrs. Croft's commonsensical speech and the nautical metaphor challenge her brother's facile assumptions about women's roles and wifely duties. For its commentary on gender and manners alone, the narrator's introductory portrait of Mrs. Croft warrants consideration in the classroom:

> Mrs. Croft, though neither tall nor fat, had a squareness, uprightness, and vigour of form, which gave importance to her person. She had bright dark eyes, good teeth, and altogether an agreeable face; though her reddened and weather-beaten complexion, the consequence of her having been almost as much at sea as her husband, made her seem to have lived some years longer in the world than her real eight and thirty. Her manners were open, easy, and decided, like one who had no distrust of herself and no doubts of what to do; without any approach to coarseness, . . . or any want of good humour. (52; vol. 1, ch. 6)

Mrs. Croft's robust physique and self-assurance appeal to most students, especially if they are invited to view Mrs. Croft in relation to other female characters in this novel. By returning to this description, students may even remark that Mrs. Croft models the kind of resolution that Anne appears to lack, at least early on in the novel, before novice readers gain a more complete sense of Anne's value. Further, Mrs. Croft's good health and intrepid spirit call for the comparative analysis honed throughout the course, since she represents a new form of womanhood, one that students may or may not recognize as belonging to Austen's social world. Specifically, Mrs. Croft is welcomed by students as a pleasing alternative to the hypochondriacal Mary Musgrove, who is always in the habit "of fancying herself neglected and ill-used" (39; vol. 1, ch. 5). Moreover, Mrs. Croft's sheer physical strength invites students to form a favorable comparison with the athletic and equally strong-willed Elizabeth Bennet in *Pride and Prejudice*. Perhaps even more important, Mrs. Croft's resourcefulness and adaptability throw the silliness and giddy enthusiasms of Louisa and Henrietta Musgrove, and the vacuity of their mother, Mrs. Musgrove, into relief.

Because the students in my course Women and Literature: Jane Austen and Her Predecessors have already read Wollstonecraft's two nonfiction works and the writer's novel, *Maria; or, The Wrongs of Woman*, I can simply ask them to recall certain key issues taken up by Austen and Wollstonecraft and points made about them in class. Inevitably, students note how *Persuasion*'s contempt for rank and Austen's oblique yet pointed commentary on women's education echo Wollstonecraft's vindications of the rights of men and of women. Seen in this way, Anne's vigilance, composure, and modesty are the markers of a truly accomplished woman and are recommended to readers in contrast to the ineptitude of some of the other female characters. The narrator's introduction of the Musgrove sisters in the family tableau aligns the girls' trajectory with that of "thousands of other young ladies," who display "the usual stock of accomplishments" and live "to be fashionable, happy, and merry" (43; vol. 1, ch. 5). Henrietta and Louisa, as it happens, are the happy-go-lucky products of what Wollstonecraft terms, in *A Vindication of the Rights of Woman*, "a false system of education" ([Vindication] 71). As the narrator's sketch of the two young women gives way to Anne's private ruminations on their happiness, what I wish students to savor most of all about this passage is how Austen's free indirect discourse intensifies Anne's sense of security, her "comfortable feeling of superiority" (*Persuasion* 43; vol. 1, ch. 5). While never smug, Anne does occupy the privileged position of a heroine who knows the distinct advantages that careful reflection affords—a position she safeguards.

In most instances when teaching the novels of Austen, I can count on the fact that students will identify easily with lively, outspoken heroines such as Elizabeth Bennet, in *Pride and Prejudice*, or even Marianne Dashwood, in *Sense and Sensibility*, so the focus on the unassuming Anne Elliot and the narrative's rendering of her consciousness in *Persuasion* require a change of pace and direction—a welcome opportunity for slow reading of the novel. Some students may even share in the assessment of Anne made by her author: "she is almost too good for me" (J. Austen, *Jane Austen's Letters* [Le Faye, 4th ed.] 335). Yet Austen's introductory portrait of Anne invites students to reassess any working definition of heroineship that they may have sketched over the course of the semester, and to evaluate their sense of Austen's progress as a novelist writing in the shadow of Wollstonecraft. Although Anne's reserved conduct and self-effacing tendencies would appear to contradict the legacy of Wollstonecraft, Anne is a revolutionary heroine in a variety of senses, which signal the evolution of Austen's art. With her experience of loss—first of an excellent mother, and then of a first love—Anne exemplifies the resilience and refusal of victim status that Wollstonecraft tied to a rational education. Anne, though given to reflection, is not a great intellectual, and students willing to go along with Austen's moral approbation of her modesty will readily understand that her intelligence is not the kind likely to meet with accolades, book tours, and international fame.

She does model grace under pressure and possesses a remarkable ability to endure the insults and complaints directed at her by a host of self-centered relations. By the end of the course, students may decide to point only to Austen's failure to embrace fully the tenor and scope of Wollstonecraftean radicalism. Seen in another way, Anne is valuable as a character because she suggests the extent to which Austen's last novel refuses to define heroineship strictly in terms of youth, beauty, and effervescence. The modesty and grace modeled by Anne may not be precisely the advantages Wollstonecraft had in mind when she urged her female readership, in the 1790s, to cultivate a keen sense of rational independence from men, but they do matter enormously in terms of the operations of Austen's moral universe.

Persuasion as Transition: From "Tawny Leaves" to the "Spring of Felicity"

Lynda A. Hall

Jane Austen's last completed novel, *Persuasion*, might be taught as a culmination of her realistic novels, as an homage to the Romantic age of literature, or as a vision of a new kind of egalitarian future. I teach an undergraduate college survey course that is supposed to introduce Anglophone literatures from 1800 to the present day. Though no one-semester course can comprehensively cover this period of time, I find teaching *Persuasion* at the beginning of the semester a good way to connect Augustan literature and Romantic poetry while looking forward to Victorian literature of the mid-nineteenth century. I explain to my students that *Persuasion* can be read both as a Romantic work and as a response to Romanticism. In this essay I highlight ways that teachers might use *Persuasion* as a transitional work. Where additional study might be needed, I also mention resources for further research.

During Jane Austen's lifetime, Europe was in political turmoil; the French Revolution might be considered the beginning of the end of aristocratic rule in Europe, and the literary movement that would become known as Romanticism evolved throughout Austen's lifetime as a reaction to these social and political changes, beginning with hope for a more egalitarian future and ending with the dark despair of the Byronic hero. Throughout the years in which Austen's novels were published, Napoleon was ravaging the continent. And though many have criticized Austen for ignoring this political turmoil, *Persuasion* is a testament to the fact that she did not. The revolutionary political and social changes of the period can be traced throughout *Persuasion*, and students can discover through a compelling love story many of the complex disruptions that Austen was observing in the world around her.

Persuasion, unlike Austen's other novels, identifies its historical period, which coincides with Napoleon's first exile, and reveals the personal turmoil within the domestic sphere during wartime, or as William Deresiewicz observes, Austen "synchronize[es] the novel's personal drama of loss and love with the national drama of war and peace" (147). More than a novel about love and marriage, *Persuasion* is a story about loss, patience, and recovery; Anne Elliot must endure a poignant loneliness just as the grounded sailors must endure what Mary A. Favret refers to as "the tedium of waiting" symptomatic of "warfare in the age of Napoleon" ("Writing" 319). In fact, when Mrs. Croft is debating with her brother, Captain Frederick Wentworth, about women on board ships, she describes the agony of waiting for news of her husband while he is at sea:

> The only time I ever really suffered in body or mind, the only time that I ever fancied myself unwell, or had any ideas of danger, was the winter that

> I passed by myself at Deal, when the Admiral (Captain Croft then) was in the North Seas. I lived in perpetual fright at that time, and had all manner of imaginary complaints from not knowing what to do with myself, or when I should hear from him next. (J. Austen, *Persuasion* 76–77; vol. 1. ch. 8)

Persuasion is more than the love story of Anne and Captain Wentworth; it is also a dramatization of a world in flux: between peace and war, between the inherited wealth of the gentry and the earned wealth of the meritocracy, and between the realistic, domestic sphere and romantic ideas of mutability and change. In fact, in this novel, "change is a condition of life," as John Wiltshire notices. "Decline and decay are a witness to the natural process of living, as Mrs. Croft's 'weather-beaten face' is a witness to the soundness and health of her marriage—because she has genuinely lived she remains adaptable and quick" ("Romantic *Persuasion*" 5). Mutability, or the natural state of change, is a common trope in Romantic poetry and might be a good way to introduce a connection between that poetry and *Persuasion*.[1]

To begin to discuss these contrasts, I find it helpful to introduce *Persuasion* to students just as Austen does to readers—with Sir Walter Elliot perusing the Baronetage, an activity that reveals his narcissism and self-importance. We learn that Sir Walter "was not very wise" (26; vol. 1, ch. 3), and though he believes that leasing his estate to an admiral "speaks his own consequence, and, at the same time, can never make a baronet look small" (27), he deplores the military "as being the means of bringing persons of obscure birth into undue distinction, and raising men to honours which their fathers and grandfathers never dreamt of" (21). Thus, even through Sir Walter's myopic perspective, this volatile period of social change is introduced.

Then we meet the Musgroves, who, "like their houses, were in a state of alteration, perhaps of improvement" (43; vol. 1, ch. 5), and the various naval officers with whom our heroine feels at home. Students begin to recognize these somewhat subtle social stratifications while also noticing the movement toward change. None of the social ranks seem stable: "Hierarchy parts company with responsibility: the landed seem peculiarly ill-fit to rule; and while society bristles with egotists, the more sociable rate as nobodies," as Peter Knox-Shaw observes ("Byron" 53). In fact those who have recently become "rich" have done so at great risk (J. Austen, *Persuasion* 66; vol. 1, ch. 7). Captain Wentworth reflects that if he had not brought his "old built sloop," the *Asp*, into Plymouth Sound when he did, a large gale would have sunk the ship: "I should only have been a gallant Captain Wentworth, in a small paragraph at one corner of the newspapers; and being lost in only a sloop, nobody would have thought about me," he declares (71; vol. 1, ch. 8). Much like the mutability considered by the Romantic poets, change in *Persuasion* is disruptive but natural.[2]

While *Persuasion* recognizes the reality of traditional patriarchal power, it also looks forward to a new era that will be filled with expanding roles for women. In addition to defending the place of women on board ships, Mrs. Croft is portrayed throughout the novel as a capable, independent woman. She is first referred to as "a very well-spoken, genteel, shrewd lady" who "asked more questions about the house, and terms, and taxes, than the Admiral himself, and seemed more conversant with business" (25; vol. 1, ch. 3). And, when Anne joins the Crofts in their gig, she observes Mrs. Croft "coolly giving the reins a better direction" so that they miss hitting a post, and "by once afterwards judiciously putting out her hand they neither fell into a rut, nor ran foul of a dung-cart." Anne concludes that this experience is "no bad representation of the general guidance of their affairs" (99; vol. 1, ch. 10). The Crofts might be understood as a new kind of married couple—companions *and* partners.

Where Mrs. Croft might be Anne's model of a woman of the future, Lady Russell might be a reflection of the past—because she focuses on marriage as a wealth builder rather than as a form of companionship. Mrs. Smith and Mrs. Clay also reflect this marriage-market mentality, and by depicting these characters' struggles, the novel reveals a kind of ambivalence about the function of marriage. Even after she has been reunited with Wentworth, Anne still believes she was right to follow the advice of Lady Russell, "in the place of a parent," though she now realizes that the advice was in error, since it was, "perhaps, one of those cases in which advice is good or bad only as the event decides." Had she continued with the engagement, she "would have suffered in [her] conscience" (268; vol. 2, ch. 11). The "event" to which Anne refers is the changes that have come with the war, including the fortune that Wentworth has gained; however, Mrs. Smith's experience shows Anne what it might have been like to have been widowed and poor, and Mrs. Clay, who flatters Sir Walter and Elizabeth and possibly ends up marrying Mr. William Elliot, reveals the precarious nature of mercenary alliances. So does Jane Austen argue for or against such marriages in this novel? Perhaps neither. As Deresiewicz explains, Austen "observed historical change without rooting for it" (157). Thus, Austen remained in her mode of realism—revealing the truth about the change she observed around her. Nevertheless, this novel also marks a subtle departure from the strict realistic mode, as her prose reveals Romantic tropes not as prevalent in her earlier fiction.

Depending on the expertise of the students, a brief definition of Romanticism might be necessary.[3] To situate this period of literary expression, in my class we briefly discuss some of the early Romantic poets and their connection to nature, the French Revolution, and the mystical. From a historical standpoint, we talk about how Romanticism as a movement or school was a reaction to the neoclassicism of the eighteenth century. Since there are no definitive dates associated with Romantic literature, however, we tend to focus on political dates to delineate the time period: perhaps Romanticism began with the American Revolution, with the earliest stages of the French Revolution, or after Maximilien Robespierre's rise and the Reign of Terror.[4]

Anne is arguably Austen's most Romantic heroine. The story follows Anne's psychological evolution, or as Ann W. Astell observes, her "experiential knowledge, mediated through the emotions, which tests her moral maturity, her psychic stamina, to the utmost" (13). When Anne and Wentworth are first reacquainted after an eight-year separation, what the narrator describes as a casual visit nearly overwhelms Anne. This might be a good place to point out Austen's use of free indirect discourse: characters within the text might think that Anne is indifferent, but the reader is aware of her dramatic inner response, as the narrator moves smoothly between objective observation ("the others appeared") and Anne's sense that "the room *seemed* full—full of persons and voices" (emphasis added), though there are most likely only five adults in the room. Once they leave, the narrator moves to Anne's inner monologue: "'It is over! it is over!' she repeated to herself again and again, in nervous gratitude" (J. Austen, *Persuasion* 64; vol. 1, ch. 7). When Wentworth talks about his possible fate if the *Asp* were lost in a storm, the narrator tells us, "Anne's shudderings were to herself alone" (71; vol. 1, ch. 8). When Anne is released from her young nephew's grasp by the gallant captain, "[h]er sensations on the discovery made her perfectly speechless. She could not even thank him," and she feels "very painful agitation," which "required a long application of solitude and reflection to recover her" (87; vol. 1, ch. 9). Though Anne may seem calm to the other characters, through this dramatic irony readers realize that she is profoundly distressed by her encounters with Wentworth. Therefore, readers are prepared for her poetic musings during her walk with Wentworth and the Musgroves to the Hayter home, when a connection between Anne's sensations and nature becomes clearer.

The autumn, a time of decay, might also point toward spring, a time of hope and renewal. Anne attempts to recover from her earlier agitation by finding solace in the natural world around her: "the view of the last smiles of the year upon the tawny leaves, and withered hedges." The narrator informs us that Anne recites "to herself some few of the thousand poetical descriptions extant of autumn" (90; vol. 1, ch. 10). But she is interrupted again when she overhears Wentworth, who speaks "with playful solemnity" about the strength and firmness of a hazelnut and predicts that Louisa's "present powers of mind" will cause Louisa to "be beautiful and happy in her November of life" (94–95). Wentworth's gentle mocking of poetic nature metaphors might be understood as a contrast to Anne's inner musings about "tawny leaves and withered hedges" (90), but perhaps it also suggests the two characters' deep affinity of temperament and their shared capacity for poetic reflection.

Since Wentworth does not know that Anne can hear him, this is another good example of Austen's use of free indirect discourse. First, we learn, "It would have surprised Anne, if Louisa could have readily answered such a speech," which retains some distance from Anne's inner thoughts. But then we move closer to Anne: "she could imagine what Louisa was feeling." Once the speakers move beyond her hearing, Anne's sensations reflect those of a gothic heroine, as "[h]er own emotions still kept her fixed. She had much to recover from, before she could move" (95; vol. 1, ch. 10). Anne's sensations are roused by her love for Wentworth, but they are sustained and heightened in a natural setting and with reference to what we might think are lines of Romantic poetry.

We perceive Austen's use of natural images again when Anne first encounters Lyme Regis and its environs. The narrator describes "its high grounds and extensive sweeps of country, and still more, its sweet, retired bay, backed by dark cliffs, where fragments of low rock among the sands, make it the happiest spot for watching the flow of the tide, for sitting in unwearied contemplation" and "green chasms between romantic rocks, where the scattered forest trees and orchards of luxuriant growth, declare that many a generation must have passed away since the first partial falling of the cliff prepared the ground for such a state, where a scene so wonderful and so lovely is exhibited" (103; vol. 1, ch. 11). Later, after this reference to the mutability of nature, we also learn that Anne's appearance changes in this environment, as the narrator tells us "she was looking remarkably well" with "the bloom and the freshness of youth restored by the fine wind which had been blowing on her complexion." And with a complicated bit of narrative maneuvering, readers observe that Anne notices Wentworth noticing "a gentleman" (her cousin, Mr. Elliot) who is noticing her. Anne believes she understands Wentworth's perspective: "He gave her a momentary glance, a glance of brightness, which seemed to say, 'That man is struck with you, and even I, at this moment, see something like Anne Elliot again'" (112; vol. 1, ch. 12). "That man" is Mr. Elliot, but the "I" is Wentworth. The narration shows readers that Anne is aware of her own transformation in the bracing air of the seaside and that she is recognized by the gaze of two men. By looking closely at the language in this passage, students can understand that the natural world around Anne and the poetic phrases she has been repeating seem to have a healing effect on her physical appearance. This moment comes right before a climax of the story, when Louisa Musgrove falls to her apparent death; it also provides a climax in the development of Anne and Wentworth's relationship. Anne is recovering her "bloom" and strength in the outdoors, and Wentworth is rediscovering his appreciation for Anne even while she embarks on a long discussion with Captain Benwick about the "benefit of struggling against affliction" (108; vol. 1, ch. 11).

These scenes might link the nature-centered poetry of William Wordsworth, John Keats, and Percy Bysshe Shelley to the more expansive poetry of Walter Scott and Lord Byron—"all the tenderest songs of the one poet [Scott], and all the impassioned descriptions of hopeless agony of the other [Byron]"—but they also reflect back on a more Augustan perspective on reading. Anne is quick to hope that Benwick "did not always read only poetry" when "he repeated, with such tremulous feeling, the various lines which imaged a broken heart, or a mind destroyed by wretchedness." Anne goes on to recommend that Benwick read "a larger allowance of prose in his daily study" (108; vol. 1, ch. 11).

Claudia L. Johnson suggests that Anne's reference to the "works of our best moralists, such collections of the finest letters, such memoirs of characters of worth and suffering" (J. Austen, *Persuasion* 109; vol. 1, ch. 11) may refer to Samuel Johnson's essays published in *The Rambler* (C. Johnson, *Jane* 159). Anne may be recommending to Benwick that "[t]he safe and general antidote against sorrow is employment" (S. Johnson 257). Clearly, Anne has read Samuel Johnson and other neoclassical or Augustan thinkers and has learned to value tempering poetic musing with active exertion. Students might recall that when she dreads "the possible heats of September in all the white glare of Bath" (J. Austen, *Persuasion* 35; vol. 1, ch. 5) she is summoned to help Mary Musgrove in the countryside, where she is "glad to be thought of some use, glad to have any thing marked out as a duty" (36); when she anticipates meeting Captain Wentworth for the first time since she broke their engagement, she volunteers to remain at the cottage with her injured nephew, knowing "herself to be the first utility to the child" (62; vol. 1, ch. 7). Anne might long to dwell on her melancholy thoughts of pain and loss, but she finds a way to employ herself and be of use. *Persuasion* may recognize the beauty of a Romantic disposition, but it does not argue for a Romantic way of facing loss.

Therefore, although Louisa's fall and illness reflect Romantic tropes, they are realistic and serious, a direct result of her overzealous nature and her desire for the sensation of falling and being caught by the rugged navy captain. Susan Allen Ford points out the "sexual component" of the Romantic heroine in this scene (Ford 85): Louisa's "face was like death" (J. Austen, *Persuasion* 118; vol. 1, ch. 12), but the narrator reminds us that the spectacle of "a dead young lady" is also interesting to passersby, and the reality of Louisa lying unconscious causes her sister to faint and her brother to hang over her body "with sobs of grief" (119). The scene is horrifying and dramatic, and this might be a good point to discuss the various tropes of horror and terror prevalent in Romantic poetry.[5] Anne, however, displays a rational response, calling for a surgeon and later being designated by Wentworth as the most "proper" and "capable" nurse for Louisa (123). Wentworth's resistance to Anne begins its reversal as the danger of Louisa's determination is revealed, and he begins to see Anne in a more realistic light.

Captain Wentworth is portrayed throughout the novel as having a strong presence, and in contrast to Benwick, who identifies with the Scott and Byron poems after the death of his fiancée, Wentworth is not shown dwelling in self-pity. Austen's narrator describes him as heartbroken but resolved to move forward: "He had not forgiven Anne Elliot. She had used him ill; deserted and disappointed him; and worse, she had shewn a feebleness of character in doing so, which his own decided, confident temper could not endure. . . . It was now his object to marry. He was rich, and being turned on shore, fully intended to settle as soon as he could be properly tempted." Wentworth is a man of action, and he intends to fall in love with "any pleasing young woman who came in his way, excepting Anne Elliot" (66; vol. 1, ch. 7). But after Louisa's accident, when he retreats to his brother's happy home in Shropshire, "lamenting the blindness of his own pride, and the blunders of his own calculations" (264; vol. 2, ch. 11), and he hears the news of Louisa's engagement to Benwick, he is determined to find happiness with Anne. Though Wentworth could have dwelled indefinitely in his loneliness, or continued to blame the nineteen-year-old Anne who had rejected him, he moves forward. He sees an opportunity to renew his suit and marries Anne. Thus, *Persuasion* argues in favor of appreciating the beauty that is romance but tempering it with the resolution of the Augustan. It is a fitting transition from the "tawny leaves" of autumn (90; vol. 1, ch. 10) to the "spring of felicity" (274; vol. 2, ch. 12).

Reading Jane Austen's last completed novel as a transition from Romantic literature to the literature of the Victorian period helps students understand not only the evolution of poetic thought but also the full import of Austen's messages. Anne moves from an upper-class family that cannot "receive and estimate [her husband] properly" to Wentworth's family—which offers her a prompt welcome (273; vol. 2, ch. 12). She is a heroine for whom "tenderness itself" is necessary to weather the "dread of a future war" (275). And she moves from an early autumn of her young life to a "spring of felicity."

NOTES

[1] Percy Bysshe Shelley's "Mutability" (88) and William Wordsworth's "Mutability" (353) might be included here.

[2] Besides William Deresiewicz, Mary A. Favret ("Writing"), and Peter Knox-Shaw ("Byron"), other resources to consult about Jane Austen's reflections on this social stratification are Margot Finn's chapter in *The Cambridge History of Romantic Literature*, where Finn considers how we might understand English homes in Romantic literature as "domestic markers of a public history" ("Homes" 293); Susan Allen Ford's paper in *Persuasions*, where Ford considers Anne and Wentworth's separation from the landed estate; and Ashley Tauchert's book, *Romancing Jane Austen*, where Tauchert discusses Sir Walter's narcissism as signaling "his loss of the 'real'" (142).

[3] Duncan Heath and Judy Boreham's *Introducing Romanticism* presents a simple overview complete with graphic illustrations. A more detailed summary of how Romanticism has been defined historically by literary theorists can be found in *Romanticism: Points of View*, edited by Robert F. Gleckner and Gerald E. Enscoe. Teachers might assign short essays by Walter Pater and Earl R. Wasserman, covering a period from 1889 to the late 1950s, to track the evolution in definitions of the age of Romanticism.

[4] At this point, a brief investigation into Wordsworth's "Lines Composed a Few Miles above Tintern Abbey" can be helpful to provide historical grounding and a definition of Romanticism (163–65).

[5] Ann Radcliffe famously describes the difference between terror and horror: "the first expands the soul, and awakens the faculties to a high degree of life; the other contracts, freezes, and nearly annihilates them" ("On the Supernatural" 149).

"The Richness of the Present Age": Romantic Allusions in *Persuasion*

Anna Dodson Saikin

When planning syllabi for my introduction to Romanticism courses, I often like to use *Persuasion* as a capstone text to reflect and refract the themes covered over the semester. It is not unheard of for students to read Austen within the context of Romantic-era writers, and her earlier novels tend to signal themselves as more obvious choices. *Sense and Sensibility*, for example, considers the emotional responses of the eighteenth-century cult of sensibility, and *Northanger Abbey* parodies Ann Radcliffe's gothic novels (e.g., *Romance of the Forest*). Yet I find that the moral and emotional complexity of Anne Elliot's developing inner life in *Persuasion* often echoes the complexity of Romantic-era thinkers and writers and thus provides fruitful applications of the social, historical, and political change that constitutes what Jerome McGann famously called the "romantic ideology." This essay, then, situates *Persuasion* within the Romantic era to provide teachers a means by which to help students understand the cultural significance of the novel's frequent allusions to poetry.

I begin the discussion in class by introducing Anne's long walk through the fields in volume 1, chapter 10, with Louisa and Henrietta Musgrove and Anne's sister Mary, joined by Captain Frederick Wentworth and Charles Musgrove. As the walkers proceed, Anne's thoughts turn inward to "musings and quotations" as Anne tries "not to be in the way of any body." Though Anne is distracted by Louisa and Henrietta's lively and flirtatious conversation with Wentworth, the narrator notes that Anne's

> *pleasure* in the walk must arise from the exercise and the day, from the view of the last smiles of the year upon the tawny leaves and withered hedges and from repeating to herself some few of the thousand poetical descriptions extant of autumn, that season of peculiar and inexhaustible influence of the mind of taste and tenderness, that season which has drawn from every poet, worthy of being read, some attempt at description, or some lines of feeling. (90; vol. 1, ch. 10)

The shift from Anne's interior reflections to the narrator's voice, hinging on the phrases beginning with "that," suggests the narrator's sympathy with the shape and color of Anne's quiet thoughts and shows how Anne is open to the "pleasure" that can arise from the November day. Early in the novel, the narrator says that Anne "learned romance as she grew older" (32; vol. 1, ch. 4): is her openness, students may be asked, an example of her having learned "romance"?

Students may initially conflate "romance" with Romanticism, and this impression requires a close reading of the passage to dispel. I follow Adela Pinch's analysis of Austen's works as enacting an epistemological framework of feeling (137–63) by asking students to read the novel's description of "tawny leaves and withered hedges" alongside selections from Samuel Taylor Coleridge and William Wordsworth's *Lyrical Ballads* or John Clare's poem "I Am" (Clare 361).[1] The closing passage of Wordsworth's "Lines Written a Few Miles above Tintern Abbey," for example, notes that the nostalgic remembrance of the speaker's sister (Dorothy) comes when the speaker views the surrounding landscape:

> Nor wilt thou then forget,
> That after many wanderings, many years
> Of absence, these steep woods and lofty cliffs,
> And this green pastoral landscape, were to me
> More dear, both for themselves, and for thy sake!
> (Coleridge and Wordsworth 118)

Such comparisons demonstrate how the mood Anne has for poetry is connected to both her emotional state and her natural surroundings.

Once my students have an understanding of poetry's value to Anne, we then move into our discussion of the key scene where Anne discusses the poetry of Lord Byron and of Walter Scott with the grieving but expressive Captain Benwick. The narrator notes that Benwick "was evidently a young man of considerable taste in reading, though principally in poetry," and Anne latches on to their shared interests with the "hope of being of real use to him in some suggestions as to the duty and benefit of struggling against affliction." Anne and Benwick's conversation not only acknowledges their shared tastes, but also provides an opening for Anne to help him recover from excessive identification with the grieving voices in Byron's and Scott's poetry. Their conversations on "poetry, the richness of the present age, and . . . opinion[s] as to the first-rate poets" situate *Persuasion* within a particular historical moment wherein Anne's appreciation of poetry provides an opportunity for her to frame her struggle with her own sad feelings as a caution for Benwick not to fall too deeply into despair. The text notes that Byron and Scott are of particular interest to them, as they discuss "whether *Marmion* or *The Lady of the Lake* [by Scott] were to be preferred, and how ranked the *Giaour* and *The Bride of Abydos* [by Byron]." The animation of their discussion is captured in their contesting view of poems known to both of them and in their enjoyment of the joke about "how the *Giaour* was to be pronounced" (J. Austen 108; vol. 1, ch. 11).

The novel's allusions to Scott's *Marmion: A Tale of the Flodden Field* and *The Lady of the Lake* and to Byron's *The Giaour: A Fragment of a Turkish Tale* and *The Bride of Abydos* would have been readily recognized by Austen's first readers but may have little significance to today's readers. Here, Linda Bree's Broadview edition of *Persuasion* excels, as it includes in its appendixes excerpts from Scott's *Marmion* and Byron's *The Giaour*. Bree's inclusion of these excerpts allows students of any level to see how different Romantic poems may reflect elements of Anne's journey as enthusiastic yet restorative.

Both of the excerpts given in Bree's edition lament the impossibility of moving on after a loss, and when read together, they help students paint a more complete portrait of Anne as a Romantic figure. Scott's poem begins with the coming of winter: "November's sky is chill and drear, / November's leaf is red and sear" (Scott, "Marmion" 297). Students will remember that this is the same month in which Anne takes her walk and will thus link her with the poem's speaker. After detailing nature's longing for spring, Scott contrasts the life of nature:

> To mute and to material things
> New life revolving summer brings:
> The genial call dead Nature hears,
> And in her glory reappears.

Then Scott turns to the fate of his defeated country: "But Oh! my country's wintry state / What second spring can renovate?" (299). Scott specifically laments the state of Scotland, but it is easy to believe that the lines might have special resonance for Anne, given that they express the finality of loss, on the one hand, and the possibility of renewal, on the other. Scott's question, "What second spring can renovate?" is given a hopeful response when Anne visits Lady Russell at Kellynch Hall and receives compliments that cause her to hope "she was to be blessed with a second spring of youth and beauty" (J. Austen, *Persuasion* 134; vol. 2, ch. 1).

In addition to Anne's personal journey, the novel's plot deals with the significance of past actions and their effects on the present. Scott's poetry provides an opportunity for students to question Sir Walter's efficacy as head of household, as Anne does when she urges her father to pay his debts in order to stay in Kellynch Hall, the Elliot family home (14; vol. 1, ch. 2). Sir Walter's obsession with the "history and rise of the ancient and respectable family" as recorded in the Baronetage (4; vol. 1, ch. 1) sharply contrasts with Anne's clear-eyed awareness of her family's financial need for "the most comprehensive retrenchments," which, Lady Russell notes, "very many of our first families have done" (14, 13; vol. 1, ch. 2). Although the narrator calls Sir Walter's obsession "[v]anity" (4; vol. 1, ch. 1), the importance of the Baronetage to the Elliott family's actions, particularly Anne's refusal of Wentworth and subsequent suitors, which affects the family's monetary health, is clearly implied. *Marmion*, then, not only appeals to Anne's and Benwick's tastes but also provides insight into the decision Anne makes to forgo her family's legacy for love.

Similarly, Lord Byron's *The Giaour* reiterates Anne's attempts to love again. One fragment concerns the loss of the speaker's lover, whose death is passionately mourned:

> 'Tis true, that, like that bird of prey,
> With havoc have I mark'd my way:
> But this was taught me by the dove,
> To die—and know no second love. (Byron, "Giaour" 301)

Whereas *Marmion* holds open the possibility for regeneration, *The Giaour* despairs that "Earth holds no other like to thee, / Or, if it doth, in vain for me" (302). Although Anne can barely admit to herself how much she continues to love Wentworth, *Persuasion*'s allusion to *The Giaour* permits her to express her deep feeling even if she cannot verbally say it. Byron's poetry, which had a scandalous reputation, complicates the common perception of Austen's novels as chaste romances. Anne's interest in *The Giaour* and in how to pronounce the title can also serve as a prompt for students to read the title and portions of the poem aloud in order to note the passion of Byron's language and to consider how that poetic excess might prompt Anne and Benwick to become friendly acquaintances on their first meeting. Anne and Benwick achieve a level of familiarity after this short meeting that allows Anne to "preach patience and resignation to a young man whom she had never seen before" (J. Austen, *Persuasion* 109; vol. 1, ch. 11) and to reflect thoughtfully that she is "amused" at her "emboldened" actions (108).

Anne's conversation with Benwick is not the novel's sole allusion to contemporary poetry. In our discussions, I emphasize to my students the similarities and differences between Anne's repeating poetry to herself during her walk and similar scenes found in novels by Radcliffe and by Charlotte Smith. Like Radcliffe, Austen sends her heroine on a walk outdoors accompanied by her knowledge of poetry, which is her primary solace and comfort. Yet the text is aware that such a movement is constructed from Anne's romantic thoughts. Whereas Radcliffe and Smith weave poetry into their novels that is supposedly written by their heroines, Austen resists attributing original poems to Anne and instead relies on poetry with which her readers would be familiar. These contemporary references show modern readers another aspect of *Persuasion*'s commitment to realism and historical circumstances.

Mary Jacobus notes that "Scott's patriotic nationalism and Byronic disaffected philhellenism allow both tragedy and a critique of imperialism to filter into the novel's political unconscious," an observation that holds water when analyzing the poetry of Byron and of Scott in relation to the novel (251). Following Jacobus's lead, I remind students of Byron's late-life obsession with Greece and Byron's role in the Greek revolution that overthrew Ottoman Turkish rule. I also discuss how Scott's poetry emphasized Scottish national pride within the context of British unification. In both cases, the poetic language echoes the language used in *Persuasion* when Anne dwells on the past even as she contemplates the future, an expansion of Anne's mind that similarly signals the novel's expanded focus from regional to national and international concerns, or as Jacobus puts it: "poetry constitutes an indirect commentary on the national background against which the novel requires to be read, given its near-contemporary time-frame of 1814" (241). Jacobus's interpretation of Byron succinctly reminds students that a preoccupation with the past was part of the Romantic project.

I find it helpful to couple Jacobus's analysis with that of Nicholas Mason, who argues that Byron's authorial persona was a creation of the poet and his publisher, John Murray, through their advertising efforts to publicize *Childe Harold's Pilgrimage* (69–77). Given this context, Austen's first readers may not have needed to know which sections of *Marmion* and *The Giaour* Anne and Captain Benwick discuss while sitting "rather apart" from others, because the poets themselves came to stand for certain Romantic concepts. This interpretation is borne out when the speaker notes that Benwick "shewed himself so intimately acquainted with all the tenderest songs of the one poet [Scott], and all the impassioned descriptions of hopeless agony of the other [Byron]" (J. Austen, *Persuasion* 108; vol. 1, ch. 11). In other words, Benwick adopts a poetic persona to express his feelings. Although the novel makes clear that Benwick's interest in poetry signifies his underlying sensibility, the tone of the passage does not necessarily distinguish which of the poets (if either) is more damaging to his psyche.

Indeed, Anne admonishes Benwick to exercise more discretion and choose texts other than poetry that would be more likely to lift his spirits: "[Anne] ventured to hope he did not always read only poetry; and to say, that she thought it was the misfortune of poetry, to be seldom safely enjoyed by those who enjoyed it completely; and that the strong feelings which alone could estimate it truly, were the very feelings which ought to taste it but sparingly" (108; vol. 1, ch. 11). The passage notes that Anne recommends for Benwick to include "such works of our best moralists" in his reading list, an implicit reference to eighteenth-century essayists such as Samuel Johnson (109). Claudia L. Johnson argues that Johnson was a favorite of Austen's and suggests that Anne "may be referring to *Rambler* 32, on patience, and *Rambler* 47, on regulating sorrow" (C. Johnson, "'Operations'" 35), and there is ample evidence in Austen's other novels of characters recommending conduct literature to each other (e.g., Mr. Collins reading aloud from James Fordyce's *Sermons to Young Women* in *Pride and Prejudice*, or Emma Woodhouse compiling appropriate reading lists in *Emma*). By providing Benwick recommendations for reading material other than poetry, Anne reveals her deliberately rational turn of mind, noting that the "strong feelings" that allow someone to enjoy poetry "truly" are the exact reason it should be consumed "sparingly." While Anne indulges in poetic musings, she attempts to control her passionate impulses by expressing concern over Benwick's "strong feelings" even as she worries whether she can follow her own advice. Byron's and Scott's poems are set apart as an indulgence, as they occupy the tenuous space between reason and emotion.

I hope to have demonstrated how teachers can help students realize that even timeless works of art such as Austen's novels are the product of the time and place in which they were made. Byron's and Scott's poetry provides an opportunity to bring into class discussions the value of overt and covert references to popular culture. Anne's knowledge of poetry allows Anne to responsibly critique characters such as Captain Benwick who show too much feeling, while also providing herself with consolation, as she does during her November walk prior to Louisa's fall. Fantasy provides a space in which to think of possible, fictive futures, but Anne's impulse is nevertheless grounded in reality. Students can practice close reading techniques to reveal Anne's imaginative futures while also analyzing the cultural influences that inform her decisions.

NOTE

[1] If taught as part of a British literature survey course, *Persuasion* can be paired with almost any selection from *Lyrical Ballads*; however, I find that Wordsworth's Lucy poems complement Anne's emotional journey particularly well. See, for example, "Song" and "A Slumber Did My Spirit Seal" (Wordsworth and Coleridge 154).

OTHER TEACHING STRATEGIES

Social Class in *Persuasion*

Catherine Engh

When she moves from Kellynch Hall to Uppercross, Anne Elliot finds the Musgrove family preoccupied with interfamilial loves and disputes. She recognizes "it to be very fitting, that every little social commonwealth should dictate its own matters of discourse," and finds it "highly incumbent on her to clothe her imagination, her memory, and all her ideas in as much of Uppercross as possible" (46; vol. 1, ch. 6). Though Anne is thinking about the challenges of orienting herself to the social discourse of a different place, she models a discipline relevant for readers of *Persuasion* who would orient themselves to the social discourse of a different time.

How much do students need to know about the attributes of the English class system in Jane Austen's time—about rank and family name, the ambiguous category of the gentleman, the winning of military prize money, and marriages between families that have cash and those that own land—in order to clothe their imaginations in the novel's discourse? In what follows, I outline strategies for bridging contemporary assumptions about social class in late capitalism and assumptions that defined the acquisitive yet heritage-oriented, postwar English society of *Persuasion*. I conclude by reflecting on how I've balanced sensitivity to Austen's moral discernment with awareness of the structural inequities that form the backdrop against which English leisured society emerges into view.

Persuasion begins with the problem of debt and the resolution of the Elliot family to move from its ancestral seat. The first chapters offer an introduction to the fundamentals of the Elliot family's ideology; Anne's consciousness, and her tendency toward virtuous self-denial, is occluded by the "strong family pride" (9; vol. 1, ch. 1) of Sir Walter and Elizabeth and the prejudices "on the side of ancestry" of Lady Russell (12; vol. 1, ch. 2). Students usually understand why Sir Walter bemoans the loss of "[j]ourneys, London, servants, horses, table" (14), but we have to spend time talking about why his "ancient and respectable family," which was afforded the "dignity of baronet, in the first year of Charles II," distinguishes him (4; vol. 1, ch. 1). I ask a volunteer to read aloud the first lines of the novel:

> Sir Walter Elliot, of Kellynch-hall, in Somersetshire, was a man who, for his own amusement, never took up any book but the Baronetage; there he found occupation for an idle hour, and consolation in a distressed one; there his faculties were roused into admiration and respect, by contemplating the limited remnant of the earliest patents; there any unwelcome sensations, arising from domestic affairs, changed naturally into pity and contempt, as he turned over the almost endless creations of the last century—and there, if every other leaf were powerless, he could read his own history with an interest which never failed. (3)

For students who don't know what a "patent" or a baronet is, it's unclear why this book holds Sir Walter's interest. I explain that the title of baronet, which was inherited from father to son, came into being in 1611. It was in the second half of that same century, during the restoration of Charles II, that the Elliots' ancestor first received his title. Baronetages list the baronets and their genealogies, and reading one calls to Sir Walter's mind the "limited remnant of the earliest patents," or the few family names that have survived over generations. Although illustrious family lines have fallen out of existence, Sir Walter believes that the Elliots retain a place in the historical record. The book consoles Sir Walter in a distressed hour because it validates his self-importance at a moment when the "unwelcome sensations" that arise from his domestic affairs do not.

The opening lines of *Persuasion* show students that Sir Walter's pride is grounded in the assumption that one's place in the world is determined by birth. This assumption runs counter to the belief often held by students today that a college degree will give access to a higher quality of life. For this reason, students are well-positioned to detect satire in the narrator's pronouncement that Sir Walter "never took up any book but the Baronetage" yet "could read his own history with an interest that never failed" (3; vol. 1, ch. 1). Ultimately, the consolation afforded by the Baronetage does not free the Elliot family from status-related anxieties about the future: Elizabeth wants to be "properly solicited by baronet-blood" (7), and Sir Walter disapproves of Anne's decision to maintain a friendship with "a mere Mrs. Smith, an every day Mrs. Smith" over an acquaintance with "her own family connections among the nobility of England and Ireland" (171; vol. 2, ch. 5). While he believes that the Baronetage affirms the Elliot family's right to social precedence, Sir Walter's desire to secure the continuous good standing of the family consigns its members to a life of social insularity that Anne cannot abide.

Because money today holds a greater claim to prestige than it did in Austen's time, it's not hard for students to comprehend Lady Russell's initial disapproval of Anne's alliance with Captain Frederick Wentworth, the "stranger without alliance or fortune" who becomes the novel's figure of self-made success (29; vol. 1, ch. 4). To help students understand how claims to wealth mix with claims to land, family name, and profession in *Persuasion*, I assign the chapter "Three Around Farnham" in Raymond Williams's *The Country and the City* (108–19), in which Williams analyzes the interlocking system of "estates, incomes and social position" that determine changes of fortune in Austen's novels (113). Williams's analysis helps students to distinguish between the various sources of wealth that support characters in *Persuasion*—landed and trading capital as well as fortunes from naval exploits and plantation slavery—and to see why Mr. William Elliot wishes to supplement his importance by becoming Sir William Elliot, a gentleman with a handle to his name. Students come to see that Austen's fictions represent a complex process of class formation. In *Persuasion*, the power and prestige of the nation's elites are not fixed but subject to ongoing conflict and negotiation. The traditional authority of Sir Walter is challenged, if not wholly upended, by characters like Wentworth and Admiral and Mrs. Croft. In this way, Austen's novel gives the lie to the Baronetage's assumption of relative class stability while at the same time illuminating the insecurities that prompt a distressed Sir Walter to adopt that form of historical consciousness in the first place.

Claudia L. Johnson has taught us to see that *Persuasion* is distinguished among Austen's novels by its depiction of "alternatives to . . . the establishment": alternatives, that is, to the moral authority of the landed gentry ("*Persuasion*" 261). Jane Austen's brothers Francis and Charles had lifelong careers in the Royal Navy, and *Persuasion* can be read as a postwar tribute to their profession. The story begins with the Crofts replacing the Elliots as residents of Kellynch Hall and ends with Elizabeth Elliot's belated acknowledgment that Wentworth will "move about well in her drawing-room" (246; vol. 2, ch. 10). The navy has its own system of rank that, though hardly immune to the influence of well-placed persons, allows Wentworth to amass a "handsome fortune" (32; vol. 1, ch. 4) without the help of "interest" (70; vol. 1, ch. 8). In Wentworth, students see a form of social esteem earned through fortitude, luck, and personal adaptability. I point out that the meritocratic values that Austen identifies with the navy are also evident in the younger generation of characters in the landed classes. This is one reason why the marriages among these classes—between Henrietta Musgrove and Charles Hayter, Louisa Musgrove and Captain Benwick, and Anne and Wentworth—are plausible and fulfill what one of *Persuasion*'s first reviewers calls the importance of "probability" in fiction.[1] Charles is distinguished by his learning as a gentleman among a family of farmers, and Benwick, who reads Lord Byron's and Walter Scott's poetry, also seems to have gentlemanly tastes. The addition of a "grand piano forte and a harp" in the Musgroves' "old-fashioned square parlour" attests to the Musgrove sisters' correspondingly "modern minds and manners." Even more refined than the improving tastes of the Musgrove sisters is Anne's discernment of mind. Anne quietly prefers her own "elegant and cultivated mind" to all the Musgroves' enjoyments (43; vol. 1, ch. 5).

Though mind, manner, and accomplishment are important forms of social and romantic currency in *Persuasion*, they are no guarantee of sincerity. Mrs. Clay's "acute mind and assiduous pleasing manners" are duplicitous (37; vol. 1, ch. 5), and she is a good final match for Mr. Elliot, the unscrupulous London lawyer whose "rational, discreet, polished" (175; vol. 2, ch. 5) appearance and "air of good sense" (115; vol. 1, ch. 12) screens a "disingenuous, artificial, worldly man, who has never had any better principle to guide him than selfishness" (225; vol. 2, ch. 9). If the naval profession is an approved avenue to wealth in *Persuasion*, it is because the naval community shares a claim to national utility; a custom of open, informal communication; and a degree of flexibility as to gender roles. Mrs. Clay and Mr. Elliot exemplify, by contrast, the insincerity of those who view wealth and "consequence" as ends in themselves (223). The dramatic uncovering of Mr. Elliot's true character allows readers to judge his ambitions by the language that he has used to support them. Reading the letter in which Mr. Elliot disparages his own kin, Anne measures the unworthiness of his aspirations by the amorality that has attended them.

Anne is an ideal heroine, one whom Austen thought to be "almost too good" ("Letters" 201) because she has a mind to measure moral criteria like "sincerity" (*Persuasion* 239; vol. 2, ch. 10) and "a strong sense of duty" (268; vol. 2, ch. 11). I've found that students like to learn about class conflict, but only then to appropriate Anne's moral insights in defense of sentimental readings of the novel. Take, for example, Mrs. Smith. They are consistently drawn to Anne's humanizing observation that, despite her misfortune, Mrs. Smith is constitutionally blessed with "that disposition to be comforted, that power of turning readily from evil to good, and of finding employment which carried her out of herself" (167; vol. 2, ch. 5). Students use this passage to support their arguments that wealth, rank, and social ornaments do not reliably align with the moral and spiritual qualities that really matter. This is good general wisdom that I hesitate to qualify. However, a careful reader will note that there are rarely innocents in Austen's social world. Mrs. Smith's material disadvantages make it desirable for her to regain her husband's West Indian property, which is surely a slave plantation. Wentworth finally does this service for Mrs. Smith, and her return to respectability is premised on a plundering of the profits of slave labor all the way across the Atlantic. If it feels liberating to note that Mrs. Smith's fallen social status does not fully define her, it's less liberating to acknowledge that she functions as a reminder of metropolitan subjects' dependency on the commodification and forced labor of slaves.

In *Persuasion*, the newly wealthy and the landed characters are entangled with nation-building processes that perpetuate social inequity. Mrs. Croft knows the difference between the West and the East Indies because Admiral Croft has been employed to protect Britain's trade monopoly in India. Wentworth first meets Anne after he is made a commander in "the action off St. Domingo" (28; vol. 1, ch. 4), a real historical event in which British forces defended their control over trade with the Caribbean island that is the present location of the Dominican Republic and Haiti. The island was then known for the riches of its sugar plantations. Saree Makdisi proposes that Austen's novels represent the "continuity of the civilizing mission both at home and overseas" (Makdisi xx). We see this continuity, and perhaps a critique of it, in *Persuasion* when it falls on Anne to visit the "afflicted tenantry and cottagers"—the "yeomen and labourers"—to whom her father offers only "condescending bows" (38; vol. 1, ch. 5). Anne describes the duty as being of a "trying nature" (41), and we might infer that this is because it entails confrontation with the cultural divides, not to mention the poverty, perpetuated by the system of agrarian capitalism of which she is a beneficiary. Though students don't always have background knowledge about the processes of imperialism that were overseen by the British Navy and the landed gentry, they are familiar with Occupy Wall Street's rhetoric of the ninety-nine percent. They understand that capitalist success in the modern era is premised on processes of financialization and privatization that tend, like the nation-building efforts of the colonial era, to disadvantage most of the world's people (Makdisi xx).

Students admire Anne for her sensitivity to the claims of social inferiors. I like to point out that this character trait is related to her readiness to learn "romance as she grew older" (32; vol. 1, ch. 4). The most valuable point that undergraduates may take from *Persuasion* at a moment in which they find themselves on the brink of adulthood could be this: that the development of a personal orientation to social class—the negotiation, for instance, of the desire for a higher quality of life with ethical and political awareness—is just as much a process now as it was in Austen's time.[2] The characters who most interest Austen are those like Anne and Wentworth who are capable of changing their minds about what ought to distinguish a person, and of confronting the moral and political compromises that sustain domestic "felicity" in their modernizing society (274; vol. 2, ch. 12).

NOTES

[1] In 1821, Richard Whately, writing a review of *Northanger Abbey* and *Persuasion* for the *Quarterly Review*, defines the new style of novel pioneered by Austen as "fictions as are quite *perfect* in respect of the probability of their story" ("New Style" 209).

[2] For an extensive analysis of privatization and financialization as aspects of neoliberal capitalism's policy of accumulation by dispossession, see Harvey.

Debating *Persuasion*

Melissa J. Ganz

"Was Anne Elliot right to listen to Lady Russell's advice and to break off her engagement with Captain Frederick Wentworth?" I ask when I teach *Persuasion*. The question results in lively debates about the tensions between duty and desire, compliance and resolution, and prudence and risk. Students tend to respond to my question, at first, by offering their own views of Anne's decision and explaining what they would have done had they been in her place. Such comments help students relate to Anne's plight while highlighting important differences between Austen's world and our own. But I lead us back to the text: "What does Austen show us about Anne's decision in the novel?" I ask. Through the discussions that follow, students learn to articulate and defend nuanced arguments while grappling with the formal and ethical implications of Austen's text. In this essay, I outline my strategies for teaching the novel through this lens.

I developed this approach in an introductory literature class for English majors. The course, Critical Practices and Processes in Literary Studies, seeks to hone students' close reading and critical writing skills while offering an overview of British literature from the late eighteenth century to the present day. Subtitled Protest and Rebellion in the British Tradition, the class is loosely organized around the motif of dissent. We consider formal and thematic rebellions in literature, and the emphasis throughout the course is on respectful dialogue and debate. The class is small (capped at twenty students) and discussion-based and meets for seventy-five minutes twice each week. We read *Persuasion* early in the semester, right after the Romantic poets. Students thus come to the text with some basic understandings of literary and cultural developments of the late eighteenth and early nineteenth centuries. The class is familiar, for example, with William Wordsworth's and Percy Bysshe Shelley's celebrations of feeling, impulse, and imagination as well as with the Romantics' critiques of the materialistic values of the day. I ask students to keep these issues in mind as we turn to Austen's novel.

In our first class on *Persuasion*, we look closely at the opening paragraphs. (I ask for volunteers to read these paragraphs aloud so that we can examine them in detail.) We consider Austen's portrait of Sir Walter Elliot and his obsession with heritage, evident in his reading and rereading of his family's history in the Baronetage. Right away, Austen exposes and undermines Sir Walter's egotism. Next, we look at Austen's account of Anne's self-absorbed sister Elizabeth and discuss the neglected position that Anne occupies in the family after her mother's death. Anne is "nobody with either father or sister," the narrator explains (6; vol. 1, ch. 1). We consider the heroine's surprisingly late appearance in the novel—although the narrator mentions Anne in passing in the first few pages, we do not hear her speak until the third chapter—and discuss how this formal choice registers Anne's lack of agency. We examine, too, Austen's satire of the Elliots' overspending as well as the comically short-sighted sacrifices that Sir Walter and Elizabeth propose to make when faced with the need to "retrench" (10). And we look at Austen's account of Anne's trusted friend and adviser, Lady Russell. Though "a benevolent, charitable, good woman, and capable of strong attachments," Lady Russell shares the Elliots' "prejudices on the side of ancestry"; her "value for rank and consequence . . . blinded her a little to the faults of those who possessed them" (12; vol. 1, ch. 2). We find, then, at the outset, a mixed assessment of Lady Russell's judgment and a sharp critique of the Elliots' vanity.

With Austen's satire of the Elliot family in mind, we turn to the romantic plot at the heart of the text. We read the narrator's account of the brief engagement between Anne and Wentworth as well as Anne's reflections on their relationship after learning that Wentworth's sister, Sophia Croft, and her husband, the admiral, are interested in renting Kellynch Hall. Eight years earlier, in the summer of 1806, when Wentworth first visited Somersetshire, he and Anne fell in love. "A short period of exquisite felicity followed," the narrator explains, "and but a short one.—Troubles soon arose":

> Sir Walter, on being applied to, without actually withholding his consent, or saying it should never be, gave it all the negative of great astonishment, great coldness, great silence, and a professed resolution of doing nothing for his daughter. He thought it a very degrading alliance; and Lady Russell, though with more tempered and pardonable pride, received it as a most unfortunate one.
>
> Anne Elliot, with all her claims of birth, beauty, and mind, to throw herself away at nineteen; involve herself at nineteen in an engagement with a young man, who had nothing but himself to recommend him, and no hopes of attaining affluence, but in the chances of a most uncertain profession, and no connexions to secure even his farther rise in that profession; would be, indeed, a throwing away, which she grieved to think of! Anne Elliot, so young; known to so few, to be snatched off by a stranger without alliance or fortune; or rather sunk by him into a state of most wearing, anxious, youth-killing dependance! It must not be, if by any fair interference of friendship, any representations from one who had almost a mother's love, and mother's rights, it would be prevented. (28–29; vol. 1, ch. 4)

This passage sets up the central conflicts of the novel, and we look closely at it: Austen here pits prudence, security, and wealth against risk, uncertainty, and love. At the same time, we consider Austen's experiments with narration and point of view. We discuss her use of free indirect discourse and examine the effects of blending third-person, omniscient narration with a limited, first-person perspective. In particular, we consider how the novel invites readers to identify with Lady Russell's perspective even as it undermines her point of view. Some students find Lady Russell's arguments compelling; they highlight the negative language that the narrator uses—a "throw[ing] . . . away," a "youth-killing dependance" (29)—to describe Anne's engagement. These students note the close connection Lady Russell has to Anne and her concern for Anne's welfare. Others, however, call attention to Lady Russell's alignment with the superficial Sir Walter, emphasizing the novel's relentless mockery of his judgment. In their reading, the passage undermines Lady Russell's interference and advice.

At this point, we consider the view that Anne takes of her decision to end her relationship with Wentworth. We carefully consider the language that Austen uses to describe Anne's changing perspective. "She was persuaded to believe the engagement a wrong thing—indiscreet, improper, hardly capable of success, and not deserving it," the narrator explains of Anne's decision to take back her pledge. It was, the narrator emphasizes, "not a merely selfish caution, under which [Anne] acted, in putting an end to [the tie]," for she imagined herself "consulting [Wentworth's] good, even more than her own" (30; vol. 1, ch. 4). Over the next eight years, though, Anne's opinion undergoes a marked shift: "Anne, at seven and twenty, thought very differently from what she had been made to think at nineteen," the narrator reveals. "She was persuaded that under every disadvantage of disapprobation at home, and every anxiety attending his profession, all their probable fears, delays and disappointments, she should yet have been a happier woman in maintaining the engagement, than she had been in the sacrifice of it" (31). When we look at these passages, we consider how Austen's use of the passive voice ("was persuaded" in the first instance and "had been made to think" in the last) evokes Anne's reluctant compliance with Lady Russell's advice. We look, too, at that crucial word "persuasion." Students note the shift in Austen's use of the word, from "persuaded" as in "swayed" to "persuaded" as in "certain." Austen's language tracks Anne's growing independence. Students comment, as well, on the deep regret Anne feels, her physical and emotional decline, and Wentworth's surprising good fortune, all of which suggest that breaking off the engagement was a mistake. We discuss, too, Austen's decision to set the novel in the summer of 1814 rather than in 1806, when Anne first meets Wentworth. Students note that this formal strategy serves to give Anne and Wentworth a second chance while inviting readers to question Anne's reliance upon Lady Russell's advice.

In the next class, we consider how Austen complicates the questions surrounding Anne and Wentworth's engagement. To prepare for this stage of the debate, I divide the class into groups and ask each group to look closely at two passages from the second half of the first volume. In particular, I ask students to examine the exchange that Anne overhears between Wentworth and Louisa Musgrove during their walk to Winthrop (chapter 10) as well as the climactic conclusion to the volume, in which the headstrong Louisa suffers a concussion after jumping from the steps on the Cobb at Lyme Regis (chapter 12). I ask all the groups to consider what these passages suggest about the value and limits of prudent decision-making and receptiveness to others' advice. After separate discussions, each group shares its ideas with the class. I keep track of the evidence by putting two columns on the board—one column for evidence indicating the problems with cautious behavior and one column for evidence suggesting its benefits.

As evidence of the problems with prudence, students point to Anne's distress as well as Wentworth's own anger and despair during the walk to Winthrop. "I see that more than a mere dutiful morning-visit to your aunt was in question," Wentworth observes to Louisa during a pause in their walk, "and woe betide him, and her too, when it comes to things of consequence, when they are placed in circumstances, requiring fortitude and strength of mind, if she have not resolution enough to resist idle interference in such a trifle as this." "It is the worst evil of too yielding and indecisive a character," he continues, "that no influence over it can be depended on.—You are never sure of a good impression being durable. Every body may sway it . . ." (94; vol. 1, ch. 10). Although Wentworth ostensibly refers here to the uncertainty that Louisa's sister, Henrietta, feels about whether to proceed with her intended visit to her suitor, Anne perceives that his comments also refer to herself, and that Wentworth, too, remains troubled by their broken engagement. His subsequent questions about Anne, after learning that she rejected Charles Musgrove's proposal of marriage, confirm his continuing interest in her, leaving her struggling to control her emotions. Through Wentworth's bitter remarks and Anne's anguished response, Austen highlights the costs of prudent behavior.

Other students argue, however, that Louisa's accident on the Cobb shows the dangers of possessing too impetuous and unyielding a disposition. Louisa insists on jumping down a steep flight of steps even though Wentworth advises her against it. The consequences are devastating: she is "too precipitate by half a second," the narrator explains, and she ends up falling on the pavement and knocking herself unconscious (118; vol. 1, ch. 12). Louisa's head injury provides a fitting reminder of the problems that result when individuals act without stopping to think. Anne alone remains calm during the crisis; Wentworth himself looks to her for advice. His opinion of her character, Anne realizes, begins to undergo an important change. In contrast to the risky and obstinate Louisa, Anne appears to possess both flexibility and fortitude. What initially appears to be weakness now begins to look like strength.

In subsequent classes we continue to debate the value and limits of prudent behavior. We focus particular attention on Austen's treatment of Lady Russell. I ask why we hear so little of Anne's influential friend in the first volume of the novel, given the central role that she plays in Anne's life. The question prompts us to consider how and why Austen undermines Lady Russell's authority. We then discuss Lady Russell's attempt to persuade Anne to marry her seemingly upstanding cousin, William Walter Elliot. In the second volume, Austen develops the central conflict of the first: Anne again faces a choice between marrying for love and marrying for wealth and status. A match with Anne's cousin, Lady Russell advises, would not only be a "most suitable connection" but would also be "a very happy one." Anne, however, thinks otherwise: "Mr. Elliot is an exceedingly agreeable man," she replies, "and in many respects I think highly of him . . . but we should not suit" (173; vol. 2, ch. 5). We consider Anne's growing willingness to disagree with her friend and to defend the importance of compatibility in marriage. We look, too, at Austen's account of Anne's walk with Lady Russell down Pulteney Street in Bath, when Anne sees Wentworth and eagerly observes her friend's reaction. Austen's irony is brilliant: Anne is "perfectly conscious of Lady Russell's eyes being turned exactly in the direction for him, of her being in short intently observing him" (194; vol. 2, ch. 7). Yet, as it turns out, Lady Russell utterly fails to notice Wentworth, so preoccupied is she with looking at the window curtains across the street. We discuss Austen's humorous commentary on Anne's absorption with Wentworth as well as the novel's keen satire of Lady Russell's limited perception. Like so many other narrow-minded people in the world of the novel, Lady Russell sees only surfaces and appearances. Previously, she judged Wentworth based on superficial markers; now she does not see him at all. Austen's satire of Lady Russell supports the argument that Anne made a mistake in listening to her friend's advice.

We contrast Lady Russell's view of Anne's rival suitors with that of Anne's old friend the invalid Mrs. Smith, who tactfully (or strategically) waits to disclose the truth about Mr. Elliot's character until she is certain that Anne has no intention of marrying him. Where Lady Russell imposes her own (misguided) views upon Anne, Mrs. Smith goes out of her way to avoid unduly influencing her friend. ("You must allow for an injured, angry woman," she explains. "But I will try to command myself. I will not abuse him. I will only tell you what I have found him. Facts shall speak" [215–16; vol. 2, ch. 9]). Unlike Lady Russell, Mrs. Smith does not rely upon superficial judgments. She presents Anne with objective evidence—a letter written by Mr. Elliot to her late husband that reveals Mr. Elliot's heartless character—and allows Anne to assess this evidence for herself. We spend time considering the differences between Anne's relationships with Lady Russell and Mrs. Smith. Austen, it seems, cautions against possessing too malleable a disposition: Anne errs when she substitutes Lady Russell's judgment for her own. But Austen does not suggest that one should completely ignore others' advice. Through Anne's exchange with Mrs. Smith, Austen shows the need to consult other people in order to test—or, at least, to verify—one's own judgment.

In our last class, we consider the renewal of the engagement between Anne and Wentworth and Anne's reassessment of her earlier decision. First, we look at Anne's debate with Captain Harville concerning men's and women's fidelity; then we read Wentworth's letter and consider its significance. "I can listen no longer in silence," Wentworth writes to Anne. "I must speak to you by such means as are within my reach. You pierce my soul. I am half agony, half hope. Tell me not that I am too late, that such precious feelings are gone for ever. I offer myself to you again with a heart even more your own, than when you almost broke it eight years and a half ago. Dare not say that man forgets sooner than woman, that his love has an earlier death. I have loved none but you" (257–58; vol. 2, ch. 11). Students suggest that the form of the letter helps to convey Wentworth's urgency and passion; indeed, it is one of the few times in the novel that Austen gives us direct access to Wentworth's consciousness. We compare Wentworth's passionate epistle with Mr. Elliot's brief quasi-proposal. ("The name of Anne Elliot," Mr. Elliot tells Anne during their exchange at a concert a few days earlier, "has long had an interesting sound to me. Very long has it possessed a charm over my fancy; and, if I dared, I would breathe my wishes that the name might never change" [204; vol. 2, ch. 8].) Whereas these remarks confirm Mr. Elliot's shallowness and egotism, the letter from Wentworth reveals his utter sincerity and devotion. We consider Anne's reaction to Wentworth's epistle as well as Anne's subsequent encounter with Wentworth in the aptly named Union Street, where the two exchange "again those feelings and those promises which had once before seemed to secure every thing, but which had been followed by so many, many years of division and estrangement" (261; vol. 2, ch. 11). The third-person narration here evokes the sense of surprise and relief that Anne and Wentworth both feel at this unexpected and much longed-for reconciliation. Anne seems, at last, to have made the right choice.

Yet while Anne now feels certain that Lady Russell's earlier advice was wrong, she suggests that she was right to listen to it. "If I was wrong in yielding to persuasion once," Anne tells Wentworth, distinguishing her previous reliance upon Lady Russell's counsel from her present rejection of her friend's advice, "remember that it was to persuasion exerted on the side of safety, not of risk. When I yielded, I thought it was to duty; but no duty could be called in aid here. In marrying a man indifferent to me, all risk would have been incurred, and all duty violated" (265–66; vol. 2, ch. 11). Anne continues:

> I have been thinking over the past, and trying impartially to judge of the right and wrong, I mean with regard to myself; and I must believe that I was right, much as I suffered from it, that I was perfectly right in being guided by the friend whom you will love better than you do now. To me, she was in the place of a parent. Do not mistake me, however. I am not saying that she did not err in her advice. It was, perhaps, one of those cases in which advice is good or bad only as the event decides; and for myself, I certainly never should, in any circumstance of tolerable similarity, give such advice. But I mean, that I was right in submitting to her, and that if I had done otherwise, I should have suffered more in continuing the engagement than I did even in giving it up, because I should have suffered in my conscience. (267–68)

I ask the class to reconsider Anne's decision with this passage in mind. Based on this evidence, some students argue that Austen shows that filial deference is, in fact, more important than individual desire—at least, in the all-important matter of marriage. Anne, in other words, was right to listen to Lady Russell and to break off her engagement. Others, however, argue that in spite of Anne's reflections, the novel shows that she was wrong to yield to her well-meaning but misguided friend. In a world filled with uncertainty, illness, and accidents, they suggest, Austen shows the necessity of love and fidelity. Anne's eventual marriage, in this reading, rectifies her earlier mistake and shows Austen to be a true Romantic. Still others argue that the novel is ambivalent and that Austen has it both ways, endorsing at once duty and desire, prudence and risk.[1]

We conclude our debates about the novel by looking at the very end of the text. Anne's "spring of felicity," the narrator explains, "was in the warmth of her heart":

> Anne was tenderness itself, and she had the full worth of it in Captain Wentworth's affection. His profession was all that could ever make her friends wish that tenderness less; the dread of a future war all that could dim her sunshine. She gloried in being a sailor's wife, but she must pay the tax of quick alarm for belonging to that profession which is, if possible, more distinguished in its domestic virtues than in its national importance. (274–75; vol. 2, ch. 12)

We consider Austen's shift to the present tense at the end of this passage and her reminder of the risks involved in Anne's match. Students note that even now, in spite of Wentworth's good fortune, the union brings with it uncertainty and danger. Marrying a man in the navy—even a successful and wealthy captain—is a perilous choice. I ask students to consider whether this ending changes their view of Anne's decision to wed Wentworth. For some, the final paragraph provides further support that Austen shows the need to accept some risk as an inevitable part of life; others, though, emphasize the novel's continuing ambivalence on this point. After we review the different interpretations, I take a vote to see which argument students find most compelling. The vote prompts everyone in the class to take a position in the debate. Our discussions about Anne and Wentworth's vexed relationship ultimately help students practice articulating and defending nuanced arguments, while prompting them to think through difficult questions at the heart of the text.

This approach works well in the introductory class that I teach, but it could also be adapted for surveys of eighteenth- or nineteenth-century fiction as well as for courses on Jane Austen, Romanticism, and the marriage plot. In such courses, students could read contextual materials alongside *Persuasion* to further examine the implications of Anne and Wentworth's engagement. For example, students might consider the novel in relation to the controversies surrounding the French Revolution, discussions about the nature and value of consensual obligations, or contemporary ideas about love, courtship, and marriage. The novel takes on new meaning when read alongside Edmund Burke's assertions concerning "the evils of inconstancy and versatility" in society (*Reflections* 194), William Godwin's radical critique of the practice of promising (87–90), and Mary Wollstonecraft's defense of women's free choice and agency in courtship (*Vindication of the Rights of Woman* [Lynch]). These materials would enable students to weigh in on longstanding debates about Austen's political and ethical commitments. To what extent does the novel support a Burkean investment in stability, tradition, and inherited wealth, and to what extent does it embrace a radical, Jacobin commitment to individual freedom? In what ways does the text endorse a traditional, patriarchal view of the family, and in what ways does it challenge that view? Such questions have sparked lively controversies among critics that would make for provocative discussions in the classroom.[2] By reading such materials, students could consider how Austen's account of Anne and Wentworth's vexed engagement contributes to the era's own social, political, and ethical debates.

NOTES

I'm grateful to the students in my Critical Practices and Processes in Literary Studies classes at Marquette University for their lively debates about *Persuasion*. Our discussions helped me think through the ideas and develop the strategies outlined in this essay.

1 Some students point to Louisa's surprising union with Captain James Benwick as further evidence that Austen shows the need to temper impulse and feeling with prudence and restraint. This union makes for an interesting comparison with the main love plot.

2 See, for example, Butler; Duckworth; C. Johnson, *Jane*; Kirkham; Knox-Shaw, *Jane*; and Poovey.

Teaching *Persuasion* with the Michell Film Adaptation

Abigail Burnham Bloom

I teach Jane Austen's *Persuasion* to undergraduates in two different discussion-based English classes at an urban liberal arts college—a course on nineteenth-century novels and their film adaptations and a course devoted to Jane Austen. There are three major film adaptations of *Persuasion*, all of which retain the novel's title: the 1971 film, directed by Howard Baker and dramatized by Julian Mitchell; the 1995 film, directed by Roger Michell and dramatized by Nick Dear; and the 2007 film, directed by Adrian Shergold and dramatized by Simon Burke.[1] All can be useful in discussions of the novel through comparisons as well as through what Laura Carroll and her colleagues call "triangulations" (Carroll et al. 226): comparisons of three versions, which in this case can be two films and the novel or two versions of the novel's ending and a film version. In both courses, I show short scenes from the different adaptations while talking about the novel. After completing discussion of Austen's work in the course on novels and films, I show the 1995 Michell film in its entirety.[2] In this essay, I focus primarily on my experiences presenting the 1995 film to my students in the course on novels and films, but I will refer to scenes in the other films as well as to Austen's original ending for the novel.

Persuasion is the first novel taught in my novels and films course. Unless they have studied the nineteenth century previously, students in this course have little understanding of the culture, the class structure, or the position of women in nineteenth-century English society and so often need assistance in understanding such things in *Persuasion* as the marriage between first cousins or the subtleties of class distinctions. The showing of films, whether just selected scenes or in their entirety, can bring a modern vantage point to elements of the novel and can be a springboard for discussions. Watching Michell's 1995 film *Persuasion* in conjunction with reading the novel leads students to a greater understanding of life in Regency England and beyond because the film combines beautiful cinematography, excellent acting, and a clear vision of how Austen's novel can be made accessible and relevant to another era. Comparison of the setting, characterization, and themes of the novel with those of the film can be an effective basis for enhanced comprehension of the novel.

Making use of the high recognition value of the literary works being adapted, BBC film adaptations of classic novels that were produced in the 1990s stayed close to their sources in terms of setting, action, dialogue, and plot. Yet all adaptations differ from their sources, and fidelity to the source does not ensure that an adaptation will be successful as a film. A film can never translate a novel onto the screen as a novel is translated into other languages; in making decisions, the director also alters the emphasis, themes, and even meaning of the work, so that the film becomes an interpretation or even a revision of the novel.

Examining the differences brings out some of the intricacies of both the novel *Persuasion* and its adaptations, and components of the novel can be made more comprehensible to students. As Julie Sanders explains in *Adaptation and Appropriation*, "[I]t is usually at the very point of infidelity that the most creative acts of adaptations and appropriation take place" (20). I draw out the opinions of students by asking for their comments on scenes from the film, and they often begin by remarking that the film is just like the novel. I point out that the film follows the plot and develops the characters in similar ways to the novel, but that there are differences, and I ask students to enumerate them. By examining the differences between the novel and the film, students can begin to understand the background assumptions of Austen's era, the skill with which Austen constructed the events of the novel, and ideas common to the era when the film was made.

Setting

Persuasion takes place in a time far different from our own. Beginning in 1814 and ending in 1815, *Persuasion* is set in preindustrial England when the country was still involved in the Napoleonic wars with France. The concerns, manners, and behavior of the characters can be difficult for students to comprehend. Watching the films can help students visualize the locations, the looks, and the expectations of a different era as well as gain a greater understanding of the structure, meaning, and resonances of the novel. Students need to be made aware of the difference between life as it was lived in the 1800s, Austen's representation of that life, and the film's representation of Austen's depiction. While Austen seldom describes the physical appearance of characters or even their clothes in detail, decisions have to be made in casting actors, dressing them, and having them speak in each scene of the film. Actors may not appear as readers picture them in their minds, while locations, costumes, and hairstyles usually acquire a certain cleanliness and becomingness that was not a regular feature of the 1800s.

The Michell film incorporates many ideas from today, particularly in regard to servants and women. Students could easily miss the meaning of the passage in the novel when the Elliots leave Kellynch Hall: "The last office of the four carriage-horses was to draw Sir Walter, Miss Elliot, and Mrs. Clay to Bath. The party drove off in very good spirits; Sir Walter prepared with condescending bows for all the afflicted tenantry and cottagers who might have had a hint to shew themselves" (38; vol. 1, ch. 5). The novel here briefly notes the wealth of the Elliots and Sir Walter's neglect of his tenants. In the film, as the Elliots enter their carriage to leave Kellynch Hall, the servants line up in their formal dress to see Sir Walter off. Their faces portray no emotion. I ask students to speculate about the significance of this emphasis. Much like the seamen who row Admiral Croft at the start of the film, the servants make the life of the Elliots possible; they are a factor of life in the past that interests people today. Unlike the sailors, the servants in the film apparently enjoy no camaraderie. For a twentieth- or twenty-first-century audience the depiction emphasizes the enormous waste of money and activity involved in the life of the wealthy landowners. In contrast to her father and sister, Anne stays behind to do chores at Kellynch Hall; she does manual labor herself, supervising and working with the servants, and visits the tenantry, while she is treated as a servant by her family. The contrast between Anne and her father and sister is exaggerated in the Michell film, as Anne travels to Uppercross in a cart with a pig and a goose, a very different conveyance from that used by her father and sister.

Characterization

Lacking a consistent narrative voice or the ability to portray directly what characters are thinking, film has difficulty conveying the interiority of characters. Important thoughts and ideas of characters in the novel are frequently expressed in dialogue in the film or through body language or facial expressions. In addition, external images may convey characterization. Michell's film uses all of these methods at different times. As Anne leaves her family in Bath to spend time with her friend Mrs. Smith, Austen writes, "Anne could have said much and did long to say a little, in defence of *her* friend's not very dissimilar claims to theirs, but her sense of personal respect to her father prevented her. She made no reply. She left it to himself to recollect, that Mrs. Smith was not the only widow in Bath between thirty and forty, with little to live on, and no sirname of dignity" (171–72; vol. 2, ch. 5). Anne directly reveals her thoughts in Michell's film by saying to her father, "I have a prior engagement, with Mrs. Smith—who is not the only widow in Bath, with little to live on, and no surname of dignity" (Dear 67). In this comment, Anne insults Mrs. Clay to her father and sister, which politeness restrains her from doing in the novel. Students have suggested that Michell made this change because the thoughts of Anne are not available on the screen, so her saying them brings them out in the open, and that by speaking directly she begins to appear as a stronger woman, capable of stating what is on her mind.

Amanda Root plays Anne in Michell's film, and the actor's body language and looks convey Anne Elliot's thoughts. When Anne first sees Captain Frederick Wentworth, a close-up shows Root's hand grasping her chair. This physical need for stability communicates Anne's insecurity. Through the course of the film, Root comes to use more facial expressions, and her entire aspect becomes brighter. The film was shot more or less in the order of the finished scenes so that as the film progresses, Root appears more lovely. Whereas Captain Wentworth claims he would almost not have known Anne when he first sees her, her cousin Mr. William Elliot appreciates her beauty with his first glance at her face. No longer repressed and unhappy, Anne shows her intelligence while in Lyme Regis and begins to reveal her emotions, and her face shows the change.

Thoughts can also become manifest through imagery. In one memorable scene of the film, as Anne packs up the contents of Kellynch Hall so that it may be rented to the Crofts, she opens the Navy List and finds a letter that has been folded into the shape of a ship. As she holds this paper boat in her hands, the words "much feeling" and "I offer myself to you" can be discerned. Anne is transported back seven years to when Captain Wentworth courted her. This external image reveals Anne's feelings about the past but also connects with the real ships that appear at the start and end of the film. The image is thereby associated with the navy, with orderliness and kindness, and with better times in the past and in the future for Anne, whose status will be changing, like that of the sailors. In Shergold's 2007 film Anne opens a locked treasure box and finds a portrait of her mother and some letters. Like the paper ship in Michell's 1995 version, the letters evoke a secret memory. Although in the 2007 version the letters look ahead to Wentworth's declaration by letter to Anne, the reverberations are less clear and effective.

Themes

During the long nineteenth century, concern was starting to be raised over what was called the woman question, a general term that covered the education, rights, manners, and occupations of women. As students immediately notice differences in the behavior of Elizabeth Elliot in the film in comparison with the novel, I ask why Michell made the choices he did. Austen writes, "Elizabeth was certainly very handsome, with well-bred, elegant manners" (*Persuasion* 151–52; vol. 2, ch. 3); but in the film Elizabeth demonstrates "indolent shrillness" (Dickson 46). For example, in the first scene inside Kellynch Hall in Michell's film, Elizabeth behaves impolitely, slumping in her seat and eating bonbons; indeed, she is rude. When questioned in the film as to why Anne would not be her companion in Bath, Elizabeth responds, "[N]o one will want [Anne] in Bath." This is not how an eighteenth- or early-nineteenth-century lady would have acted or talked. Elizabeth, in the novel, is caught up in her father's idea of social class and would ignore someone rather than behave with deliberate hostility. Students note that Elizabeth's uncouth behavior quickly reveals the family's opinion of Anne and that Elizabeth's selfishness creates a foil for Anne. It may also explain why Elizabeth has not married despite having been on the marriage market for so long.

Both Elizabeth and Anne behave in the film more like twentieth- or twenty-first-century women than like nineteenth-century women. In another scene in the film Anne leaves her chair at the musical performance in Bath abruptly, in order to prevent Captain Wentworth from exiting the event. No woman at the time could have done this without giving herself a bad reputation. Presumably, Michell has Anne behave this way to show that Anne has become her own woman and no longer considers herself bound by the rules of her family or society, and that she wants to make her feelings for Wentworth known. Since she behaves more like a modern woman in the film and has been created from a twentieth-century "protofeminist" perspective (Dickson 49), students may identify more with her and her situation. When asked whether they identify with Anne as she is portrayed in the film or the book, and if so, why, students have sometimes said that they do because she doesn't feel a part of her family, because her family and Lady Russell make marital decisions for her (some of my students are first-generation Americans whose families want to select their spouses), because Anne made a decision that has influenced her life negatively, and because she is older and, at first, apparently less glamorous (especially in the Michell film) than most of the heroines my students have encountered.

The Opening of **Persuasion**

I draw students' attention to the opening of Austen's novel and Michell's film as well as to the endings of both, for often important themes and meanings can be discerned there. I ask them what they think will be the emphasis of the novel after reading the first chapter and the emphasis of the film after watching the early scenes. After we read chapter 1, including Austen's invented Elliot entry in the Baronetage, and discuss why the novel would start with this and what can be anticipated from it, we then watch the first scene of the 1971 film directed by Baker, which begins with Sir Walter reading the entry in the Baronetage and uses that moment as a means of introducing his three daughters, giving each a small scene that encapsulates her personality. Michell's 1995 film interweaves scenes of sailors rowing Admiral Croft to a meeting, in which the end of the war is announced, and of the Elliots' lawyer and his daughter arriving at Kellynch Hall and disputing with the Elliots' creditors. By contrasting the navy with wealthy landowners, the film's opening makes two factors stand out. First, the sailors work together with precision and concern for each other, while Sir Walter and Elizabeth are at odds with Anne and in need of changing their style of living. And second, now that peace is upon England, sailors will be taking their place among members of a traditionally higher class. Admiral Croft has the money and the ability to assume the situation once available only to those with inherited wealth. Nick Dear comments on this as a major theme of the film in his introduction to the screenplay: "The story essentially describes an old order fading away into decadence, and a new tribe, a meritocracy, coming to the fore. In other words, it marks the turning point between the eighteenth century and the nineteenth" (ii). What happens among a small group of characters depicted in the novel represents a general trend of the rise of the military and of the middle class in general. The opening of the film can bring this out more clearly than Austen's novel does because it directly contrasts the navy with the Elliots.

The start of Shergold's 2007 film features Anne, list in hand, racing around Kellynch Hall while servants place white sheets over the furniture to ready the house for the arrival of the Crofts. The covered furniture perhaps suggests that Anne is also, as it were, under wraps. The placing of white sheets over the furniture occurs in the 1995 film as well, offering an example of how films may be indebted to both earlier films and the novel.

The Ending of Persuasion

Students read Austen's original, canceled ending of *Persuasion* as well as the published version. After Austen thought she had finished writing the novel, she rewrote the last two chapters, changing the events that lead to the uniting of Anne and Captain Wentworth. In Austen's original ending, in chapter 10, Admiral Croft has heard gossip that Anne will be marrying her cousin, Mr. Elliot. He enlists Wentworth to ask Anne if she would like the Crofts to leave Kellynch Hall so that it will be available for her to occupy as a bride. When Anne denies the truth of the rumor, "they were restored to all that had been lost" (transcription; 318). In the rewritten ending, the Musgroves come to Bath, and Anne visits the Musgroves and Captains Harville and Wentworth at the White Hart Inn at Bath. Captain Harville explains to Anne that Captain Benwick commissioned him to have a miniature, which would have gone to Harville's sister, Fanny, who was Benwick's former fiancée, reset for the woman Benwick will marry, Louisa Musgrove. Captain Harville, upset that Benwick seems to have forgotten Fanny, talks with Anne about the ability of men and women once in love to move on. Ultimately Anne, thinking of her own situation with Wentworth, states that "[a]ll the privilege I claim for my sex, is that of loving longest, when existence or when hope is gone" (256; vol. 2, ch. 11). Wentworth overhears her words and leaves a letter of proposal for her. In this ending, Anne's own voice and ideas bring about her ultimate union with Captain Wentworth. Rather than relying on a chance piece of gossip and a request from Admiral Croft, the reunion of Wentworth and Anne in the published ending results from Anne's beautiful expressions of her reasoning, from her speaking her mind clearly and being partially overheard by the man she loves. Her sentiments bring Wentworth to a place where he can get past his anger at her earlier rejection of him and propose again. Anne and Wentworth become more happy in their reunion, "more tender, more tried, more fixed in a knowledge of each other's character, truth, and attachment" (261). Rather than returning to their old relationship, their new relationship is stronger and better, and the novel implies that it was worth waiting for.

Michell's film uses parts of both endings, and students enjoy considering why he included aspects of the canceled ending. At Admiral Croft's contrivance, Captain Wentworth asks Anne about her engagement to Mr. Elliot, but before she can respond, Lady Russell interrupts them. Finally, at the White Hart, while overhearing Anne's conversation with Captain Harville, Wentworth writes Anne the letter asking for an answer. By examining the ending of the novel as published with the canceled ending and the film's ending, a closer understanding of each can be achieved through "triangulation." Carroll and her colleagues explain that the object of this form of comparison is "to highlight adaptation as an act of interpretation and translation across media, which opens the primary source text and the adaptation to new readings" (Carroll et al. 226). Students may have difficulty comprehending that different decisions might have been made by the author and the filmmakers. Their belief in inevitability can be combated by "complicat[ing] ideas about the naturalness of both the novel and the film as well as the simplicity and obviousness of their relationship with each other" (229). The Michell film draws out the efforts by Anne to find her voice and suggests that Lady Russell again parts the couple, although in this case only for a brief time. Anne must experience another disappointment before reuniting with Wentworth. Thus the film provides a larger role for Lady Russell and extends Anne and the audience's anticipation of resolution.

The voiceover of the reading of Wentworth's letter in Michell's film provides a lovely symbol of Wentworth and Anne's reconciliation. Wentworth's voice begins the voiceover of the letter, while Anne's voice concludes the reading, suggesting the couple's inevitable union. Once the couple comes to an understanding in the Michell film, Wentworth and Anne walk along a street and stop to kiss while a circus walks by. No such couple in Austen's world would have kissed on the street. Indeed, according to Rebecca Eaton, a producer of the film, at her insistence two versions of the ending of *Persuasion* were shot, one without the kiss and one with, the latter to be released in the United States, where viewers expect a Hollywood ending (Eaton 109; Davies 12). However, with the circus there, and other passersby following the circus, Anne and Wentworth appear more alone than they did in the society of the Elliots. They make space for themselves in the crowd similarly to how they will create their marital home on board a ship.

While the novel situates them in no specific place at the end, the final scene of the film reveals Anne and Wentworth living on board his ship. Anne has found happiness outside of a repressive society and in the midst of adventure. The film both begins and ends with a ship, bringing together the themes of class and the relationship between Anne and Wentworth. The ship has become an image for the orderliness of the navy; the ascendency of Anne in the eyes of Wentworth, who previously said he would not have a woman on board his ship; the superiority of the Crofts' marriage, which has been spent aboard ship; and Anne's devotion to Wentworth.

Austen's final sentence subtly suggests that the future is uncertain: "She [Anne] gloried in being a sailor's wife, but she must pay the tax of quick alarm for belonging to that profession which is, if possible, more distinguished in its domestic virtues than in its national importance" (*Persuasion* 275; vol. 2, ch. 12). The novel underscores the "domestic virtues" while glossing over the "tax of quick alarm," whereas Michell's film emphasizes the continuance of war when, toward the end of the film, Admiral Croft announces that Napoleon has left

Elba and raised an army, and his neighbor remarks that he may be going back to war. As Anne's engagement did earlier, the peace slips out of hand and must be achieved again once and for all. Andrew Macdonald and Gina Macdonald point out that "The final shot of the Bounty . . . adds a satiric touch worthy of Austen though outside her novel: the dark underside of naval virtues, the result of harsh punishments and deprivations" (285).[3] The presence of the replica *Bounty* provides the opportunity to bring out this reflection of the darker themes present in the film. Just as it illuminates the position of servants and women, a twentieth- or twenty-first-century perspective points out the limitations of Austen's world. Regret for the past is changed to immersion in an exciting present in Michell's film, in which Anne has come to the fore through her own intelligence and strength. According to Caryn James, in Michell's version of *Persuasion*, "the camera becomes the visual equivalent of Austen's rich, commenting voice."[4]

Students find that analyzing the differences between the novel and the film provides a valuable means of exploring the meaning of both. Imelda Whelehan writes, "Perhaps encouraging more flexibility in analyses of literary texts through the study of adaptations will enable the audience to be more self-conscious about their role as critics and about the activities of reading/viewing that they bring to bear in an academic environment" (19). While students may believe that there is a meaning to a novel that their professor can reveal to them, they often watch films noncritically without reflecting on the meaning of what they see. They may even think that adaptations require no choice on the part of the filmmakers, as they follow the novel. On the contrary, adaptations involve making many choices and therefore provide a valuable means of examining the intricacies of a novel.

NOTES

[1] Adaptations of Jane Austen novels have been popular for both television and movie theater audiences in recent decades. The characters are endlessly fascinating, and the action flows from the ordinary business of life involving universally understood situations. Audiences enjoy that the heroine in each story learns from her mistakes, has a second chance, and ends up with the man she loves. Unlike a solitary author writing a book, many hands are at work in creating a film. I use the names of the directors here as shorthand for anyone who may have influenced the decisions made about the films.

[2] In addition to the films, students enjoy watching the *YouTube* video *Eric Cochrane Presents:* Persuasion *by Jane Austen*. This parody brings up and exaggerates several ideas that students enjoy discussing: the similarity of the Musgrove sisters, Anne's desire to be rid of Louisa Musgrove, and the marriage of first cousins. The foul language of the project, which gives it a modern tone far removed from Austen, reveals how characters feel directly. Anne's declaration at the end, "I love you, Mr. Rochester," is perhaps a nod to the fact that Ciarán Hinds plays Captain Frederick Wentworth in Michell's film and Rochester in a 1997 film of *Jane Eyre*, or perhaps it places *Persuasion* as one novel among many in which the heroine eventually gets her man. Showing the *YouTube*

parody allows students to laugh at some of the aspects of the novel that they have found repetitive or ridiculous. But it also can open up an introduction to theories of parody and humor and ways that Austen used these elements in her writing.

[3] Austen provides no details of where the Wentworths would live, but the couple's life at sea depicted in Michell's film would have had its dangers. The replica *Bounty*, built in 1960 for the 1962 film *The Mutiny on the Bounty*, sank at sea with loss of life during Hurricane Sandy in 2012. Shergold's 2007 film shows Wentworth giving Kellynch Hall to Anne as a wedding present, which suggests that he has purchased the estate from Mr. Elliot, an unlikely proposition.

[4] Gottlieb; Groenendyk; and Macdonald and Macdonald, among others, examine Michell's attempt to replicate Austen's effects in a different medium.

Nursing in *Persuasion*: The Value of Women's Work

Sylvia A. Pamboukian

Persuasion is haunted by morbidity and mortality. The novel mentions the illnesses and deaths of Lady Elliot, Mr. Clay, Mrs. Elliot, and Lord Dalrymple and more directly addresses those of Mr. Smith, Dick Musgrove, and Fanny Harville. For example, the attractive widower Mr. Elliot wears black crepe after the death of his low-born but wealthy wife, and the task of resetting the late Fanny Harville's portrait of Captain Benwick precipitates a conversation that fundamentally alters Anne Elliot's relationship with Captain Frederick Wentworth. To paraphrase *Mansfield Park*, Jane Austen's pen may not dwell on mortality (533; vol. 3, ch. 17), yet *Persuasion* repeatedly reminds readers that people sicken and die, leaving behind parents, children, siblings, spouses, lovers, and friends.[1] It is against this background that little Charles's dislocated collarbone, Louisa Musgrove's head injury, and Mrs. Smith's invalidism must be interpreted.

Persuasion is unusual in that it includes not only illness but also nursing, making the usually taken-for-granted work of domesticity visible. In novels of the long eighteenth century, illness is common but nursing is rare.[2] For example, Victor in Mary Shelley's *Frankenstein* suffers extended illnesses in Ingolstadt and in Ireland. Clerval visits Victor in Ingolstadt during Victor's convalescence, and Alphonse visits him in Ireland, but nursing is handled invisibly by nurse-servants such as the crude Irishwoman who taunts Victor with Clerval's murder.

Persuasion offers students an opportunity to realize how different Regency nursing was from our notion of nursing as a hospital-based profession and to acknowledge the work of domesticity often hidden from readers.[3] In Austen's time, the word *nurse* described a variety of people, in addition to nursery maids and wet nurses, who cared for the sick: they might be trained or untrained, skilled or unskilled, domestic or institutional, and paid or unpaid. Nurses might be amateur caregivers, hospital nurses, entrepreneurial servant-handywomen, religious nursing sisters, or professionally trained home-care nurses.[4] As *Persuasion* shows, Regency nursing encompassed various levels of social class, wealth, knowledge, experience, and personal commitment. *Persuasion* therefore has a place in courses on health and illness, the professions, gender, and domesticity. Although the depictions of an era's medical practices in novels, including realist ones, ought not to be considered factual, *Persuasion* offers readers an often-overlooked window into one popular image of nursing at this time and is a corrective to the stereotype that Austen is concerned only with upper-middle-class love and marriage.

Persuasion asserts that nursing is a valuable activity that is entertaining and practical, "something that makes one know one's species better" (169; vol. 2, ch. 5). That nursing entertains or occupies sensible women is evident in the contrast between Anne and her two sisters. Elizabeth is no more able to change her lifestyle than her father is, and Austen is scathing about "the nothingness of her scene of life . . . the vacancies which there were no habits of utility abroad, no talents or accomplishments for home, to occupy" (9; vol. 1, ch. 1). Neither Elizabeth nor Mary manages her household, servants, or tenants according to "method, moderation, and economy" as Lady Elliot used to do (10). Despite her social rank as the second lady of the county, Elizabeth is dismissed by the narrative: she is untalented, unaccomplished, and unoccupied (9). Similarly, the character of Mary recalls the overly nervous fine ladies of eighteenth-century comedy (akin to Frances Burney's Lady Louisa Larpent in *Evelina* and *Pride and Prejudice*'s Mrs. Bennet). When her son, little Charles, dislocates his collarbone, Mary goes to a dinner party claiming that nursing is not appropriate for mothers because it strains their too-tender feelings. Conversely, Mary later insists on staying behind in Lyme Regis ostensibly to nurse Louisa, on the grounds that she is Louisa's sister-in-law, while claiming that Anne is "nothing" to Louisa (124; vol. 1, ch. 12). But Mary avoids the work of nursing Louisa in pursuit of her own pleasures: "She [Mary] had been taken to Charmouth, too, and she had bathed, and she had gone to church . . . all this joined to the sense of being so very useful, had made really an agreeable fortnight" (141; vol. 2, ch. 2). In the depiction of Mary and Elizabeth, Austen seems to echo Mary Wollstonecraft's critique of upper-class women as "a swarm of ephemeron triflers" and Wollstonecraft's call for women to spend time "exercising the understanding" and following a "noble pursuit" (*Vindication of the Rights of Woman* [*Bartleby .com*]). Through the Elliot sisters, Austen criticizes the selfishness and idleness of fine ladies who cling to outmoded values.

Austen champions instead the notion of a lady as an active and useful member of society, a role often associated by critics with Mrs. Croft. Anne and Mrs. Harville also exemplify this useful work through nursing. These instances in *Persuasion* may be located alongside examples in other novels that explore the nature of domestic, middle-class female work, including work as a music teacher in Frances Burney's *The Wanderer*, as a governess in Charlotte Brontë's *Jane Eyre*, as an artist in Anne Brontë's *The Tenant of Wildfell Hall*, and as an amanuensis in George Eliot's *Middlemarch*. Anticipating Florence Nightingale's famous dictum "every woman is a nurse," Anne asserts that nursing "does not belong to a man, it is not his province" (J. Austen, *Persuasion* 61; vol. 1, ch. 7). When little Charles dislocates his collarbone, Anne rises to the challenge:

> Anne had every thing to do at once—the apothecary to send for—the father to have pursued and informed—the mother to support and keep from hysterics—the servants to control—the youngest child to banish, and the poor suffering one to attend and soothe;—besides sending, as soon as she recollected it, proper notice to the other house, which brought her an accession rather of frightened, enquiring companions, than of very useful assistants. (57–58)

The dashes in this one sentence capture the quick-thinking nature of the home-care nurse, who must manage multiple housekeeping, medical, and interpersonal tasks at once. The apothecary Mr. Robinson only "felt and felt, and rubbed, and looked grave," then left (58). But Austen's readers knew that nursing involved day-and-night bedside vigils and regular administration of prescribed medicines and diet (such as beef tea or gruels) by the spoonful or, for those unable to swallow, by enema. It meant providing assistance during vomits, purges, and blisters (and care of the ensuing wound); administering poultices; changing soiled sheets, clothes, and dressings; and helping patients to use the chamber pot, as well as other physically arduous tasks often associated with servants.[5] At this time, *nurse* and *servant* could be used interchangeably, but a home-care nurse was also a manager who constantly evaluated the patient without medical (or possibly any) support. Readers see this when Anne kneels on the floor next to little Charles's sofa, more like a servant than a mistress (85; vol. 1, ch. 9). When little Walter toddles into the room, he assumes that Charles is being (laboriously) spoon-fed, but Anne is so occupied she cannot spare a hand to shake off little Walter when he climbs on her back. Captain Wentworth removes little Walter forcibly, then distracts him in another area of the room, "until Anne can make over her little patient" to the Miss Musgroves, giving them the task of amusing the invalid during the long convalescence typical of this period (87). This implies that men like Captain Wentworth can, at best, only remove burdens from the nurse's shoulders, not serve as nurses themselves.

Similarly, Anne competently handles Louisa's care when Louisa falls and hits her head on the Cobb at Lyme. Anne instructs Benwick and Wentworth to "rub her hands, rub her temples" and gives them her salts (118; vol. 1, ch. 12). Then Anne instructs the men to carry Louisa to the inn and sends Benwick for a surgeon. Anne's responsibility is relieved when Captain Harville instructs them to bring Louisa to his house, having exchanged a look previously with Mrs. Harville (120). Once there, Mrs. Harville takes over as "a very experienced nurse; and her nursery-maid, who had lived with her long and gone about with her every where, was just such another. Between those two, she [Louisa] could want no possible attendance by day or night." Such attendance is undoubtedly burdensome for Mrs. Harville and her minimal staff, for Louisa cannot sit up for several weeks and thus needs around-the-clock care (122). Anne offers to sleep on the floor of Louisa's room for the night shift but is sent away by a jealous Mary (124). Instead, Anne sends the Musgroves' nursery maid, Sarah, to Lyme because Sarah is a "far more useful person" than either Charles or Mr. Musgrove (131; vol. 2, ch. 1), who would only "multiply trouble to the others." Austen's readers would realize clearly what an extra nurse-servant means in Mrs. Harville's lower-middle-class household, which has few servants to help with the cleaning, washing, and cooking. Slightly vulgar Mrs. Musgrove also realizes the burden of nursing, so, while Mary amuses herself, Mrs. Musgrove cares for the Harville children (132), as Captain Wentworth removes the burden of little Walter from Anne's back (87; vol. 1, ch. 9).

Close reading the details about little Charles's and Louisa's accidents can lead students to a discussion of social class, gentility, work, and gender. Nursing in these cases relies on a female network of caregivers from several social positions and with different levels of skill. The Musgroves' nursery maid, Sarah, the Harvilles' unnamed nursery maid, and Mary's nursery maid, Jemima, are paid servants, but they take their turns with Anne and Mrs. Harville, who are unpaid and a class above them, in caring for the sick or injured. Anne, Mrs. Harville, the Harvilles' nursery maid, and Sarah are represented as experienced and knowledgeable. Mrs. Harville states that her nursery maid has been with her for a long time and has traveled about with her (122; vol. 1, ch. 12), and Sarah's charges range from school-aged children to adults, indicating Sarah's many years of experience. Conversely, Jemima appears to be younger and less experienced, since her charges are still young children, and since Mrs. Musgrove complains about Jemima's being "upon the gad" rather than hard at work in her nursery (49; vol. 1, ch. 6). While Anne and Mrs. Harville are amateurs, Jemima, Sarah, and the Harville nursery maid may be considered semiprofessional, since nursing is not their primary duty but a skill set that may increase their employability.

The connection Austen makes between nursing by mothers and by nursery maids implies that parenthood is the stage of life when middle-class women gain nursing skills, Anne forming an exception as an unmarried woman of that class. The range of experience possessed by the characters who nurse implies that this network is self-perpetuating; for instance, young Jemima acquires knowledge from Anne and Sarah, just as Henrietta and Louisa acquire experience with children when they visit their nephews and when Henrietta returns to Lyme during her sister's recovery, presumably to help during the convalescence. *Persuasion* highlights the active, amateur, and often taken-for-granted work of middle-class women in the domestic sphere, something readers glimpse in other Austen novels, such as in *Mansfield Park* when Mrs. Grant worries about preserving a turkey in the hot weather. In that case, Mrs. Grant is quickly silenced by her husband, since domestic work ought not to be publicly acknowledged (252; vol. 2, ch. 4). In *Persuasion*, readers see female nurses successfully function without male interference or much medical supervision. The network of female caregivers (mistresses and maids who are young and old, married and single, paid and unpaid, and experienced and novice) is well able to restore Louisa and little Charles to health.

The Musgrove sisters also offer a way to understand the work of a lady through their role as visitors to the convalescent. Lady visitors to the sick or suffering appear in other Austen novels, from *Pride and Prejudice*'s Lady Catherine's scolding her tenants into better health, to Emma Woodhouse and Harriet Smith's gifts of soup to the invalid poor before they encounter Mr. Elton in *Emma*. Mrs. Norris in *Mansfield Park* is perhaps Austen's most self-serving caregiver, since she parades her offer of a remedy for Sotherton Court's groom before the assembled party and takes the leftover jellies from the ball at Mansfield Park home with her "to nurse a sick maid" (328; vol. 2, ch. 11). Readers may suspect that she is taking the jellies for herself, just as she sponges a cheesecake from Sotherton's housekeeper, takes the theater's green baize, and instructs Fanny Price to carry two batches of the park's roses to her house. Anne Brontë's eponymous governess in *Agnes Grey* does the hard work of visiting the poor and reading to the blind while her charge, idle Miss Murray, takes the credit, just as Mary wants to take credit for nursing Louisa. Several nineteenth-century novels emphasize the value of lady visitors, as in Margaret Hale's lifesaving visits to the striking workers in *North and South*, by Elizabeth Gaskell, and the Marches' visits to the German family with scarlet fever in *Little Women*, by Louisa May Alcott. The value of a visitor is shown in *Persuasion* when the Musgrove sisters visit little Charles and offer Anne a respite from both him and Captain Wentworth.

Anne's conversations with Captain Benwick offer significant instances of Anne's role as a caregiver. Benwick is not convalescent, but he is suffering from melancholy after the death of his fiancée, Fanny Harville. Anne notes the similarity between her dejection and Benwick's, but she asserts the value of work for men and women alike when she says to herself that he is younger than she is and has more opportunities for action (J. Austen, *Persuasion* 104–05; vol. 1, ch. 11). She does not say that he also has the advantage of her in being more valued by his friends. Fighting her own melancholy, Anne rallies to help Benwick. She goes through the "trouble" of overcoming his shyness and discusses the "duty and benefit" of activity and of reading less poetry and more uplifting moralists and prose writers (108). Although she may not always follow her own advice, her actions help lift both his depression and hers. Visiting is not limited to women: we learn that Captain Wentworth stayed with Benwick after breaking the news of Fanny Harville's death, just as Edmund Bertram visits with Tom Bertram during his long illness in *Mansfield Park*, and Colonel Brandon visits Marianne Dashwood after her illness in *Sense and Sensibility*. Like Brandon, Benwick finds love (for a second time) by reading to a convalescent, Louisa (*Persuasion* 237; vol. 2, ch. 10). To distinguish between characters Austen satirizes and those she admires, students may discuss the real benefits of visiting the sick and analyze whose visits in *Persuasion* are serious business and whose merely allow the characters to play at work or steal the social credit of visiting.

Austen clearly lauds work as a positive activity for all sorts of people, from male naval officers (such as net-making Captain Harville) to naval wives (such as nurse Mrs. Harville and financially astute Mrs. Croft) to servant-nurses (such as the Musgroves' nursery maid, Sarah). Nurse Rooke perhaps best encapsulates Austen's vision of the entrepreneurial handywoman-nurse who is both a paid professional outside of the household (i.e., not a household servant) and a part of the female network of care.[6] When the invalid Mrs. Smith becomes acutely ill, she worries about being sick "among strangers," or outside her network of unpaid family caregivers. But Mrs. Smith is ably nursed by Nurse Rooke, who is "a nurse by profession." Austen emphasizes Nurse Rooke's status through her title and through the word "profession," which indicates the impropriety of expecting her to work without pay. Far from criticizing Nurse Rooke as greedy, Austen praises her financial acumen through Mrs. Smith's comment that Nurse Rooke is a "shrewd, intelligent, sensible woman" (168; vol. 2, ch. 5). Anne concurs, "Women of that class have great opportunities, and if they are intelligent may be well worth listening to" (169). Nurse Rooke engages in a side business selling handicrafts to her wealthier patients, since she "has a large acquaintance, of course professionally, among those who can afford to buy" (168). In this respect, Nurse Rooke resembles the navy men who rise according to merit and who mix social and professional acquaintances across established social ranks (and whose activity and mobility are condemned by Sir Walter; 21; vol. 1, ch. 3). Austen values financial acumen both in working-class Nurse Rooke and in upper-class women, as when Anne and Lady Russell ably comprehend Sir Walter's need to retrench and when Mrs. Croft enters into negotiations regarding Kellynch Hall (25). Austen favorably links the entrepreneurial handywoman-nurse and the financially savvy lady in contrast to financially helpless fine ladies and gentlemen who "know nothing worth attending to" (169; vol. 2, ch. 5).

Austen plays on the meaning of the word *profit* when Mrs. Smith says that Nurse Rooke "is sure to have something to relate that is entertaining and *profitable*" (emphasis added). Readers should pay close attention to the various configurations of profit in the section of the novel that features Mrs. Smith. At first, Anne seems to embrace the notion that nursing is self-abnegating and profitless, as when she expects Nurse Rooke to tell stories of "ardent, disinterested, self-denying attachment, of heroism, fortitude, patience, resignation" (169; vol. 2, ch. 5). But in Austen's work, neither nurses nor patients are angels; instead, Austen emphasizes the ways that both Nurse Rooke and Mrs. Smith profit emotionally from the patient-nurse relationship through sharing amusing stories and teaching and learning skills such as knitting.

Students may wish to discuss in what ways—spiritual or psychological, among others—Anne profits from her amateur nursing as well. In addition to its emotional benefits, professional nursing offers women an avenue for financial profit. For Nurse Rooke, the profit lies in using her acquaintance to find more paid work as a nurse, as when she attends Mrs. Smith at the request of her sister (who is Mrs. Smith's landlady) and then hopes to attend the next lady Elliot on Mrs. Wallis's recommendation (225; vol. 2, ch. 9). For Mrs. Smith, profit lies in Nurse Rooke's selling pincushions to Mrs. Wallis and, more significantly, in her friendship with Anne, which leads to her recovering her property in the West Indies. Mrs. Smith hesitates to reveal the true motives of Mr. William Elliot in his courtship of Anne in order to profit from knowing his future wife, saying, "I want your interest with him," just as a naval officer might use his "interest" or connections to forward his career (211). As in her depiction of the navy, Austen does not criticize either Nurse Rooke or Mrs. Smith for using connections for financial profit. On the contrary, Austen joins the sickroom and the schoolroom (where Mrs. Smith and Anne had met years earlier) as semiprofessional spaces in which women build mutually profitable relationships outside of the male-dominated network of the baronetage.

Mrs. Smith's hesitation to reveal Mr. Elliot's true nature is the most controversial incident in the novel, and it is significant that it takes place in the sickroom. Through sickroom gossip, Nurse Rooke creates an opportunity for Mrs. Smith to use her connection with Anne to goad Mr. Elliot (her husband's executor) to recover property of hers that he is currently refusing to administer (227; vol. 2, ch. 9). In doing this, Mrs. Smith faces a conflict between different kinds of profit. If she approves of Mr. Elliot's courtship of Anne, Mrs. Smith will profit financially at Anne's emotional expense because Anne will marry a man whom Mrs. Smith knows is dishonorable. This selfish deceit recalls the behavior of Mrs. Clay, who cultivates a friendship with Elizabeth in order to marry Sir Walter and thus to supplant Elizabeth as the lady of Kellynch Hall. Of course, Anne's marriage to Mr. Elliot could also be viewed as financially and socially profitable for Anne because of her increase in rank as a married woman and a baronet's wife (211). Lady Russell and Anne (briefly) are entranced at the prospect of Anne becoming the next lady Elliot (173; vol. 2, ch. 5). Mrs. Smith seems to refer to this kind of profit when she says, "One hates to be officious, to be giving bad impressions, making mischief. Even the smooth surface of family-union seems worth preserving . . ." (215; vol. 2, ch. 9). Readers of the novel will identify this value for smooth surface over emotional connection with Mrs. Clay's hollow friendship with Elizabeth, the Baronetage's emotionally empty descriptions of family, and the Elliots' emotionally barren relationship with the Dalrymples.

In contrast, Nurse Rooke, Mrs. Wallis, Mrs. Smith, and Anne (as Mrs. Smith's sickroom visitor) are part of a network of care with a different configuration of profit. By withholding what she knows, Mrs. Smith is not giving Anne the correct return on Anne's emotional investment in coming to visit her, nor is she paying back Mrs. Wallis's and Nurse Rooke's frankness by using their sickroom gossip as a kind of insider trading. In the end, Mrs. Smith chooses to honor the sickroom's unspoken code of mutual profit and emotional reciprocity by telling Anne what she knows (221; vol. 2, ch. 9). During Mrs. Smith's confession, Anne repeatedly condemns Mr. Elliot's "selfishness and duplicity" but notably never Mrs. Wallis's, Nurse Rooke's or Mrs. Smith's (225). On the contrary, Mrs. Smith's confession becomes a critique of the dominant values that require a male executor to act on behalf of a widow, a husband to act financially for his wife, and a woman to uphold a notion of family codified in a book that dismisses women as so many "Marys and Elizabeths" (4; vol. 1, ch. 1). That Mrs. Smith has made the right choice becomes clear when Austen depicts her recovering her health and Anne's new husband recovering her property (274; vol. 2 ch. 12).

Persuasion offers readers a positive image of nursing nearly forty years prior to Florence Nightingale's rise to prominence, in an era in nursing later demonized as disorganized, exploitative, and ineffective.[7] Although male medical practitioners appear briefly in *Persuasion*, the novel credits female caregivers with saving little Charles, Louisa, and Mrs. Smith in defiance of the deaths that haunt the narrative. Austen uses Anne, Sarah, Jemima, Mrs. Harville, and Nurse Rooke to highlight her appreciation for nursing as an active role for women that defies many of the traditions (represented by Sir Walter, Elizabeth, and Mary) that limit women to frivolity and dependence, while avoiding romantic stereotypes about the angelic self-sacrifice and self-abnegation of nurses. Like the navy, nursing is an example of Austen's value for work and for merit-based reward.

This is an unexpected view of nursing since, for some critics, Sarah (Sairy) Gamp from Charles Dickens's *Martin Chuzzlewit* is the epitome of the pre-Nightingale nurse: alcoholic, ignorant, and selfish. Other critics interpret Sairy's vices as Dickens's endorsement of contemporary stereotypes of handywomen-nurses that were perpetuated by the male-dominated medical establishment in order to undermine women in medicine. In Sairy Gamp, Dickens differentiates sharply between the paid handywoman-nurse and the amateur lady-caregiver, condemning the former as greedy and ignorant and praising the latter as angelic and self-sacrificing. These two stereotypes have long masked Austen's more nuanced depiction of pre-Nightingale nursing in *Persuasion* through Anne and Nurse Rooke, neither of whom is greedy and ignorant or angelic and self-sacrificing. As a form of work, nursing in *Persuasion* is part of a mutually beneficial and justifiably profitable occupation for middle-class and working-class women in a world in which women have few options to occupy their time meaningfully or to support themselves financially. Reading *Persuasion* with an eye to the figure of the nurse invites readers to consider the realities of nursing, illness, and death during the Regency period and to enrich their notions of class, work, gender, and social change in this most nuanced of Austen's novels.

NOTES

1 For the primacy of the body, including illness, in Austen's work, see Wiltshire, *Jane Austen*.

2 For examples, consider the unexplained fever of Frances Burney's eponymous *Cecilia*, Lady Delacour's quack treatment for cancer in Maria Edgeworth's *Belinda*, and Eleanor Joddrell's self-inflicted stab wounds in Burney's *The Wanderer*.

3 The word *profession* is used in this essay only to describe a socially recognized occupation in the Regency period, without the connotations of standardized education, practitioner registration, and centralized authority that the word carried in later periods. Prior to the Medical Act of 1858, medicine in the United Kingdom was only marginally professional in this later sense. See Pamboukian, *Doctoring the Novel*, on the professionalization of medicine.

4 For more information on nursing in the nineteenth century, see Madsen; Rafferty; Helmstadter and Godden; and Summers.

5 Helmstadter and Godden discuss the ways in which nineteenth-century nurses were treated as servants and the importance of cleanliness in some models of medicine at this time (4–5).

[6] Cohen views Nurse Rooke as an early figure of female professionalism.

[7] Florence Nightingale attained international prominence during the Crimean War and established a school of nursing at St. Thomas' Hospital in 1860. She is sometimes credited with founding the profession in its modern form. However, the figure of the Nightingale Nurse, a woman trained in nursing in a hospital setting who works according to sanitary standards, is also conceived as maintaining ladylike personal conduct and submitting to the medical hierarchy.

The Medical Context: Disability, Injury, Illness, and Nursing in *Persuasion*

Talia Schaffer

Students often want to identify with characters, but they may have trouble engaging with Austen's sad, silent, and exhausted Anne Elliot.[1] I stress to them that we need to investigate Anne's sense of depletion, not fight against it. I remind my students that Austen could have written Anne any way she liked. Why might she have chosen to stress that Anne's "bloom had vanished early"? How could it actually serve the novel for Anne to be, at the beginning, "faded and thin" (6; vol. 1, ch. 1)?

One answer is that Anne's decline makes her identifiable. Bodily debility is, in Jasbir Puar's words, "the debilitating ongoingness of structural inequality and suffering," a somatic expression of hopeless economic life (149). It makes sense to attribute the somatic decline of dependent single women in the early nineteenth century to economic disempowerment, "the physical wearing out of a population," but this explanation also resonates with the experiences of modern working-class American adults (Berlant 754). I teach in an urban commuter school with immigrant, first-generation college students. Everyone in my classroom either has a disability or has a friend or family member with one—as is common in populations that often get substandard health care. Many students have experienced a traumatic injury like a broken limb, while others cope with chronic conditions like diabetes. Some vividly remember trying to navigate public transit when they were pregnant, some have had serious illnesses, some have learning disabilities, and some are medicated for anxiety or depression. Many of my students are simply heavier, smaller, or taller than the bodily configurations allowed for by standardized furniture designs. In other words, my students are real people, in a world in which everyone is expected to emulate unrealistic body types.

One of the fundamental tenets of disability studies is that we will all develop disabilities if we live long enough. Activists talk about being temporarily able-bodied.[2] Disability is a fluid, universally shared experience, and humans naturally have a wide range of capacities. Lennard Davis notes: "the 'problem' is not the person with disabilities; the problem is the way that normalcy is constructed to create the 'problem' of the disabled person" ("Introduction" 1). The concept of normalcy developed between 1840 and 1860 as part of the newly developing fields of statistics and eugenics. Thus, *Persuasion,* published in 1817, gives us a precious glimpse of a culture without the concept of the "normal" (Davis, "Introduction" 2).

Virtually everyone in this novel has some experience of a condition: debility, injury, nervousness, depression, broken collarbone, brain damage, or obesity. Interestingly, having a handsome body and functional mind often seems to be associated with emotional coldness, as in the cases of Sir Walter Elliot, Elizabeth Elliot, Mr. William Elliot, and Mrs. Clay. As John Wiltshire points out, "Sir Walter thinks he and his like are immune from time," whereas the novel actually emphasizes "the changes and vicissitudes wrought by time, and of the human body as an object besieged by its onslaughts" (*Jane Austen* 164). These characters seem well preserved because they have exiled themselves from the historical changes that have weathered the Crofts, faded Anne, depressed Benwick, irritated Mary, immobilized Mrs. Smith, aggrieved Mrs. Musgrove, and taught Wentworth tenderness for the weak.

Persuasion shows that ordinary people live in ways that require care. After all, in the early nineteenth century, everyone needed care. The causes and prognoses of most illnesses remained largely mysterious, treatments were haphazard, and the lack of germ theory, antiseptics, and diet information meant that ill health was widespread, while a moment's disaster could be fatal. Impairments were not only more common but also much more visible than they are today, since patients were not consigned to hospital but continued to mix in general society.

Bodies are important in Austen, but their meaning changes as her work develops.[3] In *Northanger Abbey*, Catherine Morland is strong and healthy. In *Sense and Sensibility*, Elinor Dashwood regards Marianne Dashwood's depression as a deliberate choice, a selfish indulgence that Marianne should and must relinquish. In *Pride and Prejudice*, the flushed cheeks and sparkling eyes of Elizabeth Bennet after her walk, her athleticism, is the subject of Mr. Darcy's admiration. A cold may keep Jane Bennet at Netherfield, but it also sidelines her; it is the healthy sister, not the sick one, to whom the narrative attends. Throughout these early novels, Austen is intrigued by bodily variation, but her interest is primarily in healthy, attractive, sexualized bodies and balanced, reasonable, and cheerful minds. Characters who lack those attributes often get scolded into compliance. Healthy bodies are more appealing, more marriageable.

However, Austen's later novels gradually move from an approbation of health towards an appreciation of disease. *Mansfield Park* features the delicate Fanny Price, and *Emma* the food-refusing Jane Fairfax. Bodily delicacy demands social attention. Whether it is Fanny's cousin insisting that Fanny ride for her health, or Jane's friends pressing food and exercise on Jane, it now seems that the vulnerable female body takes on a new value. Ill health places the women in social relation to others, making them grateful recipients of tender kindnesses (or, alternatively, resentful victims of others' meddling); it generates social situations, the very material of the novels. In Austen's last (unfinished) novel, "Sanditon," an entire town is structured around illness, offering a particularly pointed example of the social advantages of debility.

The feminist theory of ethics of care helps explain this caregiving sociality.[4] Care ethicists argue that humans are, in Virginia Held's words, "relational and interdependent, not the individualistic autonomous rational agents of the perspective of justice and rights" (72). We have to depend on others to survive. The disabled person and the caretaker—or the parent and the child, or the teacher and the student—offer examples of the kind of intimate dependency in which we are all enmeshed. A penniless orphan child, an elderly woman, an infant, a second-language learner, and a person who feels sad would all be legitimate recipients of care and can give care as well—nobody is stuck in one role. For instance, Anne's conversation soothes Captain Benwick, while Benwick's attentions flatter Anne. This is a relationship of mutual care.

Care is so widespread in nineteenth-century fiction that a person who needs help often acquires a kind of retinue: a shifting cadre of miscellaneous volunteers. Louisa's care community, for instance, includes Lyme Regis locals who met her only once before her fall, her old nurse, her parents, her romantic interest, and her sister-in-law's sister. Contrast this heterogeneous group with Sir Walter's chosen community in Bath, a rigidly hierarchical organization of affiliates chosen solely for status. These divergent social worlds disorient Anne, who decidedly prefers the care community to the status-based social scene.[5]

Care communities punctuate *Persuasion*, becoming successively larger and more abstract. The first and smallest such community forms when Anne visits her querulous sister Mary, who demands that Anne "come to Uppercross Cottage, and bear her company as long as she should want her" (J. Austen 35; vol. 1, ch. 5). Care, in this case, merely means amusement and companionship. Nineteenth-century people found "the creation of small, select societies around their bedsides one of the greatest advantages of illness," Miriam Bailin explains (20). Indeed, *Persuasion* insists on caregiving as the stuff of ordinary life, not the heroic exception.[6] But it also insists that caregiving can realign social relations. Initially, Mary's connections are mutually discontented, but the moment Mary's nephew Charles dislocates his collarbone, the Musgroves briefly achieve intense communion—although they will soon lose interest and revert to squabbling once it turns out the child is not in danger.

The second care community Anne encounters is determined by affinity rather than biological relations. Captain Benwick lives with the kindly Harvilles, and Captain Harville, the brother of Benwick's deceased fiancée, Fanny, has, in turn, befriended Captain Wentworth because Wentworth cared for Benwick when Fanny died. The community formed by the Harvilles, Benwick, and Wentworth deeply attracts Anne, accustomed as she is to the Elliot family's formality. She yearns to be part of the group, musing wistfully, "These would have been all my friends" (J. Austen, *Persuasion* 105; vol. 1, ch. 11).

Louisa's accident both incorporates Anne into the community she yearns to join and extends it. Once again, a traumatic injury rearranges social patterns. Louisa's caregivers are quite diverse and include her family—parents, brother, and sister and those siblings' connections (Charles Hayter, Anne, and Mary)—Captain Wentworth; virtual strangers such as Captain Benwick and the Harvilles; the Crofts, who function as concerned but not directly involved connections; and Sarah, the Musgroves' old nursery maid.

This social organization operates according to tacit rules that may seem unusual if we assume the Baronetage represents the period's social norms. First, the members of this community care for one another, not just for their patient. "Mrs. Musgrove had got Mrs. Harville's children away as much as she could, every possible supply from Uppercross had been furnished, to lighten the inconvenience to the Harvilles, while the Harvilles had been wanting them to come to dinner every day; and in short, it seemed to have been only a struggle on each side as to which should be most disinterested and hospitable" (140; vol. 2, ch. 2). Second, unlike the static upper-class hierarchy, which is recorded in a published volume, this community is a fluid group, as members move in and out of the circle, negotiating, for instance, whether Mary or Anne should stay with Louisa at the Harvilles' home (124; vol. 1, ch. 12). Third, whereas the Elliot family values etiquette, this care community valorizes tender feeling, as expressed through both hospitality and poetry. Whereas the Elliot family identifies people through a lineage, the care community emphasizes reciprocity, the mutual exchange of assistance. Within the alternative social vision of the care community there is space for relationships not possible elsewhere, such as nurturing same-sex ties (Captain Benwick's and Captain Wentworth's mutual devotion), and for an unmarried woman to suddenly be seen as valuable (in Wentworth's words, "no one so proper, so capable as Anne!" [123]). My point here is that from young Charles to Captain Benwick to Louisa, catastrophe creates the kind of social world that allows Anne an alternative to the stratified, formal hierarchy of her upbringing.

Anne takes this liberating alternative with her when she is exiled to Bath, rebelling against her father's and sister's rules by seeking out Mrs. Smith, whose social circle is even more radically fluid, egalitarian, and decentralized than Louisa's. Mrs. Smith monitors information that moves through the laundress, the servant, the nurse, and her patients. Her society includes people whom the Elliots do not even condescend to notice. As Sir Walter sputters, she is "a mere Mrs. Smith, an every day Mrs. Smith, of all people and all names in the world, to be the chosen friend of Miss Anne Elliot, and to be preferred by her, to her own family connections among the nobility of England and Ireland! Mrs. Smith, such a name!" (171; vol. 2, ch. 5). Mrs. Smith holds the power of information; her disability enables her to act as a kind of proto-reporter, or novelist (see Schaffer 180; Miller 73). While "the nobility of England and Ireland" occupy one kind of social space, the laborers, nurses, and sick people compose an alternative, interconnected, networked version of Bath, and Mrs. Smith's information economy will one day supplant the status economy of the Baronetage.

These care communities contrast not only with Sir Walter's strictly hierarchical social world but also with Mr. William Elliot's self-interested marketplace model. Mr. Elliot is the *Homo economicus* of classic liberalism and modern capitalism. He has no ties, refusing to care for Mrs. Smith in spite of his personal and legal responsibilities. Mr. Elliot's idea of liberal autonomy was powerfully attractive in the period in which Austen wrote. Captain Wentworth endorses it when he begs Louisa to be as firmly impervious to outside influence as a glossy hazelnut (*Persuasion* 94–95; vol. 1, ch. 10). However, Wentworth's attempt to assume an impenetrable persona does not last, for his real sympathies are with suffering, as he is drawn to Anne's weary body. Moreover, through Louisa's trauma and recovery, Austen demonstrates that the self is not a closed, autonomous monad but is rather tremblingly permeable, dependent, and interrelated with others.[7] Louisa learns the hard lesson that when you jump, you must make sure someone is there to catch you, perhaps the most elemental example of interrelationality.

It is a lesson that the two handsome and lonely Elliots have not learned. They lead an utterly stagnant life. Sir Walter, "at fifty-four, was still a very fine man" (4; vol. 1, ch. 1), while Elizabeth, stuck for thirteen years in the same round of balls and visits, was "still the same handsome Miss Elliot that she had begun to be thirteen years ago" (6). The Elliots have created this stasis because they regard physical signs of experience, aging, and feeling as disadvantages. Only when one admits the possibility of bodies changing—aging, weakening, and hurting—and of loving a person through those changes can one admit the idea of historical change, which is perhaps *Persuasion*'s great subject, as Deidre Shauna Lynch argues (Introduction x–xvi; and Wiltshire, *Jane Austen* 163–64). Sailors become weather-beaten; women lose their bloom. "It is a period, indeed! Eight years and a half is a period!" exclaims Wentworth (J. Austen, *Persuasion* 244; vol. 2, ch. 10). Bodily decline and disability make history visible. If Elizabeth has remained unchanged for thirteen years, Anne and Mrs. Smith have a different somatic reality: "twelve years were gone since they had parted, and each presented a somewhat different person from what the other had imagined," as two strong, glowing, and healthy teenagers have become a pale lady and "a poor infirm, helpless widow" (166; vol. 2, ch. 5).

Anne begins the book alone: "only Anne" (6; vol. 1, ch. 1). It is, interestingly, illness that changes that situation. I remind students that Anne has no access to any of the modern ways people create social networks—by joining teams, taking classes, or participating in community activities. In this context, it is only crises of health that can make change possible. For a health crisis provokes caring, which is the feeling that flowers into all other relationships, whether marital or familial ties or friendships, including the avuncular trust of Admiral Croft, the kind maternal fussing of Mrs. Musgrove, the poetic ministrations of Captain Benwick, and the romantic passion of Wentworth. Elizabeth never finds a suitor—perhaps because she allows herself no weakness, and weakness is the site to which love can affix itself in this novel.

Persuasion makes real the modern theoretical recognition that disability is universal. Everyone gets tired, gets distressed, develops blisters, gets fat, sobs; everybody hurts, sometimes. But care is bigger than disability. Everyone in this novel needs help with the children, an invitation to dinner, a fellow driver to help pull the reins, or a sympathetic listener to complaints about the in-laws' disrespect. *Persuasion* recognizes that we live in a relational world where, as Mary writes in her letter, "we love her the better for having nursed her" (179; vol. 2, ch. 6).[8] This caregiving opposes both Mr. Elliot's experience of cutthroat capitalism and Sir Walter's hierarchical regime based on birth, not to mention the "slow death" of structural inequality (as Lauren Berlant names it) that many of my students endure today. Today it is easy to resent others' impairments as departures from the norm, but for Austen, writing before the invention of normality, suffering was simply what happened over time. *Persuasion*'s radical social vision, its lesson of tender, mutual regard for normative, widespread human frailty, may come out of Anne's fadedness, but it is something that should never lose its bloom.

NOTES

[1] See Wiltshire, *Hidden Jane* 147, for an account of the reader's experience of inhabiting Anne's sorrow.

[2] An excellent introduction to disability studies issues is Davis, *Disabilities*. Foundational texts include Garland-Thomson *Freakery* and *Staring*; Siebers; McRuer; and, for Victorian studies, Stoddard Holmes.

[3] For different but important views on this subject, see Wiltshire, *Jane Austen*; Heydt-Stevenson.

[4] Major scholarship on the ethics of care includes Held; Kittay; and Noddings.

[5] When Lady Russell reminds Anne of her family in Bath, "Anne would have been ashamed to have it known, how much more she was thinking of Lyme, and Louisa Musgrove, and all her acquaintance there, how much more interesting to her was the home and the friendship of the Harvilles and Captain Benwick, than her own father's house . . ." (J. Austen, *Persuasion* 134; vol. 2, ch. 1).

[6] When Anne imagines dramatic mortal illness and heroic interventions in the sickroom, Mrs. Smith immediately punctures her illusions (J. Austen 169; vol. 2, ch. 5).

[7] As Adela Pinch puts it: "Louisa is now the opposite of the hazelnut Wentworth held up to her as an image of firmness of mind. She has no 'baked crust of consciousness to parry sensations from the outside world'" (157).

[8] Mary makes this claim in the letter in which she announces Louisa's engagement to Captain Benwick—another love that develops through nursing.

Organizing Bodies: Teaching Metaphors of Space in *Persuasion*

Rebecca Posusta

The classes in which I teach Austen are composed largely of students who are not English majors. Most of my courses are introductory literature courses that have a broad focus on the three major genres. I teach *Persuasion* in a course exclusively for first- and second-year nonmajors. These students from across the disciplines often come into the course with only a cursory knowledge of what literature is and how to read it effectively. The name Jane Austen may sound familiar to them, but few of them have ever read her novels. Finding ways to make Austen's novels relevant and interesting to them is certainly a challenge, so I begin with the premise that Austen's remarkably intuitive use of space in her novels is a gateway for understanding the deeper nuances of her narrative. By mapping the spaces in her novels, students have a tangible and visual way to explore these subtleties. In drawing scenes, they become active participants in the novel's landscape. They use this visual exercise as a way to understand what the position of each person within a given space suggests about the physical, or exterior, and mental, or interior, shape of Austen's stories.

Making Austen accessible to students through mapping is a process that is multilayered. Students first need a primer in the geographic, historical, social, and literary contexts of *Persuasion*. This primer begins with a look at the specific locations mentioned in the novel (e.g., Bath, Lyme Regis, etc.), using photographs, maps, and film adaptations. We use interior and exterior photographs of great houses and cottages in England that might have been the model for Kellynch Hall and the houses at Uppercross in order to understand how Austen's audiences would have imagined the spaces that Austen presents and how her characters interact in them.

With this contextual knowledge, students are next able to set the physical parameters of spaces from the novel in their drawings. The physical mapping of scenes either on the board or on paper provides a visual illustration of the characters' implied movement within the spaces Austen describes. We begin mapping the novel with the scene in chapter 3 in which Anne Elliot first speaks. In these pages, the Elliots are in conference with Mr. Shepherd about their best options for retrenchment. Students begin by determining who is in the room. Through the dialogue, we know that Sir Walter Elliot, Mrs. Clay, Mr. Shepherd, and Anne are present. Students are certain that, although Austen does not name them and they do not speak, Elizabeth Elliot and Lady Russell are also in the room because they have been an integral part of the prior discussions. Austen also does not specify in exactly which room the conversation takes place. We can assume that since Sir Walter is a vain man, enamored of his ancestral past, he would likely entertain in a formal style in a large drawing room.

Students take their responsibility for understanding the context of this scene seriously. When I draw the figure of Sir Walter on a settee near the fireplace, students often question this choice and tend to point out that Sir Walter is walking around in this scene; and indeed, Sir Walter begins seated but gets up, "rising and pacing the room" after Mr. Shepherd proposes that he take a navy man as a tenant (20; vol. 1, ch. 3). Students have also felt strongly that Lady Russell, in her advisory capacity, should sit separately from the family group, though she is not as neglected and forgotten as Anne is before she makes her contribution to the conversation. When we begin discussing the novel, I ask students to talk about how the central characters are described by Austen in the first couple of chapters. That Austen describes Anne as "nothing" to her family plays a part in where they place Anne in this scene. They note that Anne speaks after a dash, which they see as a pause or hesitation; after all, it has been her tendency to "give way" (6; vol. 1, ch. 1). They point out that it is Mr. Shepherd who responds to Anne, not her father or sister. Despite the fact that what Anne says is clear, thoughtful, and more helpful to the discussion than either her father's or sister's comments, she is ignored. Students are often quick to volunteer that they have a new understanding of the scene after the class maps it. They generally realize as they read that Anne's relationship with her family is a problem, but the map helps them to see how Austen uses space to illustrate the nature of Anne's physical and emotional position in her family. Metaphorically at least, they often say, Anne is removed from the center of the family group.

As part of our discussion of the novel, I show Roger Michell's 1995 BBC film adaptation (*Persuasion*). Because of time constraints, we watch the film over the course of two or three class meetings. Watching the film during and after our discussion allows students to focus on particular scenes. I ask students to think about how they mapped the space in these scenes and to note if the adaptation captured the scene in the way they had imagined it. The scene in which the Elliots confer with Mr. Shepherd is of particular interest to the students because the film handles it quite differently than the novel does. In the film, Anne enters the room midway through the conversation and is only acknowledged by Lady Russell, who sits apart from the group. Oddly, Anne does not utter her first words here. It is in another scene from later in the chapter that she speaks and must explain who Admiral Croft is. This alteration is particularly striking to students because our mapping of the scene focuses on how Austen uses Anne's first words to be very clear about how Anne thinks. What Anne says about "all the comforts and all the privileges which any home can give" being the "claim" of sailors (21; vol. 1, ch. 3) is an even more overt demonstration of her thinking than her account of Admiral Croft's service in the later scene.

As we work through this early part of the novel, I also ask students to draw a map of the neighborhood around Kellynch Hall. I tell them to include in their maps Kellynch Hall, the great house at Uppercross, Uppercross cottage, Lady Russell's home, and Winthrop. Delving into Anne's impressions after her arrival at Uppercross at the start of chapter 6, students note that Anne talks about "the art of knowing our own nothingness beyond our own circle." They also note that the only information provided about the neighborhood in this paragraph is that Kellynch Hall is "a distance of only three miles" from Uppercross (45; vol. 1, ch. 6). Taking this paragraph into account, students tend to draw a circle on the board and then place Kellynch Hall at the center. In doing so, they typically suggest that placing Kellynch at the center makes sense because from Sir Walter's point of view, the Elliot name, as it is represented by Kellynch, is of central importance to the neighborhood.

Once we map our initial impressions of Anne and her confined world at Kellynch Hall, I ask my students to focus their attention on Anne's movement particularly after she is reintroduced to Captain Frederick Wentworth. Descriptions of Wentworth are often filtered through Anne's impressions of him, so it is in their interaction that we learn more about him. When students are mapping these scenes they are able to see beyond the love story and understand the narrative more fully.

The first scene of this kind that students map is the one in which Captain Wentworth lifts little Walter from Anne's back in chapter 9. The room in Uppercross cottage is small and very different from the room at Kellynch Hall in the earlier scene that we map. Unlike Kellynch Hall, the cottage is a home with small children. Austen describes the drawing room as "pretty" but says, "[T]he once elegant furniture . . . had been gradually growing shabby" (39; vol. 1, ch. 5). Anne looks after the injured little Charles Musgrove in this small, informal space. Students tend to draw it as rather cramped and cluttered. They also focus on the tension between Anne and Wentworth and between Wentworth and Charles Hayter. All three seem to be waiting for something.

While they wait, they turn to various occupations as distractions. Anne hovers over little Charles, Wentworth stands looking out of the window, and Charles Hayter reads the newspaper. Invariably, at least one student will wonder what could be so exciting at that window to make Wentworth so determined to remain planted in front of it. This comment prompts a little laughter. The comedy of the three people in this small room so assiduously avoiding interaction often has not occurred to the students before. Their experience with Anne has up until this point prepared them to expect sadness rather than humor. We then look at how Wentworth is "not ill-disposed" (86; vol. 1, ch. 9) for conversation and turns away from the window twice, and we draw an arrow to indicate him turning to greet Anne and Charles Hayter.

Their drawings suggest to the students that it is not what Wentworth sees outside that matters; the window is just a distraction. He is actually aware of what is going on in the room. Students often suggest that in the drawing of this scene, Wentworth should be placed at a slight angle, so that while from Anne's point of view he may seem to be looking out of the window, he actually has a very good view of the room. When he "step[s] forward to [Anne's] relief" (87; vol. 1, ch. 9), he seems to have been watching her all along. Students are also certain that at this moment Anne is resolutely turned away from him. They look at the diction used here: Anne "finds herself in the state of being released" and experiences "sensations on the discovery" (86, 87). Students believe that this means that Anne does not actually turn around but merely *feels* that it is Wentworth who has just "released" her. They suggest that Anne's stubborn grief is more palpable here and that Wentworth may be more interested in her than Anne is ready to believe.

Her persistent sorrow is again apparent when we next turn our attention to the scene in which Anne overhears Captain Wentworth and Louisa's conversation behind the hedgerow in chapter 10. In this scene, Anne has successfully managed "not to be in the way of any body" throughout the walk. She has kept herself distracted by "repeating to herself some few of the thousand poetical descriptions extant of autumn" (90; vol. 1, ch. 10). Yet she cannot stop herself from noticing the attention Wentworth pays Louisa or overhearing what the two have to say about her. In drawing this scene, students again get to think about exterior space as they did when mapping the neighborhood of Kellynch Hall. Winthrop looms in the distance, and Charles Musgrove and Henrietta Musgrove head off in that direction. Mary, agitated by being left behind, leaves Anne to go in search of Louisa, who has walked off with Wentworth.

Anne sits alone on one side of the hedge while Wentworth and Louisa are on the other side. Again, a little laughter begins as the students try to work out how Anne, sitting still, hears such a long conversation between Louisa and Wentworth. They note that Anne first hears Louisa and Wentworth as they are "making their way back" (93: vol. 1, ch. 10). Are they continuing to walk in a straight line past Anne? Are they walking back and forth or in a circle? If they are walking in a straight line, then Anne will have to shift her position to catch the entire conversation. Students note that at one point Wentworth pulls a nut from a tree, and they are often convinced that this action suggests that Wentworth and Louisa have stopped. Typically, students wonder if it is just coincidence that they happen to stop right behind Anne or if Wentworth is aware that Anne can hear them. What she hears is that Wentworth believes she is too easily guided by the opinions of others (though he is actually talking about Henrietta). Students suggest that because Wentworth focuses on Henrietta's lack of firmness, he may indeed have spied Anne through the hedge and be trying to communicate his feelings to her. I point out that the text does not suggest that Wentworth is aware that Anne overhears him or that he has deliberately stopped near her. I suggest, instead, that Austen uses Wentworth's conversation with Louisa as a sort of check for Anne. Having avoided Wentworth, Anne does not see until now how deeply her decision eight years ago has affected him.

We next tackle the climactic scene at Lyme Regis. I ask students to consider what differences they can detect in Anne's behavior. Often, when we begin mapping the scene, students want to focus on the unconscious Louisa and the panicking Wentworth. I ask them to focus instead on the movements of the characters. Students notice that Anne is the only one who seems to be moving at first. They use arrows to indicate Anne's movement while the rest of the characters they have drawn remain fixed in place.[1] They note that there is a clear shift as Anne gives directions, employing "strength, zeal and thought" (119; vol. 1, ch. 12). They then note that the other characters turn their attention to her and begin to move at her prompting. This is significant because it suggests not only that Anne has developed but also that the other characters view her differently. In drawing this scene, students can better see that Louisa's fall is not as important in the novel as the real change happening in Anne. Drawing her movements allows them to see that she has turned her former habit of tractability into one of self-confidence.

We get our next hint of the significance of this shift when Anne encounters Admiral Croft in Milsom Street. Here Anne must make a conscious decision and deliberate movement to engage the admiral in a conversation. The admiral, engrossed in "contemplating some print" in a shop window, his back to the street, does not see Anne pass. Anne "might have passed him unseen," and she is "obliged to" both touch and address him to get his attention (183; vol. 2, ch. 6). Students notice that here, as in the early scene with little Walter at Uppercross cottage, a window engrosses the attention of a character. Identifying the difference between the two scenes, they note that it is Anne who makes the move in this one. They can compare the drawings of the earlier scene to the drawings of the Milstrom Street one to see the way Anne is now physically engaging rather than turning away and avoiding interaction.

When Anne greets Captain Wentworth at the musical assembly, she makes a similarly conscious choice. I again ask students to look at the language Austen employs. They note that Anne's father and sister are "behind" Anne. She moves "forward" toward Wentworth. Wentworth is "brought out of the straight line to stand near her" (197; vol. 2, ch. 8). Again, it is the motion in this scene that the students pay attention to. When we draw the way Anne's and Wentworth's paths intersect on the board, the image looks like some sort of mathematical graph. I also ask students to compare this scene in the novel with the scene in the Michell film. The central difference they detect is that the scene in the film seems slower-paced. Anne is first seen milling about outside the Assembly Rooms as if she has been waiting for Wentworth a long time. When he enters and talks with Anne, there are several pauses that make the "reluctant and ungracious" acknowledgment of him by Sir Walter and Elizabeth seem dramatically longer than the quick one sentence in the text (197). Revisiting our map of this scene after we watch the film, students seek a way to make the movement appear less hasty. Instead of representing Anne and Wentworth with a pair of solid lines that head directly toward each other, students prefer to use a dotted line for Anne that provides some idea of the hesitation she feels until she sees that Wentworth is "in no hurry to leave her" (198).

The final scene that we map is the one in which Wentworth writes the fateful letter to Anne as she speaks to Captain Harville. Much as in the scene in Uppercross cottage, students note that each character or group of characters in the room is turned away from the others and engrossed in conversation or another activity. Mrs. Croft and Mrs. Musgrove are "only a buzz of words . . . at the other end of the room" (252; vol. 2, ch. 11), Anne and Harville stand at the window facing away from the room, and Wentworth is bent over the letter he is writing. We draw this space as a triangle on the board with Harville and Anne at the apex. As Anne divulges the secrets of her heart in the form of generalities to Harville, Wentworth seems to be occupied with his letter about resetting Benwick's portrait. Anne does not think Wentworth is near enough to hear what she says, and she is even "startled at finding him nearer than she supposed" when he drops his pen. As we read through the scene, students ask to move our little stick-figure Wentworth closer and closer to Anne. They recognize his anxiety to hear what Anne is saying and note that he must "strive . . . to catch sounds" (254). I point out that he does not actually move but does hear some of what she says because in his letter he pleads, "[D]are not say that man forgets sooner than woman" (257). When the party breaks up and Wentworth and Harville leave, the students draw lines showing their movement away from Anne, but Wentworth's line makes an abrupt U-turn just outside the door, as he must return to retrieve his forgotten gloves. The students draw him once again "crossing the room" to stand near Anne. His small gesture of "standing with his back toward Mrs. Musgrove" and drawing out the letter "from under the blotter" is the work of mere moments (257). Trying to account for time in our drawings is often difficult, but hastily moving the pen back and forth across the page generally suffices for representing this momentary movement of Wentworth's.

Over the years many students have commented, just as we were finishing up our discussion of the novel, that mapping out these scenes in *Persuasion* was really helpful because they could better see the intent behind what they read when it was illustrated. Many of my students have claimed that they are visual learners. A jumble of words on a page, for them, was far less effective in conveying meaning than the illustrations we did in class. This is the benefit of teaching the metaphorical language of Jane Austen's fiction in this way. Austen might not have imagined that her work would be read in this manner two hundred years after her death, but she was clever enough to provide the spatial clues that not only enabled contemporary readers but also enable modern students to navigate her narrative.

NOTE

[1] I often tell my students that their drawing skills need not be refined. They can use stick figures, *X*'s, check marks, or circles to indicate different characters.

Placing *Persuasion*

Catherine J. Golden

Notions of space and place have been influential to literary studies since Gaston Bachelard's 1957 publication *The Poetics of Space* (translated into English in 1964). Particularly relevant to my teaching of nineteenth-century literature is the work of Tim Cresswell, who asserts in *Place: A Short Introduction*, "When humans invest meaning in a portion of space and then become attached to it in some way (naming is one such way) it becomes a place" (10), and "place is not just a thing in the world but a way of understanding the world" (11). Jane Austen intuits how attachment turns a space into a place in *Mansfield Park* when Edmund Bertram, believing that Fanny Price will quit Mansfield to live with her Aunt Norris, reassures her: "The place, Fanny, is what you will *not* quit, though you quit the house" (31; vol. 1, ch. 3; emphasis added). Place theory, a concept from human geography, illuminates *Persuasion* even more, for much of the novel is set in recognizably real places—Bath and Lyme Regis. The attachment Austen has to these locations where she lived or traveled deepens and complicates the novel's plot and characterization. Austen strategically places volume 2 of *Persuasion* in Bath, a city in which, in the eighteenth century, prosperity and social class were closely aligned with architecture and location. A keen observer of geographically precise locales, Austen uses Lyme Regis and the dramatic landscape of the Cobb, in contrast to Bath's grand and secluded streets, to detach and reunite characters in the novel's love triangles.

This essay offers two ways to place *Persuasion* in the built and natural environments of Bath and Lyme Regis: actual and virtual. Travel seminars bring students to living classrooms, and this essay draws upon my experience teaching *Persuasion* on location.[1] During a ten-day residence in Bath with field trips to Steventon, Chawton, Winchester, and Lyme Regis, students read biography and fiction; create an analytic booklet to connect Austen's fiction to literary criticism, tourist sites, and museum displays; and participate in a two-part blog assignment about places central to *Persuasion*. Prior to the seminar, students write in their blogs about how they imagine specific locations based on their reading; for the second blog entry, students visit the locales they have written about, take and post photographs, and write a response after literally standing where Austen placed her characters. The weblog format also allows travel seminar students to comment upon one another's posts, which deepens their analytic engagement in *Persuasion* and place theory. Students' posts and comments illustrate how Austen used places she knew intimately for her own fictional purposes.

Persuasion can also be taught in relation to place theory when instructors have students visit locations virtually rather than in person; students' responses demonstrate how this approach helps them imagine the places Austen thought about in specific ways. In our increasingly technological world, we can follow in Austen's footsteps by using digital mapping to tour places she visited and incorporated into *Persuasion*. Both approaches—actual and virtual—illustrate how Austen rooted *Persuasion* in built and natural environments to situate her last completed novel within the social and moral contexts of Regency England.[2]

Bath and Hierarchies of Place

Although Bath claims her as its most famous resident, Austen—like Anne Elliot—never liked living there. The city is known for its "hierarchies of dwelling-place," notes critic Gillian Beer, "where streets and houses act as social coin" (xvii). The various Bath addresses where the Austens lodged from 1801 to 1806 show the family's downward spiral before and after the death of Jane's father, Rev. George Austen, in 1805.[3] Through on-site walking tours or, virtually, through *Google Earth Web*, students can trace where Jane Austen lived, from her first, well-placed residence at No. 4 Sydney Place, across from the majestic Sydney Gardens, to suitable lodgings at No. 3 Green Park Buildings East, and then to No. 25 Gay Street, and finally to an undisclosed address on Trim Street, a narrow lane that is still hard to find and that was at the time remarkable for its alehouses and disreputable inhabitants. Austen's intimate knowledge of Bath's high- and low-class dwelling places informs *Persuasion*.

In the novel, the Bath residence chosen by Sir Walter Elliot for his family reflects his desire to join chic society, as he says: "Their house was undoubtedly the best in Camden-place. . . . Every body was wanting to visit them" (148–49; vol. 2, ch. 3). Picturing the Elliots' lodgings prior to visiting Bath, one student notes: "Austen writes that 'Vanity was the beginning and the end of Sir Walter Elliot's character; vanity of person and of situation' (4; vol. 1, ch. 1). A man of such account would not seek a humble dwelling."[4] The Elliot abode, presumably situated in the triangular pediment in the center of Camden Place, now called Camden Crescent, perches above the city center, far from the River Avon, which had a noxious odor in Georgian times. Seeing the actual location, students come to understand how the geographic markers of Sir Walter's dwelling point to his high social class standing. But Austen plays a trick on class-conscious Sir Walter by lodging him in a very new building that is as unstable as his precarious finances. Terry Old reveals in *Bath as Jane Austen Knew It*: "So steep is [the hill] that the two end houses on the right hand side of the crescent fell down the hill when they were under construction[;] . . . the crescent is off balance" (17–18). Learning of this architectural joke while studying Austen on location, the same student observes in a second entry: "This seems exactly the kind of place Sir Walter would have chosen—beauty before practicality." Rather, it is more status than beauty or practicality that Sir Walter seeks.

Laura Place, the most prestigious location in Regency Bath, is where the dowager viscountess Dalrymple and the Honorable Miss Carteret, the Elliots' titled cousins, are "living in style" (J. Austen, *Persuasion* 161; vol. 2, ch. 4). Laura Place also offers visitors a perfect view of Great Pulteney Street, the longest and broadest street in Bath, "said to be wide enough to turn a coach and four around in one go without having to back it up" (Old 20). Sir Walter frequently refers to "[o]ur cousins in Laura-place" (J. Austen, *Persuasion* 162; vol. 2, ch. 4), showing how characters become synonymous with their impressive locations; Anne—herself referred to as one of the "Camden-place ladies" (189; vol. 2, ch. 7)—must put off a "visit in Rivers-street" (249; vol. 2, ch. 11), meaning a visit to Lady Russell, who lives on that desirable street. Austen never tells us the dowager's exact address, so one student placed Lady Dalrymple's residence at the corner of Henrietta Street and Laura Place because, in the student's words, "she would be able to see what was going on outside her windows on both streets" and "who is around and if they are worthy of her company"—that is, worthy of her location.

When I stood at the intersection of Russell Street and Rivers Street on one of the walking tours, I realized how Austen's literary imagination worked. Did Austen chuckle to herself when she decided to house Anne's special friend, Lady Russell, on Rivers Street, which runs perpendicular to Russell Street? Before visiting the site, one student predicted that this location must be attractive because "Lady Russell clearly possessed a horse and carriage, meaning that the street she lives on must be wide enough for at least one carriage to pass through." In a second entry written on location, the student concludes that Rivers Street is still "a trendy place to live because Johnny Depp bought a house there. . . . I tried to imagine Johnny Depp walking around Bath as though he was part of a Jane Austen novel and found myself wondering if he knew Lady Russell lived here." In our world, where celebrities have a status akin to Georgian Bath socialites, the streets of Bath still "act as social coin" (Beer xvii).

It is hard for students to anticipate the grandeur of the Georgian Assembly Rooms that John Wood the Younger designed in 1769.[5] As one travel seminar student comments: "When I saw the Assembly Rooms I felt simultaneously as if I had gotten my description right and as if I had been way off. I had pictured the Rooms as large, but not so grand." Another student likewise notes: "my idea of the Assembly Rooms was vastly underestimated. In my defense, however, it would be difficult for anyone to accurately imagine the splendor of these rooms. I had not thought the chandeliers would be so large or ornate, especially in the Octagon Room (card room)." The student likely did not think the chandeliers would be so elaborate because Austen does not describe the Assembly Rooms in detail, although she might have assumed that her Regency readers would be familiar with this fashionable Georgian locale. The nine chandeliers that light up the Assembly Rooms were made for the building in 1771 with crystal from the Whitefriars Glassworks of London. They are, on average, eight feet high and are now lit with light bulbs in place of candles. In a setting almost too dazzling to "accurately imagine," Austen sets a pivotal scene, which travel seminar students act out on location. Captain Wentworth enters the Octagon Room to find Sir Walter, Elizabeth, and Anne Elliot as well as Mrs. Clay waiting for the Elliots' titled cousins.[6] Wentworth "was preparing only to bow and pass on, but [Anne's] gentle 'How do you do?' brought him out of the straight line to stand near her" (*Persuasion* 197; vol. 2, ch. 8). Reproducing this scene, in which Anne literally and metaphorically steps forward in her relationship with the man she was persuaded to refuse eight years before, prepares students for the couple's reunion on the "gravel-walk" (261; vol. 2, ch. 11).

In direct contrast to these desirable locations is Westgate Buildings, a place Sir Walter considers to be of "low company, paltry rooms, [and] foul air" (171; vol. 2, ch. 5). Viewing the novel through the lens of place helps students understand how exclusionary forms of xenophobia, such as classism, operate in *Persuasion*. Well known is Sir Walter's tirade: "Westgate buildings! . . . and who is Miss Anne Elliot to be visiting at Westgate-buildings?—A Mrs. Smith. A widow Mrs. Smith" (170). Lodging determines the suitability of a visit, and Austen uses the verb "to place" quite consciously in the novel; for example, "[t]he Crofts had placed themselves in lodgings in Gay-street, perfectly to Sir Walter's satisfaction" (182; vol. 2, ch. 6), whereas Mrs. Smith has been forced to rent in Westgate Buildings, to Sir Walter's dissatisfaction. As one student notes in the pretravel blog post: "Lady Russell's carriage could only be 'drawn up near its pavement' [171; vol. 2, ch. 5], so I envision the street is so narrow that it cannot allow a carriage to pass."

Nonetheless, "[i]t is at Westgate Buildings that Austen challenges social class assumptions," another student states in a pretravel blog entry: "Indeed, what distinguishes Anne from her superficial family is her understanding and compassion, which allows her to cross class boundaries and step into Westgate Buildings." In the follow-up post, this student recognizes that "people of a lower class station still reside in this part of the city. Unlike [the goods in] Milsom Street, the goods in Westgate Buildings are affordable." Milsom Street is a fashionable shopping street, where Anne and Wentworth meet by chance at Molland's (a sweetshop that is no longer there), and Westgate Buildings is an inferior one. This same student bought an inexpensive rain jacket at Westgate Buildings, and the zipper broke immediately; having caught a cold, this student concludes in his second post that "I now understand how terrible it is for Mrs. Smith to be ill, but also to live in the cheapest part of magnificent Bath." Seeing the streets on location makes palpable for students how location in Bath is still a marker of social class.

Of all the Bath locations, the Gravel Walk is especially pivotal to *Persuasion*'s plot. Located just below the Royal Crescent, this secluded path was designed in 1775 for wealthy residents who would have been carried in sedan chairs from the crescent to the baths. At the Gravel Walk, Anne and Wentworth "exchanged again those feelings and those promises which had once before seemed to secure every thing" (J. Austen 261; vol. 2, ch. 11). "In my mind, I pictured them walking along a long, slightly bending gravel path, which had fine gray stones of all shapes and colors," notes one travel seminar student in a post prior to the trip. "The foot traffic would be fairly light. When they walk the gravel path, I imagine they could hear birds chirping with the noise of the city fading in the background." This quiet setting in an otherwise bustling Bath provided Austen an opportunity to give Anne and Wentworth an intimate moment to reveal their true feelings. After having acted out Anne and Wentworth's reunion on location, the student observes how visiting this location reaffirmed her first impression: "it was so quiet that we could hear birds chirping just as I had imagined in my first post."

The two-part writing assignment, in which students produce a blog post after reading the novel and another post after visiting sites from the novel, can be adapted for classes that do not incorporate travel. Although there are a number of Web sites available that can help sharpen students' observations about place,[7] I could not find one site that would allow students to view all the places in Bath where Austen lived, walked, and set *Persuasion*, so I constructed one. Two members of Academic Technologies at Skidmore College and I created an annotated tour, Jane Austen's *Persuasion* in Bath, using *Google Earth Web*, for assignments that involve virtual visits to the locations; that tour is available through Google Chrome to students and instructors.[8] Students write their initial posts about locations after reading *Persuasion*, but they compose their follow-up posts after their virtual visit to chosen locales through *Google Earth Web*.

The Bath virtual tour includes the central places where Austen set *Persuasion*—the Gravel Walk, the Assembly Rooms, Laura Place, and so forth—and marks these sites with a *P*. Places marked with an *R* are the four residences in Bath where Austen lived between 1801 and 1806, which students can visit virtually as well. The virtual tour also allows viewers to visit Lyme Regis. Each place on the list, when clicked, opens up a window that explains the significance of the location to *Persuasion* or to Austen's life. One can also go through the tour in Street View by dragging Pegman, the small icon of a person, to a specific place or residence marker. The instructor can zoom in to the exact spot where a character stands or Austen herself lived. For example, students can look around fashionable Milsom Street, still a prime shopping area in Bath, and the less desirable Westgate Buildings. One student remarks in her follow-up post, after viewing these sites virtually: "where Mrs. Smith lived, Google Earth shows many buses and cars littering the small street . . . there was some shopping but they were primarily charity shops and discount stores"; in contrast, "Milsom Street was wide with plenty of room to turn a carriage around in. There were expensive chocolate shops and luxury clothing stores, among other things. It was busy with higher class cars and a visible lack of public transportation." After the virtual tour, students can easily imagine how in Austen's day, Milsom Street could have accommodated a carriage with ease, unlike Westgate Buildings.

A virtual tour has limitations for understanding place in Austen's Regency world. It takes practice to navigate Street View smoothly. The lines on the map of Bath restrict where one can travel virtually. *Google Earth Web* allows entrance only to some buildings; viewers can enter the Assembly Rooms to view the magnificent chandeliers in the Octagon Room, where Anne steps forward to greet Wentworth. To give students access to even more interiors of Bath, instructors can create PowerPoint slides, using photographs, to show students, for example, the inside of the Cross Bath, where Mrs. Smith takes the waters, or the length of the Gravel Walk that is not accessible on *Google Earth Web*. I also recommend using Old's illustrated walking tour *Bath as Jane Austen Knew It* in conjunction with *Google Earth Web*. Old, a longtime tour guide for the Jane Austen Centre, keys his tour to important *Persuasion* (and *Northanger Abbey*) locations as well as to Austen's residences in Bath.[9] Students appreciate this guidebook chock-full of historical information, visual material, and humorous anecdotes as another, old-school way to place Austen's characters in the geography and architecture of Bath without travel.

Advantages also abound with the virtual tour. It allows students to revisit places in their own time. Aerial views help students grasp, more easily than touring on location can, how Austen took Anne and Wentworth on a circuitous route from Union Street to Camden Place via the Gravel Walk to grant them time and privacy to come to their mutual understanding. While an actual walking tour of the major *Persuasion* sites in hilly Bath takes four to five hours—which some of my students have found exhausting—a virtual tour allows students to visit all pertinent places and Austen's residences in just one class period. Students can move from Rivers Street to Russell Street to appreciate the humor in Austen's choice of Lady Russell's address; zip to Bond Street, where Sir Walter "had counted eighty-seven women go by, one after another, without there being a tolerable face among them" (153; vol. 2, ch. 3); visit Gay Street, where Admiral Croft and his wife reside; skip to majestic Laura Place, where the Elliots' titled cousins live; and then swiftly reach Camden Place on its hilltop to see where the pretentious Elliots place themselves in new lodgings.

Enthusiastic responses posted by students after a virtual tour approximate the feedback from students who actually walked the streets of Bath.[10] One student was amazed by the Assembly Rooms: "I didn't think there would be chandeliers in the rooms. It's insane that the chandeliers are original!" Another notes "a drastic visible difference between social classes," adding, "I almost overlooked the Cross Bath where Mrs. Smith takes the waters"; it is "a very small building, nowhere near the size or grandeur of the Kings' and Queen's Bath," which Admiral Croft visits to cure his gout. Another student was able to appreciate the hilliness of Bath only after the virtual tour and observes that Camden Place "is extremely high up . . . with a view of the city and green space" and far from the River Avon with its noxious smell. Two additional student comments encapsulate the benefits of teaching using the virtual tour. One student writes: "While of course it would be more awe-inspiring to visit these places in person, the virtual tour gave me a greater sense of Austen and a chance to experience Bath over a computer." The other, who had spent a semester in Bath, remarks: "The virtual tour of Bath widens the classroom in a really beautiful way. For me, it felt as though I were still walking around the city, as I was last fall. . . . It is with a renewed excitement that I revisit it on the virtual tour, following the same streets that I, and Jane Austen, walked."

Lyme Regis and the Cobb Scene

Anne and Wentworth's happiness in volume 2 hinges on a crucial place in volume 1—the Cobb in Lyme Regis. This large stone pier of two levels extends into the sea between Devon and Dorset. Austen uses Lyme, a seaside resort, and its famous Cobb harbor, which she visited in 1804, to engineer an accident to detach Wentworth from a supposed engagement with Louisa Musgrove, elevate Anne's worth in his eyes, and move the romantic plot along. The dramatic landscape lends insight into how Austen utilizes the built environment to disentangle Wentworth from a romantic misstep and redirect his attachments back to Anne.[11]

Anyone who has walked along a windy seawall can attest to the danger of Louisa's imprudent leap from the one at the Cobb onto hard pavement, and visiting the Cobb in person confirms just how foolish Louisa's action is. The southern arm of the Upper Cobb, rebuilt in 1793, shields the harbor against raging winds and joins the Lower Cobb via Granny's Teeth—a steep flight of weather-beaten, narrow steps that connect the two levels and that Louisa insists on being "jumped down" from (*Persuasion* 118; vol. 1, ch. 12). Reading this passage aloud while standing at the base of Granny's Teeth makes palpable how Louisa jumps too impetuously for Wentworth or anyone else to catch her:

> There was too much wind to make the high part of the new Cobb pleasant for the ladies, and they agreed to get down the steps to the lower, and all were contented to pass quietly and carefully down the steep flight, excepting Louisa; she must be jumped down them by Captain Wentworth. . . . The hardness of the pavement for her feet, made him less willing upon the present occasion; he did it, however; she was safely down, and instantly, to shew her enjoyment, ran up the steps to be jumped down again. He advised her against it, thought the jar too great; but no, he reasoned and talked in vain; she smiled and said, "I am determined I will:" he put out his hands; she was too precipitate by half a second, she fell on the pavement on the Lower Cobb, and was taken up lifeless! (117–18; vol. 1, ch. 12)

Even on a sunny day, there is "too much wind," and large waves crash against and sometimes break over the Upper Cobb. Not all of my students are willing to climb Granny's Teeth, and some even try to persuade me not to. But those who have navigated the "steep flight" of twelve jagged, hard steps made of rough-hewn stones that resemble crooked teeth embedded in the seawall understand through their own experience why Wentworth advises Louisa not to jump down again. We shield our eyes from the near-blinding sun, brace against the whipping wind, and sensibly do not act out the fall, although one student staged the aftermath to heighten the melodrama. Seeing "Louisa" sprawled out "lifeless!" on the Lower Cobb, students fully grasped the character's folly and understood that Mary Musgrove is for once not being melodramatic when she screams, "She is dead! she is dead!" (118).

Viewing the Cobb virtually also helps students approximate the lived experience of steep steps and glaring sun—architectural and geographic elements that contribute to Louisa's accident. In class, one or two students read aloud the pivotal scene while the entire class visits the Cobb virtually. After viewing Lyme on "Panoramas of Lyme Regis," my students gain a deeper understanding of the height of the Cobb and of the narrow steps that Louisa climbs. One ponders, "[H]ow could Louisa even climb the stairs so quickly in her full-length dress?" Another student observes, "Austen writes that Lyme Regis must be visited to appreciate its beauty," but then adds: "It is also true that we cannot fully appreciate the Cobb and Louisa's fall without seeing it virtually."

I recommend that when viewing Lyme on "Panoramas of Lyme Regis," students use the full-screen option, which makes the stones of the harbor wall and the brilliant blue of the English Channel particularly vivid. Navigational buttons on the *Google Earth Web* tour, which includes Lyme Regis in its list of places, allow the viewer to bring the scene of the accident into view slowly or more speedily, depending on the desired effect, and to pause at the place where "determined" Louisa jumps (J. Austen, *Persuasion* 118; vol. 1, ch. 12). The footage on both "Panoramas of Lyme Regis" and *Google Earth Web*, shot on a sunny day, shows the dazzling sun and the unforgiving pavement, though not the harsh wind or the sounds or the smells of the Cobb. However, the images also highlight the distinct curvature of the semicircular stone pier, which is designed to repel the powerful waves that crash against the harbor—a feature that is less visible when actually walking on the Cobb. Other online resources can also help students experience this setting virtually. "A Tour of the Cobb and Lyme Regis" brings students up close to the treacherous steps of Granny's Teeth and to another flight of steps further along the seawall, which this resource proposes as a possible site for Louisa's accident (Bebris). "Where Exactly Did Louisa Musgrove Fall," an entry in the blog *Jane Austen Today*, includes a photographic montage of the Cobb scene from the 1971, 1995, and 2007 film adaptations of *Persuasion*, all of which show Louisa making her foolhardy leap onto hard pavement (Sallaberry). Seeing actors in period costume in the films (as opposed to watching tourists stroll the Cobb in contemporary dress in the panorama) helps students imagine Louisa's jump in Jane Austen's time rather than in our own.[12]

In *Persuasion*, Austen uses real places to dramatic effect. She invests literary meaning in the Cobb and the streets of Regency Bath, a heritage city that preserves the hierarchies of dwelling place, which are made palpable to students through the use of place theory and location-based teaching. Through travel seminars and virtual tours, students can visit the spaces that Austen turns into potent places (in Cresswell's terms [10, 11]). Following in Austen's footsteps—actually or virtually—students place Austen's novel in the built and natural environments that literally and metaphorically take root in *Persuasion*.

NOTES

[1]The Jane Austen travel seminar is listed in the Skidmore College curriculum and entitled Jane Austen in Bath. In the course, we also examine *Northanger Abbey* on location, since its first volume is set in Bath.

[2] Wiltshire makes a similar argument in "Exploring *Mansfield Park*," where he notes that locations "can make us see details in the novel more sharply and, therefore, as they accumulate, read the novel differently" (83). Parker also illuminates settings in Bath and their importance to *Persuasion* and includes a map of Bath from Austen's day.

[3] Bath had lost most of its luster as a winter spa for wealthy socialites when the Austens moved there in 1801, but its luxury shops and amenities still made it appealing.

[4] This essay quotes from or is informed by the work of Skidmore students who participated in travel seminars and have given their permission for their writing to be included: Rebecca Rawling, Samantha Bush, Anna Millhauser Pishko, Ashley Grossman McLean, David Steinberger, Emily Harvey Lacroix, and Jessada Mahatthananchai.

[5] The building was intact until World War II; it was reconstructed with the original chandeliers and reopened in 1963.

[6] Austen does not state which of the four fireplaces in the Octagon Room the group stands in front of, so when students reenact this scene on location, I let them decide where to stand.

[7] Virtual sources include "In the Footsteps of Jane Austen," which is keyed to a downloadable map of Bath as Jane Austen knew it, and which includes some extracts from Jane Austen's novels and letters; "Bath, Somerset, England," which provides panoramas of the Cross Bath and the Assembly Rooms; and *Panoramic Earth*'s 360-degree virtual tours of Bath (Robertson), including Queen's Square, where Austen stayed on her first visit to Bath in 1797 (www.panoramicearth.com/11712/Bath/).

[8] Aaron Kendall and Alex Chaucer of Academic Technologies at Skidmore College and I created a tour for location-based virtual teaching of Jane Austen's *Persuasion* using *Google Earth Web*. With Aaron Kendall, I updated the virtual tour in 2019. The tour can be used by uploading it into *Google Earth Web* by following these steps: (1) Enter this URL in a Google Chrome browser window: goo.gl/1c79Da. (2) Download the zipped .kmz file when prompted on the preview screen. (3) Unzip the .kmz file, and save it. (4) Navigate to *Google Earth Web* (earth.google.com/web) using the Chrome browser. (5) In *Google Earth Web*, click on Projects (through the menu button), select New Project, open the drop-down menu and click on Import KML File from Computer, and then select the unzipped.kmz file. (6) Click on Jane Austen's *Persuasion* in Bath to access the tour's list of places.

[9] Illustrated guidebooks that show Bath as a seat of culture in late-eighteenth- and early-nineteenth-century England also bring the architecture of Jane Austen's novel to life. While Old is the most useful for teaching, Reeve offers four separate walking tours that illuminate *Persuasion* and *Northanger Abbey* as well as the places where Austen lived between 1801 and 1806.

[10] This essay quotes from or is informed by the work of Skidmore students who participated in courses using the virtual tour of Bath or other online resources and have given permission for their responses to be included: Christy Bottomley, Miller Y. Fina, Hannah Sacks, and Jessica Shapiro.

[11] Anne rises in Wentworth's esteem after the accident; Wentworth proclaims, "[I]f Anne will stay [in Lyme], no one so proper, so capable as Anne!" (*Persuasion* 123; vol. 1, ch. 12).

[12] Lyme Regis's Upper and Lower Cobb, the scene of Louisa's fall in *Persuasion*, also come to life virtually through the "Live Cobb Webcam" (www.lymeregis.org/webcam.aspx).

NOTES ON CONTRIBUTORS

Abigail Burnham Bloom teaches Victorian literature at Hunter College, City University of New York. She has published *The Literary Monster on Film*, coedited *Victorian Literature and Film Adaptation*, and written articles on George Eliot, Robert Louis Stevenson, Jane Carlyle, Geraldine Jewsbury, and the Brontës.

Julia Prewitt Brown is professor emeritus at Boston University and the author of *Jane Austen's Novels: Social Change and Literary Form* (1979), *A Reader's Guide to the Nineteenth Century English Novel* (1987), *Cosmopolitan Criticism: Oscar Wilde's Philosophy of Art* (1997), *The Bourgeois Interior: How the Middle Class Imagines Itself in Literature and Film* (2008), and *The Films of John Schlesinger* (2019). She has been the recipient of a Mellon Foundation Grant at Harvard University and the North American Scholar Award, given by the Jane Austen Society of North America. She is currently working on a book on the films of Mike Leigh.

Peter J. Capuano is associate professor of English and director of the nineteenth-century studies program at the University of Nebraska, where he has won the College of Arts and Sciences Distinguished Teaching Award. He is also a federated faculty member of the University of California's Dickens Project. He is the author of *Changing Hands: Industry, Evolution, and the Reconfiguration of the Victorian Body* (2015) and the editor of *Victorian Hands: The Manual Turn in Nineteenth-Century Body Studies* (2019). His current book project is entitled *Dickens's Idiomatic Imagination: The "Inimitable" and Victorian Body Language*. He has been named a faculty fellow in the Center for Digital Research in the Humanities at the University of Nebraska.

Margaret Case is professor of English and chair of the Department of English Literature and Creative Writing at Roger Williams University. She is the author of essays on eighteenth- and nineteenth-century women writers and is coeditor of *"Fantomina" and Other Works*.

Monica F. Cohen is lecturer in the Department of English and Comparative Literature at Columbia University and adjunct lecturer at Barnard College. She is the author of *Professional Domesticity in the Victorian Novel: Women, Work and Home* (1998) and *Pirating Fictions: Ownership and Creativity in Nineteenth-Century Popular Culture* (2018). Her essays on the nineteenth-century novel have appeared in *Dickens Studies Annual*, *Novel*, *SEL*, *Studies in the Novel*, *Texas Studies in Language and Literature*, and *Victorian Literature and Culture*.

Sheryl Craig is an emeritus faculty member at the University of Central Missouri and has lectured on Jane Austen in the United States and Canada and in England, Scotland, New Zealand, and Australia. She has published articles in *Persuasions*, *Persuasions On-line*, *The Explicator*, and *Jane Austen's Regency World* magazine, and film reviews for the Jane Austen Centre in Bath's Web site. Her book, *Jane Austen and the State of the Nation*, was published in 2015.

Gillian Dooley is an honorary senior research fellow in English at Flinders University, Australia, and a visiting fellow in music at Southampton University. Her wide-ranging literary interests include various twentieth-century novelists and Jane Austen, especially music in her novels and her world. Dooley was coconvenor of the July 2017 Immortal Austen conference in Adelaide, and as a singer she has been curating and presenting programs of music from Austen's personal collection since 2007. One of her ongoing projects is creating a detailed index of each of the five hundred to six hundred items in the Austen family music collections.

Catherine Engh received her PhD in English from the Graduate Center, City University of New York, in 2019 and has worked for five years as an adjunct instructor of English at Hunter College. She has expertise in British Romanticism, Enlightenment philosophy, and environmental criticism. An essay from her dissertation, on Mary Wollstonecraft's critique of Jean-Jacques Rousseau in *Maria; or, the Wrongs of Woman*, was published in *ELN* in fall 2019.

Marcia McClintock Folsom is professor of literature emeritus at Wheelock College, where she also served for many years as department chair of Humanities and Writing. She is the editor of *Approaches to Teaching Austen's* Pride and Prejudice and *Approaches to Teaching Austen's* Emma. With John Wiltshire, she is editor of *Approaches to Teaching Austen's* Mansfield Park. Many of her essays have appeared in *Persuasions* and *Persuasions On-line*, including "The Final Chapters of *Persuasion*: Austen's Passionate Revision" in 2019.

Melissa J. Ganz is associate professor of English at Marquette University. Her book, *Public Vows: Fictions of Marriage in the English Enlightenment* (2019), offers a new account of the marriage plot, arguing for the centrality of nuptial law to novels and of novels to nuptial regulation. She has published essays on legal and ethical questions in texts by Daniel Defoe, Frances Burney, George Eliot, Henry James, and Robert Louis Stevenson. Her research and teaching interests include eighteenth- and nineteenth-century British literature and culture, law and literature, gender studies, and the history of the novel.

Catherine J. Golden is professor of English and the Tisch Chair in Arts and Letters at Skidmore College. She is author of *Serials to Graphic Novels: The Evolution of the Victorian Illustrated Book* (2017), *Posting It: The Victorian Revolution in Letter Writing* (2009), and *Images of the Woman Reader in Victorian British and American Fiction* (2003). She is editor or coeditor of five additional books on topics ranging from Charlotte Perkins Gilman to Victorian illustration, literature, and culture and is a regular contributor to *Illustration Magazine*, a British arts journal.

Lynda A. Hall is associate professor of English at Chapman University in Orange, California. She has published several papers on Jane Austen, as well as the monograph *Women and "Value" in Jane Austen's Novels: Settling, Speculating and Superfluity* (2016). Hall teaches a literature survey course regularly, which she begins by teaching *Persuasion*.

Sheila Johnson Kindred formerly taught in the Philosophy Department of Saint Mary's University, Canada. She is the author of *Jane Austen's Transatlantic Sister: The Life and Letters of Fanny Palmer Austen* (2017). Her essays about Jane Austen's family and fiction have been published in *Persuasions*, *Persuasions On-line*, *The Jane Austen Society Report*, and *Royal Nova Scotia Historical Society Journal*.

Julie Ann Melnyk taught for nine years at Central Methodist College in Fayette, Missouri, where she was a tenured associate professor. She served from 2001 to 2012 as associate director of the University of Missouri's Honors College, organizing and teaching a multidisciplinary humanities sequence. In 2012 she became assistant teaching professor in the University of Missouri's English Department, teaching a wide range of courses, including Nineteenth-Century British Women Writers, Jane Austen and Her Contemporaries, and The Musician in Literature. She published essays on themes in Victorian literature and religion and a book, *Victorian Religion: Faith and Life in Britain* (2008). She was promoted to associate teaching professor in June 2017. She wrote her essay for this volume shortly before she died of cancer, in December 2017, at the age of fifty-three, leaving her husband and two sons.

William Nelles is professor of English at the University of Massachusetts, Dartmouth, where he has taught since 1995. His numerous publications on narrative theory include articles on Austen's novels in such journals as *Narrative* and *Interdisciplinary Literary Studies* and a chapter on Austen's juvenilia in *Jane Austen and Sciences of the Mind* (2018).

Magdalena Nerio teaches literature and women's studies courses at the University of Texas, San Antonio. Her recent publications include an essay on nineteenth-century biographies of Lady Mary Wortley Montagu for the edited volume *Biographical Misrepresentations of British Women Writers* (2017) and "'This Epistolary Medium': Friendship and Civil Society in Margaret Fuller's Private Letters," which appeared in *The Edinburgh Companion to Nineteenth-Century American Letters and Letter-Writing* (2016). Her research on British literature of the long eighteenth century focuses on women's writing and the epistolary form.

Magdalena Ostas is associate professor of English at Rhode Island College, where she teaches in the areas of Romantic-era literature, literature and philosophy, and literary theory and criticism. She has written essays on a range of figures situated at the intersection of these interests, including William Wordsworth, John Keats, Jane Austen, Emily Dickinson, Emmanuel Kant, Friedrich Nietzsche, Ludwig Wittgenstein, and Michael Fried. She is currently at work on a book-length study on inner life in Romantic-era writing and thought.

Sylvia A. Pamboukian is professor of English at Robert Morris University near Pittsburgh, Pennsylvania. She is the author of *Doctoring the Novel: Medicine and Quackery from Shelley to Doyle* and recent articles on Arthur Conan Doyle, Mary Elizabeth Braddon, and Agatha Christie. Her current work examines poisoning in literature from the Victorian period to the present.

Timothy Peltason teaches at Wellesley College, where he is professor of English and Class of 1949 Professor in Ethics. He has written extensively about Victorian poetry and fiction and published recent articles on Mark Twain, Oscar Wilde, and Donald Westlake. His essay "Mind and Mindlessness in Jane Austen" was published in the *Hudson Review* in 2015, and he is currently at work on an essay entitled "Jane Austen and the Wrong Man."

Rebecca Posusta is senior instructor of English at the University of Colorado, Colorado Springs, and has published an article, "Architecture of the Mind and Place in Jane Austen's *Persuasion*," in the spring 2014 special issue of *Critical Surveys* on Jane Austen. She teaches a variety of literature courses, including introductory courses and courses on eighteenth- and nineteenth-century literature, postcolonial literature, sustainability in literature, Austen, and Charles Dickens. Her research focuses on the depiction of interior, or mental, and exterior, or physical, landscapes in the novels of Austen and Dickens.

Anna Dodson Saikin is an English teacher at Episcopal High School in Houston, Texas. Her poetry chapbook, *Dear Caro* (2019), reimagines Lord Byron's letters through a feminist lens. She is currently working on a book-length project that examines the role of didactic silence in British Romantic novels written between the Gagging Acts of the 1790s and the 1832 Reform Act.

Talia Schaffer is professor of English at Queens College and the Graduate Center, City University of New York. She is the author of *Romance's Rival* (2016), *Novel Craft* (2011), and *The Forgotten Female Aesthetes* (2001). Books she has edited include *Literature and Culture at the Fin de Siècle* (2006), Lucas Malet's 1901 novel *The History of Sir Richard Calmady* (2003), and *Women and British Aestheticism*, coedited with Kathy A. Psomiades (1999). She has published widely on Victorian familial and marital norms, disability studies, women writers, material culture, popular fiction, and aestheticism.

Paul Westover is associate professor of English at Brigham Young University. He is the author of *Necromanticism: Traveling to Meet the Dead, 1750–1860* (2012), coeditor of the Romantic Circles edition of William Wordsworth's *Guide to the Lakes* (2015), and editor with Ann Weirda Rowland of *Transatlantic Literature and Author Love in the Nineteenth Century* (2016). His essays have appeared in such journals as *European Romantic Review* and *Studies in Romanticism* and in edited collections on literary tourism, reception, and geography. His current research projects center on literary relics and the writings of Dorothy Wordsworth.

John Wiltshire is emeritus professor at La Trobe University, Melbourne, Australia. He has published widely on Jane Austen, and his books include *Jane Austen and the Body* (1992); *The Cinematic Jane Austen*, with David Monaghan and Ariane Hudelet (2009); and *The Hidden Jane Austen* (2014), and he edited the Cambridge University Press edition of *Mansfield Park* (2005). Beginning with *Samuel Johnson in the Medical World: The Doctor and the Patient* (1991, 2005), he has also published widely in the field of literature and medicine. His most recent book is *Frances Burney and the Doctors: Patient Narratives Then and Now* (2019).

SURVEY PARTICIPANTS

Kimberly VanEsveld Adams, *Elizabethtown College*
Henry Alley, *University of Oregon*
William Baker, *Northern Illinois University*
Janine Barchas, *University of Texas, Austin*
Lisa Berglund, *University at Buffalo, State University of New York*
Troy Boone, *University of Pittsburgh*
Caroline Breashears, *St. Lawrence University*
Mary Burgan, *Indiana University, Bloomington*
Mark Canuel, *University of Illinois, Chicago*
Sheryl Craig, *University of Central Missouri*
LuAnn Fletcher, *Cedar Crest College*
Catherine J. Golden, *Skidmore College*
Dashielle Horn, *Lehigh University*
Joan Lescinski, *St. Ambrose University*
Devoney Looser, *Arizona State University*
Claudia Martin, *Binghamton University, State University of New York*
Marie McAllister, *University of Mary Washington*
Juliet McMaster, *University of Alberta*
Kim Ian Michasiw, *York University (Toronto)*
Amy Montz, *University of Southern Indiana*
Christopher Nagle, *Western Michigan University*
Shawn Normandin, *Sungkyunkwan University (Republic of South Korea)*
Magdalena Ostas, *Rhode Island College*
Sylvia A. Pamboukian, *Robert Morris University*
Paula Reiter, *Mount Mary University*
Daniel Robinson, *Widener University*
Emily Rohrbach, *University of Manchester (United Kingdom)*
Yasmin Solomonescu, *University of Notre Dame*
Sue Sorensen, *Canadian Mennonite University*
Betsy Winakur Tontiplaphol, *Trinity University*
Linda Troost, *Washington and Jefferson University*
Katie Trumpener, *Yale University*
Lisa Wilson, *State University of New York, Potsdam*

WORKS CITED

Alcott, Louisa May. *Little Women*. 1868. Penguin Classics, 1989.

Anderson, Benedict. *Imagined Communities*. 1983. Revised ed., Verso, 2006.

Aristotle. *The Nicomachean Ethics*. Translated by David Ross, edited by Lesley Brown, revised ed., Oxford World's Classics, 2009.

Astell, Ann W. "Anne Elliot's Education: The Learning of Romance in *Persuasion*." *Renascence*, vol. 40, 1987, pp. 12–14.

Austen, Charles. Journal entry. 31 July 1826. Charles Austen's Journal, AUS/118, National Maritime Museum, London, England.

Austen, Henry. "Biographical Notice of the Author." *A Memoir of Jane Austen and Other Family Recollections*, by J. E. Austen-Leigh, edited by Kathryn Sutherland, Oxford UP, 2002, pp. 135–41.

———. "Biographical Notice of the Author." J. Austen, *Novels*, vol. 5, pp. 3–9.

———. "Biographical Notice of the Author." J. Austen, *Persuasion* [Todd and Blank], pp. 326–32.

Austen, Jane. *The Annotated* Persuasion. Edited by David M. Shapard, Anchor Books, 2010.

———. *Emma*. Edited by Richard Cronin and Dorothy McMillan, Cambridge UP, 2005.

———. *Jane Austen's Letters*. Edited by R. W. Chapman, 2nd ed., Oxford UP, 1952.

———. *Jane Austen's Letters*. Edited by Deirdre Le Faye, 3rd ed., Oxford UP, 1995.

———. *Jane Austen's Letters*. Edited by Deirdre Le Faye, 4th ed., Oxford UP, 2011.

———. "Letters about *Persuasion*." Austen, *Persuasion* [Spacks], pp. 198–202.

———. *Mansfield Park*. Edited by John Wiltshire, Cambridge UP, 2005.

———. Northanger Abbey *and* Persuasion. John Murray, 1818.

———. *The Novels of Jane Austen*. 1933. Edited by R. W. Chapman, 3rd ed., Clarendon Press, 1987. 6 vols.

———. *Persuasion*. 2003. Edited by Gillian Beer, Penguin Classics, 2015.

———. *Persuasion*. Edited by Linda Bree, Broadview Press, 1998.

———. *Persuasion*. Edited by James Kinsley, with introduction and notes by Deidre Shauna Lynch, Oxford World's Classics, 2004.

———. *Persuasion*. Edited by Patricia Meyer Spacks, Norton Critical Edition, 2nd ed., W. W. Norton, 2013.

———. *Persuasion*. Edited by Janet Todd and Antje Blank, Cambridge UP, 2006.

———. *Persuasion: An Annotated Edition*. Edited by Robert Morrison, The Belknap Press of Harvard UP, 2011.

———. *Pride and Prejudice*. Edited by Pat Rogers, Cambridge UP, 2006.

———. *Sense and Sensibility*. Edited by Edward Copeland, Cambridge UP, 2006.

———. *The Works of Jane Austen*. Edited by R. W. Chapman, 3rd ed., Oxford UP, 1987. vol. 6.

Austen-Leigh, James E. *A Memoir of Jane Austen, by Her Nephew*. Edited by R. W. Chapman, with an introduction by Fay Weldon, Folio Society, 1989.

Bachelard, Gaston. *The Poetics of Space*. 1957. Beacon, 1992.

Bailin, Miriam. *The Sickroom in Victoria Fiction: The Art of Being Ill*. Cambridge UP, 1994.

Barbauld, Anna Letitia. *Eighteen Hundred and Eleven*. *Anna Letitia Barbauld: Selected Poetry and Prose*. Edited by William McCarthy and Elizabeth Craft, Broadview Press, 2002.

Barchas, Janine. *Matters of Fact in Jane Austen: History, Location, and Celebrity*. Johns Hopkins UP, 2012.

Barnes, Julian. *Through the Window: Seventeen Essays and One Short Story*. Vintage, 2012.

"Bath, Somerset, England: Virtual Tour and Guide to the City." *VRbath*, Red Door VR, 4 June 2013, www.vrbath.co.uk/.

Bebris, Carrie. "A Tour of the Cobb and Lyme Regis." 2017, www.carriebebris.com/excerpts/Deception_research_tour.pdf.

Beer, Gillian. Introduction. Austen, *Persuasion* [Beer], pp. vii–xxxiii.

Benjamin, Walter. *Berlin Childhood around 1900*. Translated by Howard Eiland, The Belknap Press of Harvard UP, 2006.

Berlant, Lauren. "Slow Death (Sovereignty, Obesity, Lateral Agency)." *Critical Inquiry*, vol. 33, no. 4, 2007, pp. 754–80.

Betham, William. *The Baronetage of England; or, The History of the English Baronets*. Burrell and Bransby, for William Miller, 1801–05. 4 vols.

The Bible. Authorized King James Version, Oxford World's Classics, 2008.

Blackstone, Wiliam. *Commentaries on the Laws of England*. 1765. Vol. 1, U of Chicago P, 1979.

Book of Common Prayer. 1662. Penguin Books, 2012.

Boswell, James. *Life of Samuel Johnson*. Vol. 1, Charles Dilly, 1791.

Bradley, A. C. "Jane Austen: A Lecture." Littlewood, vol. 2, pp. 199–217.

Bree, Linda. Introduction. Austen, *Persuasion* [Bree], pp. 7–37.

Brontë, Anne. *Agnes Grey*. 1847. Edited by Robert Inglesfield et al., Oxford World's Classics, 2010.

———. *The Tenant of Wildfell Hall*. 1848. Edited by Lee A. Talley, Broadview Press, 2009.

Brontë, Charlotte. *Jane Eyre*. 1847. Edited by Deborah Lutz, Norton Critical Edition, 4th ed., W. W. Norton, 2016.

Brontë, Emily. *Wuthering Heights*. 1847. Penguin Classics, 2009.

Brown, Julia Prewitt. *The Bourgeois Interior: How the Middle Class Imagines Itself in Literature and Film*. U of Virginia P, 2008.

———. *Jane Austen's Novels: Social Change and Literary Form*. Harvard UP, 1979.

Burke, Edmund. "From *Reflections on the Revolution in France*." Lynch, *Romantic Period*, pp. 197–203.

———. *Reflections on the Revolution in France*. 1790. Edited by Conor Cruise O'Brien, Penguin Books, 1986.

Burke, Michael C. "A Mathematician's Proposal." specctoolkit.carnegiefoundation.org/2009/01/11/a-mathematicians-proposal/.

Burney, Frances. *Cecilia; or, Memoirs of an Heiress*. 1782. Edited by Peter Sabor and Margaret Anne Doody, revised ed., Oxford World's Classics, 1999.

———. *Evelina; or, The History of a Young Lady's Entrance into the World*. 1778. Edited by Stewart J. Cooke, Norton Critical Edition, W. W. Norton, 1998.

———. *The Wanderer; or, Female Difficulties*. 1814. Edited by Margaret Anne Doody et al., Oxford World's Classics, 1991.

Butler, Marilyn. *Jane Austen and the War of Ideas*. Clarendon Press, 1975.

Byron, George Gordon. "The Giaour: A Fragment of a Turkish Tale." Austen, *Persuasion* [Bree], pp. 301–303.

"The Cambridge Companions to Literature and Classics." *Cambridge Companions*, Cambridge University Press, 2020, www.cambridge.org/core/what-we-publish/collections/cambridge-companions/the-cambridge-companions-to-literature-and-classics.

Cantor, Paul A. "A Class Act: *Persuasion* and the Lingering Death of the Aristocracy." *Philosophy and Literature*, vol. 23, no. 1, Apr. 1999, pp. 127–36.

Carroll, Laura, et al. "Austen's and Michell's *Persuasion*." *Victorian Literature and Film Adaptation*, edited by Abigail Burnham Bloom and Mary Sanders Pollock, Cambria, 2011, pp. 225–41.

Chandler, James, editor. *The Cambridge History of Romantic Literature*. Cambridge UP, 2009.

Chapman, R. W. "Chronology of *Pride and Prejudice*." *The Novels of Jane Austen*, edited by Chapman, 1st ed., vol. 2, Oxford UP, 1923, pp. 400–08. 5 vols.

———, editor. Preface to "Lady Susan." Austen, *Works*, p. 243.

Clare, John. *John Clare*. Edited by Eric Robinson and David Powell, Oxford UP, 1984.

Cohen, Monica F. "Persuading the Navy Home: Austen and Married Women's Professional Property." *Novel*, vol. 29, no. 3, Spring 1996, pp. 346–66.

Cohn, Dorrit. *Transparent Minds: Narrative Modes for Presenting Consciousness in Fiction*. Princeton UP, 1978.

Coleridge, Samuel Taylor, and William Wordsworth. *Lyrical Ballads, 1798 and 1800*. Edited by Michael Gamer and Dahlia Porter, Broadview Press, 2008.

Colley, Linda. *Britons: Forging the Nation, 1707–1837*. Yale UP, 2009.

Collins, Arthur. *The Baronetage of England*. John Stockdale, 1806.

Conrad, Joseph. *Heart of Darkness*. 1899. Norton Critical Edition, 5th ed, W. W. Norton, 2016.

Copeland, Edward. "*Persuasion*: The Jane Austen Consumer's Guide." *Jane Austen Society of North America*, www.jasna.org/persuasions/printed/number15/copeland.htm.

Copeland, Edward, and Juliet McMaster, editors. *The Cambridge Companion to Jane Austen*. 1st ed., Cambridge UP, 1997. *Cambridge Companions*, www.cambridge.org/core/books/cambridge-companion-to-jane-austen/DF2FE1BFFA5937D2F7C5C117B75B5CE7.

———, editors. *The Cambridge Companion to Jane Austen*. 2nd ed., Cambridge UP, 2011. *Cambridge Companions*, www.cambridge.org/core/books/cambridge-companion-to-jane-austen/DC0152B323BB47D990DB0CB90395C504.

Cresswell, Tim. *Place: A Short Introduction*. Wiley-Blackwell, 2004.

David, Saul. *Prince of Pleasure: The Prince of Wales and the Making of the Regency*. Grove Press, 1998.

Davies, Tristan. "To Kiss or Not to Kiss." *The Guardian*, 7 Jan. 1995, pp. 12–13.

Davis, Lennard J, editor. *The Disabilities Studies Reader*. 4th ed., Routledge, 2013.

———. "Introduction: Normality, Power, and Culture." Davis, *Disabilities Studies Reader*, pp. 1–14.

Dear, Nick. *Screenplay for* Persuasion *by Jane Austen*. Methuen Film, 1996.

Debrett's. "The Baronetage." *Debretts.com*, www.debretts.com/expertise/essential-guide-to-the-peerage/the-baronetage/.

Defoe, Daniel. *Robinson Crusoe*. 1719. Oxford UP, 2009.

De Quincey, Thomas. "The English Mail-Coach." *"The English Mail-Coach" and "Joan of Arc."* 1905. *Project Gutenberg E-book*, www.gutenberg.org/files/6359/6359-h/6359-h.htm.

Deresiewicz, William. *Jane Austen and the Romantic Poets*. Columbia UP, 2004.

Dickens, Charles. *Martin Chuzzlewit*. 1863. Penguin Classics, 1999.

Dickson, Rebecca. "Misrepresenting Jane Austen's Ladies: Revising Texts (and History) to Sell Films." *Jane Austen in Hollywood*, edited by Linda Troost and Sayre Greenfield, UP of Kentucky, 1998, pp. 44–57.

Duckworth, Alistair M. *The Improvement of the Estate: A Study of Jane Austen's Novels*. Johns Hopkins UP, 1971.

Duneier, Mitchell. *Slim's Table: Race, Respectability, and Masculinity*. U of Chicago P, 2015.

Eaton, Rebecca. *Making* Masterpiece*: Twenty-Five Years Behind the Scenes at* Masterpiece Theatre *and* Mystery! *on PBS*. Viking, 2013.

Edgeworth, Maria. *Belinda*. 1801. Edited by Kathryn J. Kirkpatrick, Oxford World's Classics, 2008.

Edgeworth, Maria, and Richard Lovell Edgeworth. *Practical Education*. 1798. 3rd ed., Harper, 1835.

Eliot, George. *Middlemarch*. 1871. Edited by Gregory Maertz, Broadview Press, 2004.

"Engagement, 5." *A Dictionary of the English Language*, by Samuel Johnson, 2nd ed, vol. 1, 1755.

"Engagement, *N.* 8." *Oxford English Dictionary*, 2020, oed.com/view/Entry/62197?redirectedFrom=engagement#eid.

Eric Cochrane Presents: Persuasion *by Jane Austen*. *YouTube*, uploaded by MyBoggy, 12 March 2009, www.youtube.com/watch?v=IcvU_RH5w58.

Farrer, Reginald. "Jane Austen, *ob*. July 18, 1817." Littlewood, vol. 2, pp. 177–98.

Favret, Mary A. *War at a Distance: Romanticism and the Making of Modern Wartime*. Princeton UP, 2010.

———. "Writing, Reading, and the Scenes of War." Chandler, pp. 314–34.

Fergus, Jan. "Biography." *Jane Austen in Context*, edited by Janet Todd, Cambridge UP, 2007, pp. 3–11.

Finn, Margot. "The Homes of England." Chandler, pp. 293–313.

Folsom, Marcia McClintock, editor. *Approaches to Teaching Austen's* Emma. Modern Language Association, 2004.

———, editor. *Approaches to Teaching Austen's* Pride and Prejudice. Modern Language Association, 1993.

———. "The Final Chapters of *Persuasion*: Austen's Passionate Revision." *Persuasions*, vol. 40, 2019, pp. 13–28.

Folsom, Marcia McClintock, and John Wiltshire, editors. *Approaches to Teaching Austen's* Mansfield Park. Modern Language Association, 2014.

Ford, Susan Allen. "Learning Romance from Scott and Byron: Jane Austen's Natural Sequel." *Persuasions*, vol. 26, 2004, pp. 72–88.

Fordyce, James. *Sermons to Young Women*. 1768. Vol. 1, Forgotten Books, 2018. 2 vols.

Forster, E. M. *Howards End*. 1910. Everyman's Library, 1991.

Franklin, Benjamin. "Letter to Sarah Bache." 26 Jan. 1784. *The Writings of Benjamin Franklin*, edited by Albert Henry Smyth, vol. 9, Macmillan, 1905–07, pp. 161–66.

Garland Thomson, Rosemarie. *Freakery: Cultural Spectacles of the Extraordinary Body*. New York UP, 1996.

———. *Staring: How We Look*. Oxford UP, 2009.

Gaskell, Elizabeth. *North and South*. 1855. Edited by Alan Shelston, Norton Critical Edition, W. W. Norton, 2004.

Genette, Gérard. *Narrative Discourse: An Essay in Method.* Translated by Jane E. Lewin, Cornell UP, 1980.

Gillray, James. *Discipline à la Kenyon*. 1797. *Lewis Walpole Library*, Yale University, findit.library.yale.edu/catalog/digcoll:976876.

Gleckner, Robert F. and Gerald E. Enscoe, editors. *Romanticism: Points of View*. Prentice Hall, 1962.

Godwin, William. *An Enquiry Concerning Political Justice*. 1793. Edited by Mark Philp, Oxford UP, 2013.

Gottlieb, Evan, and Ian Duncan, editors. *Approaches to Teaching Scott's Waverley Novels*. Modern Language Association, 2009.

Gottlieb, Sidney. "*Persuasion* and Cinematic Approaches to Jane Austen." Austen, *Persuasion* [Spacks], pp. 301–11.

Graham, Peter W. *Jane Austen and Charles Darwin: Naturalists and Novelists*. Ashgate, 2008.

Green, Sarah K. "'A State of Alteration, Perhaps of Improvement': New Social Structures in *Persuasion*." *Jane Austen Society of North America*, www.jasna.org/essaycontest/2003/undergraduate.html.

Grey, J. David, et al., editors. *The Jane Austen Companion*. Macmillan, 1986.

Groenendyk, Kathi L. "The Importance of Vision: 'Persuasion' and the Picturesque." *Rhetoric Society Quarterly*, vol. 30, no. 1, Winter 2000, pp. 9–28.

Harding, D. W. *"Regulated Hatred" and Other Essays on Jane Austen*. Athlone, 1998.

Harris, Jocelyn. *A Revolution Almost beyond Expression: Jane Austen's* Persuasion. U of Delaware P, 2007.

Harvey, David. *The New Imperialism.* Oxford UP, 2003.

Haywood, Eliza Fowler. *Fantomina*. 1725. Fantomina *and Other Works*, by Haywood, edited by Alexander Pettit et al., Broadview Press, 2004, pp. 41–71.

Heath, Duncan, and Judy Boreham, editors. *Introducing Romanticism*. Totem Books, 2000.

Held, Virginia. *The Ethics of Care: Personal, Political, and Global*. Oxford UP, 2006.

Helmstadter, Carol, and Judith Godden. *Nursing before Nightingale, 1815–1899*. Ashgate, 2011.

Heydt-Stevenson, Jillian. *Austen's Unbecoming Conjunctions: Subversive Laughter, Embodied History*. Palgrave Macmillan, 2005.

Hill, Richard. *The Prizes of War: The Naval Prize System in the Napoleonic Wars, 1793–1815*. Sutton, 1998.

Holy Bible: New Living Translation. Tyndale House Publishers, 2015.

Honan, Park. *Jane Austen: Her Life*. Fawcett Columbine, 1987.

Hubback, J. H., and Edith C. F. Hubback. *Jane Austen's Sailor Brothers*. 1906. Biolife, 2011.

Hunter, J. Paul. *Before Novels*. W. W. Norton, 1990.

"In the Footsteps of Jane Austen Audio Tour." *Visit Bath*, 2020, visitbath.co.uk/things-to-do/jane-austens-bath/in-the-footsteps-of-jane-austen/.

Ireland, K. R. "Future Recollections of Immortality: Temporal Articulation in Jane Austen's *Persuasion*." *NOVEL: A Forum on Fiction*, vol. 18, no. 2, 1980, pp. 204–20.

Jacobus, Mary. "Between the Lines: Poetry, *Persuasion*, and the Feelings of the Past." *Recognizing the Romantic Novel: New Histories of British Fiction, 1780–1830*, edited by Jillian Heydt-Stevenson and Charlotte Sussman, Liverpool UP, 2008, pp. 237–66.

James, Caryn. "Austen Tale of Lost Love Refound." *New York Times*, 27 Oct. 1995, p. C18.

"Jane Austen in Austin: A Regency Display on View." *Ransom Center Magazine*, 16 Apr. 2014, sites.utexas.edu/ransomcentermagazine/tag/david-steel/.

"Jane Austen Information Page." *The Republic of Pemberly*, 2018, pemberley.com/janeinfo/janeinfo.html.

Johnson, Claudia L. *Jane Austen: Women, Politics, and the Novel*. U of Chicago P, 1988.

———. "The 'Operations of Time, and the Changes of the Human Mind': Jane Austen and Dr. Johnson Again." *Modern Language Quarterly*, vol. 44, no. 1, March 1983, pp. 23–38.

———. "*Persuasion:* The 'Unfeudal Tone of the Present Day.'" Austen, *Persuasion* [Spacks], pp. 257–81.

Johnson, Samuel. *The Rambler*. Edited by W. J. Bate and Albrecht B. Strauss, 1969. *The Works of Samuel Johnson*, vol. 3, Yale UP, 1958–2019.

Kavanagh, Julia. "Miss Austen's Six Novels." Littlewood, vol. 1, pp. 356–74.

Kidd, Charles, et al. *Debrett's Peerage and Baronetage*. 147th ed., Debrett's, 2012.

Kindred, Sheila Johnson. "Charles Austen: Prize Chaser and Prize Taker on the North American Station, 1805–1808." *Persuasions*, vol. 26, 2004, pp. 180–94.

———. "Charles Austen's Capture of the French Privateer *La Jeune Estelle*." *Jane Austen Society Report for 2006*, pp. 50–53.

———. "The Influence of Naval Captain Charles Austen's North American Experiences on *Persuasion* and *Mansfield Park*." *Persuasions*, vol. 31, 2009, pp. 115–29.

———. *Jane Austen's Transatlantic Sister: The Life and Letters of Fanny Palmer Austen*. McGill-Queen's UP, 2017.

Kirkham, Margaret. *Jane Austen, Feminism and Fiction*. Methuen, 1986.

Kittay, Eva Feder. *Love's Labor: Essays on Women, Equality, and Dependence*. Routledge, 1999.

Knox-Shaw, Peter. "Byron, and the Turkish Tale." *The Review of English Studies*, vol. 44, no. 173, 1993, pp. 47–69.

———. *Jane Austen and the Enlightenment*. Cambridge UP, 2004.

Kundera, Milan. *Testaments Betrayed*. Translated by Linda Asher, HarperCollins, 1995.

Lavery, Brian. *Life in Nelson's Navy: The Ships, Men and Organization, 1783–1815*. Conway Maritime, 1994.

Le Faye, Deirdre. *A Chronology of Jane Austen and Her Family*. Cambridge UP, 2013.

———. *A Family Record*. 2nd ed., Cambridge UP, 2004.

[Lewis, G. H.] "Extract from 'The Lady Novelists.'" Littlewood, vol. 1, pp. 337–38.

———. "The Novels of Jane Austen." Littlewood, vol. 1, pp. 339–55.

Libin, Kathryn L. Shanks. "Music, Character and Social Standing in Jane Austen's *Emma*." *Persuasions*, vol. 22, 2000, pp. 15–30.

Littlewood, Ian. *Jane Austen: Critical Assessments*. Helm Information, 1998. 4 vols.

Litz, A. Walton. *Jane Austen: A Study of Her Artistic Development*. Oxford UP, 1965.

———. "*Persuasion*: Forms of Estrangement." *Jane Austen: Bicentenary Essays*, edited by John Halperin, Cambridge UP, 1975, pp. 221–32.

Lodge, David. "Jane Austen's Novels: Form and Structure." Grey et al., pp. 165–78.

Loesser, Arthur. *Men, Women and Pianos: A Social History*. Simon and Schuster, 1954.

Lukács, Georg. *The Historical Novel*. 1962. Translated by Hannah Mitchell and Stanley Mitchell, U of Nebraska P, 1983.

Lynch, Deidre Shauna. *The Economy of Character: Novels, Market Culture, and the Business of Inner Meaning*. U of Chicago P, 1998.

———. Introduction. Austen, *Persuasion* [Kinsley], pp. vii–xxxiii.

———, editor. *The Romantic Period. Norton Anthology of English Literature*, vol. D, 10th ed., W. W. Norton, 2018.

Macdonald, Andrew, and Gina Macdonald. "Visualizing Empire in Domestic Settings: Designing *Persuasion* for the Screen." *Women, Popular Culture, and the Eighteenth Century*, edited by Tiffany Potter, U of Toronto P, 2012, pp. 417–33.

Madsen, Wendy. "The Age of Transition: Nursing and Caring in the Nineteenth Century." *Journal of Australian Studies*, vol. 78, no. 27, 2003, pp. 39–45.

Makdisi, Saree. *Making England Western: Occidentalism, Race, and Imperial Culture*. U of Chicago P, 2014.

Martin, Emmie. "Nearly 70% of Americans Consider Themselves Middle-Class—Here's How Many Actually Are." *CNBC*, 26 Sept. 2018, www.cnbc.com/2018/09/26/how-many-americans-qualify-as-middle-class.html.

Mary Poppins. Directed by Robert Stevenson, Walt Disney, 1964.

Mason, Nicholas. *Literary Advertising and the Shaping of British Romanticism*. Johns Hopkins UP, 2013.

Matsuoka, Mitsu. "A Hyper-concordance to the Works of Jane Austen." *The Victorian Literary Studies Archive*, victorian-studies.net/concordance/austen/.

McGann, Jerome J. *The Romantic Ideology: A Critical Investigation*. U of Chicago P, 1983.

McRuer, Robert. *Crip Theory: Cultural Signs of Queerness and Disability*. New York UP, 2006.

Miller, D. A. *Jane Austen; or, The Secret of Style*. Princeton UP, 2003.

Monaghan, David. "'A Cheerful Confidence in Futurity': The Movement Motif in Austen's Novel and Dear/Michell's Film Adaptation of *Persuasion*." *The Cinematic Jane Austen: Essays on the Filmic Sensibility of the Novels*, by Monaghan et al., McFarland, 2009, pp. 129–47.

Moody, Ellen. "A Calendar for *Persuasion*." *Ellen Moody's Website*, 3 Jan. 2003, www.jimandellen.org/austen/persuasion.calendar.html.

———. "Jane Austen and Time: A Study of Her Uses of the Almanac." *Ellen Moody's Website*, 4 June 2012, www.jimandellen.org/austen/emcalendars.html.

Mosley, Charles. *Burke's Peerage, Baronetage and Knightage*. 107th ed., Burke's Peerage and Gentry, 2003.

Nelles, William. "Omniscience for Atheists; or, Jane Austen's Infallible Narrator." *Narrative*, vol. 14, no. 2, 2006, pp. 118–31.

Nelles, William, and Linda Williams. "Narrative Order in the First-Person Novel." *Poetics Today*, vol. 39, no. 1, 2018, pp. 131–58.

The New Baronetage of England. W. Miller and E. Lloyd, 1804.

Newman, John Henry. "Letter to Mrs. John Mozley, 10 January 1837." *Jane Austen: The Critical Heritage, 1811–1870*, edited by Brian C. Southam, vol. 1, Routledge / Kegan Paul, 1968, p. 117.

Nightingale, Florence. *Notes on Nursing: What It Is and What It Is Not*. *A Celebration of Women Writers*, edited by Mary Mark Ockerbloom, digital.library.upenn.edu/women/nightingale/nursing/nursing.html.

Noddings, Nel. *Caring: A Feminine Approach to Ethics and Moral Education*. U of California P, 1984.

Old, Terry. *Bath as Jane Austen Knew It: A Walking Tour of the City*. Trail Publishing, 2011.

Paine, Thomas. "From *The Rights of Man*." Lynch, *Romantic Period*, pp. 209–12.

Pamboukian, Sylvia A. *Doctoring the Novel: Medicine and Quackery from Shelley to Doyle*. Ohio UP, 2012.

Pankhurst, Emmeline. *Suffragette: My Own Story*. 1914. Hesperus, 2015.

"Panoramas of Lyme Regis." 360° *Interactive Panoramas*, 20 Apr. 2018, www.360panoramas.co.uk/lymeregis/.

Parker, Keiko. "'What Part of Bath Do You Think They Will Settle In?' Jane Austen's Use of Bath in *Persuasion*." *Persuasions*, vol. 23, 2001, pp. 166–76.

Parsons, G. S. *Nelsonian Reminiscences: Leaves from Memory's Log: A Dramatic Eye-Witness Account of the War at Sea, 1795–1810*. 1843. Chatham Publishing, 1998.

Pater, Walter. "Postscript [On Classical and Romantic]." Gleckner and Enscoe, *Romanticism*, pp. 1–6.

Peltason, Timothy. "Mind and Mindlessness in Jane Austen." *Hudson Review*, vol. 67, no. 4, Winter 2015, pp. 609–33.

Persuasion. Directed by Howard Baker, written by Julian Mitchell, performance by Ann Fairbank, BBC, 1971. Film.

Persuasion. Directed by Roger Michell, written by Nick Dear, performance by Amanda Root, BBC, 1995. Film.

Persuasion. Directed by Adrian Shergold, written by Simon Burke, performance by Sally Hawkins, BBC, 2007. Film.

Piggott, Patrick. *The Innocent Diversion: Music in the Life and Writings of Jane Austen*. Douglas Cleverdon, 1979.

Pinch, Adela. *Strange Fits of Passion: Epistemologies of Emotion, Hume to Austen*. Stanford UP, 1996.

Polwhele, Richard. *The Unsex'd Females: A Poem, Addressed to the Author of the Pursuits of Literature*. 1800. Gale, 2018.

Poovey, Mary. *The Proper Lady and the Woman Writer: Ideology as Style in the Works of Mary Wollstonecraft, Mary Shelley, and Jane Austen*. Chicago UP, 1984.

Puar, Jasbir. "Coda: The Cost of Getting Better." *Gay/Lesbian Quarterly*, vol. 18, no. 1, 2012, pp. 149–58.

Radcliffe, Ann. "On the Supernatural in Poetry." *New Monthly Magazine*, vol. 16, no. 1, 1826, pp. 145–52.

———. *Romance of the Forest*. 1791. Oxford UP, 1998.

Rafferty, Anne Marie. "The Seductions of History and the Nursing Diaspora." *Health and Nursing*, vol. 7, no. 2, 2005, pp. 2–16.

Ramsay, Steve. *Reading Machines: Toward an Algorithmic Criticism*. U of Illinois P, 2011.

Reeve, Katharine. *Jane Austen in Bath—Walking Tours of the Writer's City*. The Little Bookroom, 2006.

Review of *Northanger Abbey* and *Persuasion*. March 1818. Littlewood, vol. 1, pp. 310–14.

Richardson, Samuel. *Pamela; or, Virtue Rewarded*. 1740. Edited by Thomas Keymer, Oxford UP, 2008.

Robertson, Stuart. "Bath (Statue in Gardens in Bath)." *Panoramic Earth*, 2017, www.panoramicearth.com/Europe/England/Somerset/Bath. Accessed 25 May 2017.

Sallaberry, Raquel. "Where Exactly Did Louisa Musgrove Fall?" *Jane Austen Today*, 11 May 2010, janitesonthejames.blogspot.com/2010/05/where-exactly-did-louisa-musgrove-fall.html.

Samuels, Lisa, and Jerome McGann. "Deformance and Interpretation." *New Literary History*, vol. 30, no. 1, Winter 1999, pp. 25–56.

Sanborn, Vic. "Teacher/Student." *Jane Austen's World*, 2010, janeaustensworld.wordpress.com/teacherstudent/.

Sanders, Julie. *Adaptation and Appropriation*. Routledge, 2006.

Schaffer, Talia. *Romance's Rival: Familiar Marriage in Victorian Fiction*. Oxford UP, 2016.

Scott, Walter. "Marmion: A Tale of the Flodden Field." Austen, *Persuasion* [Bree], pp. 297–300.

———. *Waverley; or, 'Tis Sixty Years Since*. 1814. Edited by Claire Lamont, Clarendon Press, 1981.

Sebald, W. G. *The Emigrants*. Translated by Michael Hulse, New Directions, 1993.

"Seniority, 2." *Oxford English Dictionary*, 2020, oed.com/view/Entry/175910?redirectedFrom=seniority#eid.

Shapard, David M. "Chronology." J. Austen, *Annotated* Persuasion, pp. 485–92.

Shelley, Mary. *Frankenstein*. 1818. Edited by Marilyn Butler, Oxford World's Classics, 2009.

Shelley, Percy Bysshe. *The Complete Poetry of Percy Bysshe Shelley*. Edited by Donald H. Reiman et al., vol. 3, Johns Hopkins UP, 2012.

Siebers, Tobin. *Disability Theory*. U of Michigan P, 2008.

Smith, Johanna M. "'I Am a Gentleman's Daughter': A Marxist-Feminist Reading of *Pride and Prejudice*." Folsom, *Approaches to Teaching Austen's* Pride, pp. 67–73.

Southam, Brian. "The Aftermath of *Persuasion*." Southam, *Jane Austen* [2nd ed.], pp. 307–21.

———. *Jane Austen and the Navy*. Hambledon and London, 2000.

———. *Jane Austen and the Navy*. 2nd ed., National Maritime Museum, 2005.

———. "*Persuasion*: The Cancelled Chapters." Grey et al., pp. 322–23.

———. "*Persuasion*: The Righting and Re-writing of History." Southam, *Jane Austen* [2nd ed.], pp. 262–305.

Stevenson, Robert Louis. *The Strange Case of Dr. Jekyll and Mr. Hyde*. Penguin Books, 2003.

Stoddard Holmes, Martha. *Fictions of Affliction: Physical Disability in Victorian Culture*. U of Michigan P, 2008.

Stone, Lawrence. *Broken Lives: Separation and Divorce in England, 1660–1857*. Oxford UP, 1993.

———. *The Family, Sex and Marriage: In England, 1500–1800*. Penguin Books, 1990.

———. *Road to Divorce: England, 1530–1987*. Oxford UP, 2002.

———. *Uncertain Unions: Marriage in England, 1660–1753*. Oxford UP, 1993.

Summers, Anne. "The Mysterious Demise of Sarah Gamp: The Domiciliary Nurse and Her Detractors, c. 1830–1860." *Victorian Studies*, vol. 32, Spring 1989, pp. 365–86.

Sutherland, Kathryn. *Jane Austen's Textual Lives: From Aeschylus to Bollywood*. Oxford UP, 2005.

Swetnam, Joseph. *The Arraignment of Lewd, Idle, Froward, and Unconstant Women; or, the Vanity of Them*. 1704. Gale, 2018.

Tauchert, Ashley. *Romancing Jane Austen: Narrative, Realism and the Possibility of a Happy Ending*. Palgrave Macmillan, 2005.

Todd, Janet. *Cambridge Introduction to Jane Austen*. Cambridge UP, 2015.

Tomalin, Claire. *Jane Austen: A Life*. Alfred A. Knopf, 1997.

Tuite, Clara. *Romantic Austen: Sexual Politics and the Literary Canon*. Cambridge UP, 2002.

Van Eerde, Katherine S. "The Creation of the Baronetage in England." *Huntington Library Quarterly*, vol. 2, no. 4, 1959, pp. 313–22.

Wasserman, Earl R. "Metaphors for Poetry." Gleckner and Enscoe, *Romanticism*, pp. 247–59.

Watt, Ian. *The Rise of the Novel*. U of California P, 1957.

Wells, Juliette. "'In Music She Had [Been] Always Used to Feel Alone in the World': Jane Austen, Solitude and the Artistic Woman." *Persuasions*, vol. 26, 2004, pp. 98–110.

[Whately, Richard]. "A New Style of Novel." Austen, *Persuasion* [Spacks], pp. 208–17.

———. Review of *Northanger Abbey* and *Persuasion*. Littlewood, vol. 1, pp. 318–34.

Whelehan, Imelda. "Adaptations: The Contemporary Dilemmas." *Adaptations: From Text to Screen, Screen to Text*, edited by Deborah Cartmell and Whelehan, Routledge, 1999, pp. 3–19.

White, Laura. "Background." *Austen Said: Patterns of Diction in Jane Austen's Major Novels*, austen.unl.edu/background.

Williams, Linda. *Time Maps: Part 1: Defining*. *YouTube*, posted by William Nelles, 7 Oct. 2015, www.youtube.com/watch?v=PtlR4EEIzxA.

———. *Time Maps: Part 2: Charting*. *YouTube*, posted by William Nelles, 7 Oct. 2015, www.youtube.com/watch?v=pM8X2eIo2WM.

———. *Time Maps: Part 3: Refining*. *YouTube*, posted by William Nelles, 7 Oct. 2015, www.youtube.com/watch?v=Pa3U096PMxM.

———. *Time Maps: Part 4: Bonus*. *YouTube*, posted by William Nelles, 7 Oct. 2015, www.youtube.com/watch?v=2YpFZDOkYX4.

Williams, Raymond. *The Country and the City*. Oxford UP, 1973.

Wilson Kimber, Marian. "Jane Austen's Playlist: Teaching Music History beyond the Canon." *Journal of Music History Pedagogy*, vol. 4, no. 2, 2014, pp. 213–30.

Wiltshire, John. "Exploring *Mansfield Park*: In the Footsteps of Fanny Price." *Persuasions*, vol. 28, 2006, pp. 81–100.

———. *The Hidden Jane Austen*. Cambridge UP, 2014.

———. *Jane Austen and the Body: "The Picture of Health."* Cambridge UP, 1992.

———. "*Persuasion*: The Pathology of Everyday Life." Wiltshire, *Jane Austen*, pp. 155–96.

———. "A Romantic *Persuasion*?" *Critical Review*, vol. 14, 1971, pp. 3–16.

Wollstonecraft, Mary. *The Collected Letters of Mary Wollstonecraft*. Edited by Janet Todd, Columbia UP, 2003.

———. "From *A Vindication of the Rights of Men*." Lynch, *Romantic Period*, pp. 204–08.

———. "From *A Vindication of the Rights of Woman*." Lynch, *Romantic Period*, pp. 219–49.

———. *A Vindication of the Rights of Men*. A Vindication of the Rights of Woman *and* A Vindication of the Rights of Men, edited by Janet Todd, Oxford UP, 1993, pp. 5–62.

———. *A Vindication of the Rights of Woman*. 1792. *Bartleby.com*, 8 Oct. 2017, www.bartleby.com/144/2.html.

———. *A Vindication of the Rights of Woman*. A Vindication of the Rights of Woman *and* A Vindication of the Rights of Men, edited by Janet Todd, Oxford UP, 1993, pp. 63–283.

———. *A Vindication of the Rights of Woman*. Edited by Deidre Shauna Lynch, W. W. Norton, 2009.

———. *A Vindication of the Rights of Woman*. Edited by Janet Todd, New York UP, 1989.

———. *A Vindication of the Rights of Woman*. Dover, 1996.

Wood, James. *How Fiction Works*. Farrar Strauss, 2008.

Woolf, Virginia. "Jane Austen." *The Common Reader: First Series*. 1925. Edited by Andrew McNeillie, Harcourt, 1984, pp. 137–49.

Wordsworth, William. *Poetical Works*. Edited by Thomas Hutchinson, Ernest de Selincourt, Oxford UP, 1978.

Wordsworth, William, and Samuel Taylor Coleridge. *Lyrical Ballads*. Edited by R. L. Brett and A. R. Jones, Routledge, 1991.

Zionkowski, Linda, and Mimi Hart. "'Aunt Jane Began Her Day with Music': Austen and the Female Amateur." *Persuasions*, vol. 37, 2015, pp. 165–85.